Complete Korean

Jaehoon Yeon and Mark Vincent

First published in Great Britain in 1997 by Hodder Education.
An Hachette UK company.

First published in US in 1997 by The McGraw-Hill Companies, Inc.

This edition published 2014

British Library Cataloguing in Publication Data: a catalogue record for
this title is available from the British Library.

Library of Congress Catalog Card Number: on file.

Paperback ISBN 978 1 444 19578 1
eBook ISBN 978 1 473 60263 2

10 9 8 7 6 5 4 3

The publisher has used its best endeavours to ensure that any
website addresses referred to in this book are correct and active at
the time of going to press. However, the publisher and the author
have no responsibility for the websites and can make no guarantee
that a site will remain live or that the content will remain relevant,
decent or appropriate.

The publisher has made every effort to mark as such all words which
it believes to be trademarks. The publisher should also like to make
it clear that the presence of a word in the book, whether marked or
unmarked, in no way affects its legal status as a trademark.

Every reasonable effort has been made by the publisher to trace the
copyright holders of material in this book. Any errors or omissions
should be notified in writing to the publisher, who will endeavour to
rectify the situation for any reprints and future editions.

Cover image © 2013 Thinkstock

Typeset by Graphicraft Limited, Hong Kong.

Printed and bound in Great Britain by CPI Group (UK) Ltd., Croydon,
CR0 4YY.

John Murray Learning policy is to use papers that are natural,
renewable and recyclable products and made from wood grown in
sustainable forests. The logging and manufacturing processes are
expected to conform to the environmental regulations of the country
of origin.

John Murray Learning
338 Euston Road
London NW1 3BH
www.hodder.co.uk

Also available
as an ebook

Acknowledgements

Unfortunately Mark Vincent was unable to participate in creating this new revised edition of *Complete Korean*. It is undoubtedly a huge project, which I would not have been able to take on alone had I not had the support of my daughter, Eo-Jin, and advisory editor, Robert Vernon. I have benefitted enormously from their contributions and would like to express my heartfelt thanks to both of them. I'm sure you'll agree they've helped make this new edition work well to offer an improved learning experience for everyone.

Jaehoon Yeon, 2014

Contents

Greeting people and saying where you are going
• ordering drinks and snacks • identifying and
constructing basic Korean sentences • making polite
requests • forming what is known as the polite style
of speech

Meeting, greeting and introducing people • finding
where you want to be • saying that something is or
isn't something else • giving your sentences subjects
and topics

Making phone calls • making arrangements to
meet people • discussing what you like and dislike
• counting (numbers and counting) • making
suggestions and saying you can't do something

Buying items in a shop • finding your way around
• saying where something is and where some activity
takes place • using classifiers when counting things

About the authors

I began studying Korean in the early 1990s at the University of London, and I have to admit that at first it was something of a shock! I'd always loved foreign languages at school, and had studied quite a few of them, including Russian, Spanish, and Greek. But that didn't prepare me for how different – and also how exciting – Korean would be! Korean works very differently from the European languages and it comes with a completely unique script to boot. And while that certainly makes things challenging, it also makes them fascinating and wonderfully enriching. The real secret is to refuse to be bewildered and put off by all the new things you will learn at the outset (even though it is indeed confusing at first!), and to stick at it, a little a day. I remember after my first week of classes I thought I would never make it but in the end I did, becoming at the time only the second British citizen to major in Korean. It was definitely worth all the effort, and in this course we do our best to give you as many tips as we can, and to provide down-to-earth explanations of the way the language works (as well as colloquial expressions that you will use all the time if you go to Korea). Koreans are enthusiastic and friendly people who will warmly welcome and encourage your attempts to speak their language. Learning Korean is certainly difficult; we wouldn't pretend otherwise. But it is also lots of fun, and will give you a real sense of achievement as well as many new friendships and an infinitely richer experience if you travel to Korea, not to mention a wider view of language and the wonder of human communication.

Mark Vincent

I have been teaching Korean since 1989 at the School of Oriental and African Studies (SOAS), University of London, and have taught many European students. They find Korean very difficult, but interesting and rewarding when they make it to the end. I met Mark Vincent as a SOAS student in the early 1990s, and he is one of the best students I have met so far. We came up with the idea of writing an interesting Korean language course for beginners, which Hodder and Stoughton accepted, and this is how this course came into being. I love learning foreign languages and have studied quite a number of them myself, including German, French, Russian, Japanese and Chinese. The regrettable thing is, however, I cannot fluently speak any of these languages, except for a little bit of Japanese – I can read them much better though! The aim of this course therefore, when we were writing it, was to make readers talk actual Korean! We tried to provide readers with up-to-date colloquial competence as well as structural reading knowledge. Mark, as a former learner himself, added many useful insights on the way you understand and learn an exotic language like Korea! We have provided you with easy-to-understand explanations of grammar and as many tips as possible. There is also a huge pool of additional online resources accessible for learners to master the language, ranging from official learning sites hosted by the Korea Tourism Organization to personal video blogs posted on YouTube. Do browse around and combine them into your learning with this course. Do not give up and try a little a day, then you will find it fun and rewarding.

Jaehoon Yeon

How the course works

All the units in *Complete Korean* are structured in the following way:

What you will learn sets the learning objectives and identifies what you will be able to do in Korean by the end of the unit.

Culture point gives an opening passage about a cultural aspect related to the unit theme, introducing some key words and phrases.

Vocabulary builder, along with its accompanying audio, brings in the key vocabulary you will learn in the unit. Look at the word lists, try to read the Korean and pronounce it independently before you listen and repeat after the speakers.

New expressions introduce the key phrases and expressions used in the dialogues for each unit. The English translations are listed also. These are the nuts and bolts of the language. Learn them and you will be on your way to speaking fluent Korean.

Dialogue. New language is presented in a recorded dialogue. First, read the background information, which sets the scene for what you are going to hear and read. An opening question focuses your attention on a particular point in the dialogue; further questions help you check your comprehension.

Language discovery draws your attention to key language points in the dialogue. Look for the icon for questions that lead you to discover how the language works, whether it is a grammar rule or a way of saying things. Read the notes and look back at the dialogue to see how the language has been used in practice to aid quicker learning.

Practice offers a variety of exercises, including speaking opportunities, to give you a chance to 'pull it all together' and make active use of the language. The speaking exercises let you use what you have learned in the unit and previously. Try to do the activity spontaneously without looking at the language notes or vocabulary lists. The reading and writing exercises mostly contain vocabulary from the unit. When doing personalized writing exercises think back to the dialogues you've studied in the unit to help you. Concentrate on the grammar points taught too as these will take your written Korean further.

Test yourself will help you assess how much you have learned. Do the tests without looking at the language notes.

Self check lets you see what you can do in Korean. When you feel confident that you can use the language correctly, move on to the next unit.

Study the units at your own pace, and remember to make frequent and repeated use of the audio.

To make your learning easier and more efficient, a system of icons indicates the actions you should take:

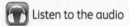 Listen to the audio

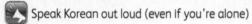 Speak Korean out loud (even if you're alone)

 Figure something out for yourself

 Culture tip

 New words and phrases

 Exercises coming up!

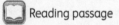 Reading passage

Write and make notes

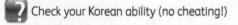 Check your Korean ability (no cheating!)

As you work your way through the course, you will also become familiar with studying on your own, looking things up, and checking your Korean ability.

You can also consult:

The Korean writing system: Hangul, at the beginning of the course, introduces the Korean alphabet, teaching you how to read and write the language. Start with this and don't be afraid to spend some significant time absorbing the information given. Once you have the foundations in place, working steadily through the rest of the course should be smooth running.

Pronunciation guide, also at the beginning of the course, is an overview of Korean sounds. We encourage you to go over it regularly.

Review units appear twice in the course to help you consolidate and remember the language you have learned over several units. Everything you need to answer the review questions has been presented previously, so checking your score will let you know if you are ready to move ahead to new material or if you ought to go back and refresh your knowledge.

Three reference sections are included:

A Translation of Dialogues is included to help you understand some of the more complex dialogues in the course.

A complete **Answer key** is given to help you monitor your performance and check your progress. It includes the answers to all the activities in the course.

The **Korean–English vocabulary** and **English–Korean vocabulary** allows you to quickly access all the vocabulary that is presented in the course.

Learn to learn

The Discovery method

There are lots of philosophies and approaches to language learning, some practical, some quite unconventional, and far too many to list here. Perhaps you know of a few, or even have some techniques of your own. In this course we have incorporated the **Discovery method** of learning, a sort of DIY approach to language learning. What this means is that you will be encouraged throughout the course to engage your mind and figure out the language for yourself, through identifying patterns, understanding grammar concepts, noticing words that are similar to English, and more. This method promotes **language awareness**, a critical skill in acquiring a new language. As a result of your own efforts, you will be able to better retain what you have learned, use it with confidence, and, even better, apply those same skills to continuing to learn the language (or, indeed, another one) on your own after you've finished this course.

Everyone can succeed in learning a language – the key is to know how to learn it. Learning is more than just reading or memorizing grammar and vocabulary. It's about being an active learner, learning in real contexts, and, most importantly, using what you've learned in different situations. Simply put, if you **figure something out for yourself**, you're more likely to understand it. And when you use what you've learned, you're more likely to remember it.

And because many of the essential but (let's admit it!) dull details, such as grammar rules, are taught through the **Discovery method**, you'll have more fun while learning. Soon, the language will start to make sense and you'll be relying on your own intuition to construct original sentences independently, not just listening and repeating.

Enjoy yourself!

Become a successful language learner

1 MAKE A HABIT OUT OF LEARNING

Study a little every day, between 20 and 30 minutes if possible, rather than two to three hours in one session. **Give yourself short-term goals**, e.g. work out how long you'll spend on a particular unit and work within the time limit. This will help you to **create a study habit**, much in the same way you would a sport or music. You will need to concentrate, so try to **create an environment conducive to learning** which is calm and quiet and free from distractions. As you study, do not worry about your mistakes or the things you can't remember or understand. Languages settle differently in our brains, but gradually the language will become clearer as your brain starts to make new connections. **Just give yourself enough time** and you will succeed.

2 MAXIMIZE YOUR EXPOSURE TO THE LANGUAGE

As part of your study habit, try to take other opportunities to **expose yourself to the language**. As well as using this course, you could try listening to the radio, watching television or reading online articles and blogs. Do you have a personal passion or hobby? Does a particular news story interest you? Do you like K-pop and other aspects of Korean culture that are currently riding the Korean **Hallyu** wave? Try to access information about them in Korean. It's entertaining and you'll become used to a range of writing and speaking styles. In time you'll also find that your vocabulary and language recognition deepen.

3 VOCABULARY

▶ To organize your study of vocabulary, group new words under **generic categories**, e.g. *points of interest*, *food*, **situations** in which they occur, e.g. under *asking directions* you can write *crossroads*, *traffic lights*, *left*, *right*, *subway/underground station*, and **functions**, e.g. greetings, parting, thanks, apologizing.

▶ Write the words over and over again. Keep lists on your smartphone or tablet and remember to switch the keyboard language so you can write in the Korean script.

▶ Listen to the audio several times and say the words out loud as you hear or read them.

▶ Cover up the English side of the vocabulary list and see if you remember the meaning of the word. Read aloud and pronounce the words on your own too without relying on the audio.

- ▶ Create flash cards, drawings and mind maps.
- ▶ Write Korean words on post-its and stick them to objects around your house.
- ▶ Look for patterns in words, e.g. adding 매 (**mae**) to a word means *every*, so 매일 (**maeil**) means *every day*, 매주 (**maeju**) means *every week*, 매달 (**maedal**) means *every month*, etc.
- ▶ Associate the words with similar sounding words in English, e.g. 많이 (**mani**), meaning *a lot*, sounds similar to *many*, whilst 배 (**pae**), meaning *pear* in Korean, sounds like its English counterpart *pear*, etc.
- ▶ **Experiment with words**. Use the words that you learn in new contexts and find out if they are correct.

4 GRAMMAR

- ▶ To organize the study of grammar, write your own grammar glossary and add new information and examples as you go along.
- ▶ Experiment with grammar rules. Sit back and reflect on how the rules of Korean compare with your own language or other languages you may already speak. Try to find out some rules on your own and be ready to spot the exceptions. By doing this, you'll remember the rules better and get a feel for the language.
- ▶ Try to find examples of grammar in conversations or other articles.
- ▶ Keep a 'pattern bank' that organizes examples that can be listed under the structures you've learned.
- ▶ Use known vocabulary to practise new grammar structures.
- ▶ When you learn a new verb form, write the conjugation of several different verbs you know that follow the same form, for example looking at verbs ending in a consonant and those ending in a vowel.

5 PRONUNCIATION

- ▶ When organizing the study of pronunciation, keep a section of your notebook for pronunciation rules and list words that give you trouble. Practise them separately.
- ▶ Repeat all of the dialogues, line by line. Listen to yourself, and try to mimic what you hear.
- ▶ Record yourself and compare yourself to a native speaker.
- ▶ Study individual sounds, then full words.
- ▶ Don't forget, it's not just about pronouncing letters and words correctly, but using the right intonation. So, when practising words and sentences, mimic the rising and falling intonation of native speakers.

6 LISTENING AND READING

The dialogues in this course include questions to help guide you in your understanding. But you can go further by following some of these tips.

▶ **Imagine the situation**. When listening to or reading the dialogues, try to imagine where the scene is taking place and who the main characters are. Let your experience of the world help you guess the meaning of the dialogue, e.g. if a dialogue takes place in a restaurant you can predict the kind of vocabulary that is being used.

▶ **Concentrate on the main part**. When watching a foreign film you usually get the meaning of the whole story from a few individual shots. Understanding a foreign conversation or article is similar. Concentrate on the main parts to get the message and don't worry about individual words.

▶ **Guess the key words; if you cannot, ask or look them up.** When there are key words you don't understand, try to guess what they mean from the context. If you're listening to a Korean speaker and cannot get the gist of a whole passage because of one word or phrase, try to repeat that word with a questioning tone; the speaker will probably paraphrase it, giving you the chance to understand it.

7 SPEAKING

Rehearse in the foreign language. As all language teachers will assure you, the successful learners are those students who overcome their inhibitions and get into situations where they must speak, write and listen to the foreign language. Here are some useful tips to help you practise speaking Korean:

▶ Hold a conversation with yourself, using the dialogues of the units as models and the structures you have learned previously.

▶ After you have conducted a transaction with a cashier or waiter in your own language, pretend that you have to do it in Korean, e.g. *buying groceries, ordering food, drinks* and so on.

▶ Look at objects around you and try to name them in Korean.

▶ Look at people around you and try to describe them in detail.

▶ Try to answer all of the questions in the course out loud.

▶ Say the dialogues out loud then try to replace sentences with ones that are true for you.

▶ Try to role play different situations in the course.

8 LEARN FROM YOUR ERRORS

▶ Don't let errors interfere with getting your message across. Making errors is part of any normal learning process, but some people get so worried that they won't say anything unless they are sure it is correct. This leads to a vicious circle as the less they say, the less practice they get and the more mistakes they make.

▶ Note the seriousness of errors. Many errors are not serious as they do not affect the meaning; for example if you use the wrong particle (-을 **-ul** instead of -를 **-lul**), wrong pronunciation (달 **tal** for 딸 **ttal**) or wrong verbal ending (-이에요 **-ieyo** rather than -예요 **-yeyo**). So concentrate on getting your message across and learn from your mistakes.

LEARN TO COPE WITH UNCERTAINTY

▶ **Don't over-use your dictionary.** When reading a text in the foreign language, don't be tempted to look up every word you don't know. Underline the words you do not understand and read the passage several times, concentrating on trying to get the gist of the passage. If after the third time there are still words which prevent you from getting the general meaning of the passage, look them up in the dictionary.

▶ **Don't panic if you don't understand.** If at some point you feel you don't understand what you are told, don't panic or give up listening. Either try and guess what is being said and keep following the dialogue or, if you cannot, isolate the expression or words you haven't understood and have them explained to you. The speaker might paraphrase them and the conversation will carry on.

▶ **Keep talking.** The best way to improve your fluency in the foreign language is to talk every time you have the opportunity to do so: keep the conversations flowing and don't worry about the mistakes. If you get stuck for a particular word, don't let the conversation stop; paraphrase or replace the unknown word with one you do know, even if you have to simplify what you want to say. As a last resort use the word from your own language and pronounce it in the foreign accent.

The Korean writing system: Hangul

History and background

The Korean alphabet is unique among all the writing systems of the world because it is the only known alphabet in the world for which the inventor and creation principles were clearly recorded in an official document.

From ancient times literacy in Korea had existed only among the ruling classes due to its complexity. Chinese characters known as 한자 (*Hanja*) had been borrowed and incorporated into the Korean language with Korean pronunciation.

However in 1443, King Sejong, the fourth king of the Joseon Dynasty created 한글 Hangul, the Korean writing system. Originally called 훈민정음 (*Hunmin Jeongeum*), meaning *the correct sounds for the instruction of the people*, Hangul was created to allow common people illiterate in Hanja to accurately, and easily, read and write the Korean language. The supposed publication date, 9 October 1446, is celebrated as 한글날 (*Hangul Day*) in South Korea.

The modern name Hangul was coined by Korean linguist 주시경 (*Ju Si-Gyeong*) in 1912. '한' (*Han*) meant *great* in archaic Korean, whilst '글' (*Gul*) denotes *script* in Korean. '한' can also be understood as the Sino-Korean word for *Korean*: 韓. Therefore Hangul's meaning is *Korean script* or *great script*. In North Korea it is known as 조선글 (*Choseongul*).

Both Koreas use Hangul as their sole official writing system, with ever-decreasing use of Hanja. South Korean newspapers now only use Hanja as abbreviations or disambiguation of homonyms, words with the same spelling and pronunciation but different meanings.

Hangul is one of the world's most scientific writing systems and has received worldwide acclaim from countless linguists. As a unique systematized phonetic alphabet, Hangul can express lots of sounds. It is perhaps the most outstanding scientific and cultural achievement of the Korean nation.

The basics of the Korean alphabet

The modern alphabet consists of 40 letters: 14 basic consonants, five double consonants, eight basic vowels and 13 complex vowels. Unlike the Latin or Greek alphabets, the alphabetical order of **Hangul** does not mix consonants and vowels. We will therefore observe the sequence of consonants and vowels separately.

CONSONANTS

There are 14 basic consonants and five double consonants. The double consonants are formed from two of the same basic consonant.

Basic consonants: ㄱ, ㄴ, ㄷ, ㄹ, ㅁ, ㅂ, ㅅ, ㅇ, ㅈ, ㅊ, ㅋ, ㅌ, ㅍ, ㅎ
Double consonants: ㄲ, ㄸ, ㅃ, ㅆ, ㅉ

VOWELS

There are eight basic vowel sounds along with 13 other complex vowel sounds. These complex vowels are combinations of no more than two vowels.

Basic vowels: ㅏ, ㅐ, ㅓ, ㅔ, ㅗ, ㅜ, ㅡ, ㅣ
Complex vowels: ㅑ, ㅒ, ㅕ, ㅖ, ㅘ, ㅙ, ㅚ, ㅛ, ㅝ, ㅞ, ㅟ, ㅠ, ㅢ

WRITING KOREAN: SYLLABLE BLOCKS

The Korean script, Hangul, is indeed an alphabet, but it has one special feature which sets it apart from most others. In English we start writing at the beginning of a word and write a sequence of letters, each one following the next, until we reach the end. Usually (apart from the case of silent letters and other peculiarities) we pronounce each letter in turn in the sequence running from left to right.

Korean, however, instead of writing a string of letters in sequence, writes its letters in syllable blocks. Each block-like shape of letters represents a syllable and each letter inside the block forms a sound. The word for person is 사람 (**saram**) and consists of two syllables.

The letters ㅅ and ㅏ make the syllable block 사 (**sa**), while ㄹ, ㅏ and ㅁ make the next syllable 람 (**ram**). The picture here shows an approximation of each of the Korean sounds contained in the word. Note that written Korean doesn't

actually draw boxes around the syllables; this is just for illustrative purposes.

Korean syllables are organized into blocks of letters that have a beginning consonant, a middle vowel and an optional final consonant. A syllable block is composed of a minimum of two letters, consisting of at least one consonant and one vowel.

Also note, if you want to only write a vowel, it must be written with the consonant ㅇ, which acts as a silent placeholder for the consonant position. Korean syllables, as previously mentioned, must consist of at least one consonant and one vowel, and also start with a consonant. If one wants to write just the vowel ㅏ, they would have to write it as 아 with the consonant ㅇ as a silent placeholder for the consonant position. An easy way to remember this is to think of the ㅇ as a zero.

Pronunciation guide

This section provides basic guidelines on how each of the 40 Hangul letter shapes should most normally be pronounced. Note, there are a few changes between the way that Korean is written and the way that it is pronounced. A couple of the basic sound changes are dealt with in the **Basic rules of pronunciation** that follows, but the majority of irregular pronunciations can be practised in the main unit lessons.

Vowels

There are eight basic vowel sounds: ㅏ, ㅐ, ㅓ, ㅔ, ㅗ, ㅜ, ㅡ and ㅣ.

Here are the eight basic vowels in syllable-block form with the consonant ㅇ. For each vowel sound we have given an example of an English equivalent.

Vowel	English parallels
ㅏ : 아	**a** as in *father, cargo*
ㅐ : 애	**a** as in *care, bare*[1]
ㅓ : 어	**o** as in *often, cot*
ㅔ : 에	**e** as in *bed, set*[1]
ㅗ : 오	**o** as in *core, tore*
ㅜ : 우	**u** as in *pull* or **oo** as in *moon*
ㅡ : 으	**u** as in *urgh*
ㅣ : 이	**ee** as in *feet, sheep*

Notes:

[1] Many native Korean speakers don't differentiate between 애 and 에, pronouncing both as a sound somewhere between the two.

Korean also has 13 complex vowel sounds: ㅑ, ㅒ, ㅕ, ㅖ, ㅘ, ㅙ, ㅚ, ㅛ, ㅝ, ㅞ, ㅟ, ㅠ and ㅢ. These can be divided into two groups depending on how they are formed and how they sound.

The first is the **y**-vowels group: ㅑ, ㅒ, ㅕ, ㅖ, ㅛ and ㅠ. These are derived from six of the basic vowel sounds with an additional short stroke and consist of a **y**-like sound. Here they are written in syllable-block form with English parallels.

Vowel	English parallels
ㅑ : 야	**ya** as in yak, yahoo
ㅒ : 얘	**ya** as in yay[1]
ㅕ : 여	**yo** as in yob, yoghurt
ㅖ : 예	**ye** as in yet, yes[1]
ㅛ : 요	**yo** as in york or **yaw** as in yawn
ㅠ: 유	**you** as in you, youth

Notes:

[1] Many native Korean speakers don't differentiate between 얘 and 예, pronouncing both as a sound somewhere between the two.

The second group of complex vowels is the **w**-vowels group: ㅘ, ㅙ, ㅚ, ㅝ, ㅞ and ㅟ. These are formed by combining two basic vowels together and consist of a w-like sound. Here they are written in syllable-block form with English parallels.

Vowel	English parallels
ㅘ: 와	**wa** as in wax, wag
ㅙ: 왜	**wea** as in wear, weather[1]
ㅚ: 외	**we** as in wet, wed[1]
ㅝ: 워	**wo** as in wonder, won
ㅞ: 웨	**we** as in wet, wed[1]
ㅟ: 위	**wee** as in weep or **wi** as in twig

Notes:

[1] Many native Korean speakers don't differentiate between 왜, 외 and 웨, pronouncing them as the same sound.

The final vowel is ─|. This complex vowel is a combination of basic vowels ─ and | and is pronounced as a quick glide from 으 (**eu**) to 이 (**i**).

Here are all 21 vowels again, listed in the order they'd appear in the dictionary:

Vowel	English parallels
ㅏ : 아	**a** as in *father, cargo*
ㅐ : 애	**a** as in *care, bare*
ㅑ : 야	**ya** as in *yak, yahoo*
ㅒ : 얘	**ya** as in *yay*
ㅓ : 어	**o** as in *often, cot*
ㅔ : 에	**e** as in *bed, set*
ㅕ : 여	**yo** as in *yob, yoghurt*
ㅖ : 예	**ye** as in *yet, yes*
ㅗ : 오	**o** as in *core, tore*
ㅘ : 와	**wa** as in *wax, wag*
ㅙ : 왜	**wea** as in *wear, weather*
ㅚ : 외	**we** as in *wet, wed*
ㅛ : 요	**yo** as in *york* or **yaw** as in *yawn*
ㅜ : 우	**u** as in *pull* or **oo** as in *moon*
ㅝ : 워	**wo** as in *wonder, won*
ㅞ : 웨	**we** as in *wet, wed*
ㅟ : 위	**wee** as in *weep* or **wi** as in *twig*
ㅠ : 유	**you** as in *you, youth*
─ : 으	**u** as in *urgh*
─| : 의	**u** (으) followed by **i** (이)
	: 이	**ee** as in *feet, sheep*

 00.01 **Read through the 21 vowels and try pronouncing them yourself. Then listen to the audio carefully and pronounce each sound as accurately as possible.**

Consonants

There are 14 basic consonants: ㄱ, ㄴ, ㄷ, ㄹ, ㅁ, ㅂ, ㅅ, ㅇ, ㅈ, ㅊ, ㅋ, ㅌ, ㅍ and ㅎ.

Here are the 14 basic consonants in syllable-block form with the vowel ㅏ. For each consonant sound we have given an example of an English equivalent.

Consonant	English parallels
ㄱ: 가	**k** as in *kill* or **g** as in *again*[1]
ㄴ: 나	**n** as in *net, now*
ㄷ: 다	**t** as in *tall* or **d** as in *idea*[1]
ㄹ: 라	**r** as in *rock* or **l** as in *let, lip*[4]
ㅁ: 마	**m** as in *mother, marry*
ㅂ: 바	**p** as in *park* or **b** as in *about*[1]
ㅅ: 사	**s** as in *sound, sky* or **sh** as in *shin*[2]
ㅇ: 아	**ng** as in *sing, song*[3]
ㅈ: 자	**j** as in *injury*
ㅊ: 차	**ch** as in *chat, chirp*
ㅋ: 카	**k** as in *kill, kite*
ㅌ: 타	**t** as in *talk, take*
ㅍ: 파	**p** as in *park, print*
ㅎ: 하	**h** as in *hack, hope*

Notes:

[1] These three consonants make a different sound, depending on their surrounding letters. The primary pronunciation is a **k**, **t** and **p** sound, but when the consonant has a vowel before and after, its pronunciation changes to a **g**, **d** and **b** sound respectively. This sounds complicating but it is an automatic process that comes naturally when talking. In fact in Korean, there are no distinctions between the sounds **k-g**, **t-d** and **p-b**.

[2] The consonant ㅅ is primarily pronounced with a **s**-sound. However when it comes before the vowel ㅣ, ㅟ or any **y**-vowel, it becomes a **sh**-sound.

[3] The consonant ㅇ, when at the start of a syllable, is not pronounced; it is a silent consonant. However when it appears as the final consonant in the syllable it is pronounced as **ng**.

[4] The sounds **l** and **r** cannot be differentiated in Korean. In terms of pronunciation, ㄹ is normally pronounced as **r**, but when it is the final consonant it is pronounced as **l**.

Korean also has five double consonants: ㄲ, ㄸ, ㅃ, ㅆ and ㅉ.

Double consonants are formed of two of the same consonant. They have no close English parallels and are rather similar to Italian double consonants (**pp**, **tt**, **cc** . . .). Here they are written in syllable-block form with the vowel ㅏ.

Consonant	English parallels
ㄲ: 까	**k** as in *sky*
ㄸ: 따	**t** as in *style*
ㅃ: 빠	**p** as in *spy*
ㅆ: 싸	**ss** as in *mass suicide*
ㅉ: 짜	**tch** as in *matching*

Here are all 19 consonants again, listed in the order they'd appear in the dictionary:

Consonant	English parallels
ㄱ: 가	**k** as in *kill* or **g** as in *again*
ㄲ: 까	**k** as in *sky*
ㄴ: 나	**n** as in *net, now*
ㄷ: 다	**t** as in *tall* or **d** as in *idea*
ㄸ: 따	**t** as in *style*
ㄹ: 라	**r** as in *rock* or **l** as in *let, lip*
ㅁ: 마	**m** as in *mother, marry*
ㅂ: 바	**p** as in *park* or **b** as in *about*
ㅃ: 빠	**p** as in *spy*
ㅅ: 사	**s** as in *sound, sky* or **sh** as in *shin*
ㅆ: 싸	**ss** as in *mass suicide*
ㅇ: 아	**ng** as in *sing, song*
ㅈ: 자	**j** as in *injury*
ㅉ: 짜	**tch** as in *matching*
ㅊ: 차	**ch** as in *chat, chirp*
ㅋ: 카	**k** as in *kill, kite*
ㅌ: 타	**t** as in *talk, take*
ㅍ: 파	**p** as in *park, print*
ㅎ: 하	**h** as in *hack, hope*

 00.02 **Read through the 19 consonants and try pronouncing them yourself. Then listen to the audio carefully and pronounce each sound as accurately as possible.**

00.03 Using the vowel and consonant tables given, try pronouncing the following words. Listen to the audio to check your pronunciation, and then repeat again to practise.

These first 12 words have syllables consisting of a single consonant and a single vowel only.

1 바보	5 고교	9 두부
2 바지	6 아버지	10 거기
3 자주	7 어머니	11 모자
4 아이	8 가구	12 모기

These next 12 words include syllables with final consonants.

13 선생님	17 과일	21 사람
14 빵	18 신발	22 점심
15 오징어	19 책	23 저녁
16 영국	20 농구	24 아침

These last 12 words are English loan words written in **Hangul**. Can you guess what they are in English?

25 호텔	29 레몬	33 오렌지 주스
26 컴퓨터	30 아이스크림	34 토마토
27 텔레비전	31 햄버거	35 테니스
28 택시	32 샌드위치	36 카메라

Some basic pronunciation rules

Korean pronunciation is simple and consistent in the sense that all letters correspond to only one sound. This means once you are familiar with the alphabet, reading Korean is really quite straightforward. Whereas the letter *a* in English could represent various sounds depending on the context and neighbouring letters, the vowel ㅏ in Korean is always pronounced **a** as in **father**, regardless of context and spelling.

In this way Korean writing is consistent. However some syllables are pronounced in different ways depending on context. The audio in this course will help you pronounce the correct sound changes, but here are a few basic pronunciation rules to help you recognize them.

RULE 1 FINAL CONSONANT SOUNDS

In Korean, the final consonant sound is never distinctly pronounced. We say the last consonant isn't released. This means you say the word as you would in English, shaping your mouth to make the final consonant sound and beginning to say it, but stopping short of releasing any air. Simply put, you slightly mute the consonant sound to sound as if the consonant has been swallowed.

However when the syllable is followed by a vowel, this final consonant sound is released and distinctly pronounced. This final consonant sound is carried over to the initial consonant position of the following syllable, as we've learned that all syllables must start with a consonant.

 00.04 **Listen carefully to the following examples and practise the pronunciation. Can you hear the consonant sounds being released when followed by the vowels?**

1 집   집에
2 앞   앞에
3 낮   낮에
4 옷   옷이
5 국   국이
6 밖   밖에
7 밭   밭에
8 꽃   꽃이

RULE 2 NASALIZATION

When the consonants ㄱ, ㄷ and ㅂ precede the consonants ㅁ or ㄴ, they are pronounced as **ng**, **n** and **m** respectively instead of the standard **k**, **t** and **p**. This process is nasalization. Look at the examples below.

학년 (**hak-nyon**) is pronounced as (항년).

닫는다 (**tat-nun-da**) is pronounced as (단는다).

합니다 (**hap-ni-da**) is pronounced as (함니다).

This sounds complex but it is an automatic process that comes naturally when talking so don't worry about it too much. You will get used to it as you learn more throughout the course.

 00.05 **Listen to the additional examples and practise the pronunciation.**

1 먹는다   (멍는다)
2 한국말   (항궁말)
3 걷는다   (건는다)
4 받는다   (반는다)
5 갑니다   (감니다)
6 십만   (심만)

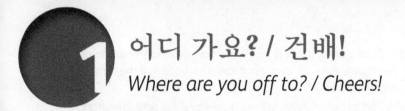

어디 가요? / 건배!

Where are you off to? / Cheers!

In this unit you will learn how to:

▶ *greet people and say where you are going.*
▶ *order drinks and snacks.*
▶ *identify and construct basic Korean sentences.*
▶ *make polite requests.*
▶ *form what is known as the polite style of speech.*

CEFR: *Can ask people for things and give people things (A1); can catch the main point in simple announcements (A2); can find specific information in simple material such as menus (A2).*

Eating and drinking in Korea

With its plentiful eating and drinking establishments, Korea is certainly never a place where you will need to go hungry . . . or thirsty! Korean cuisine is very different to the Western cuisines that we are used to. However, with Seoul being the buzzing metropolitan city that it is, you won't need to search far before you bump into a familiar restaurant or coffee chain.

Koreans love to get together and drink, and the most popular drink, particularly among men, is 소주 (*Korean vodka*). With an alcohol content of about 20 per cent, it doesn't have a particularly strong taste, but it is frequently drunk mixed with 맥주 (*beer*), to create 소맥 (소주+맥주). 맥주 on its own is also very popular, with Korean beers being typically sweeter and lighter than their Western counterparts. Another favourite is 막걸리, which is made from rice, and has a thick, milky consistency. It is the kind of drink that you will probably either love or hate.

When eating and drinking with Koreans, always wait for the eldest or most senior person to start eating before you dig in. Koreans also like to pour alcoholic drinks for each other. When doing this, make sure you hold the bottle or glass with both hands to pour or receive fill-ups from superiors or from those with whom you're drinking for the first time.

What are the names of the two traditional Korean alcoholic beverages mentioned?

Vocabulary builder 1

TALKING ABOUT WHERE YOU ARE GOING AND WHY

01.01 **Listen to the words and try to pronounce them.
Try to imitate the speaker.**

잘	*good, well* (adverb)
어디	*where?*
가-	*go* (verb stem)
가요	*go* (stem plus polite ending -요)
시내	*town centre*
-에	*to* (particle, attaches to nouns)
뭐	*what?*
하-	*do* (verb stem)
해요	*do* (stem plus polite ending -요, irregular form)
(verb stem)-러	*in order to* (verb)
하러	*in order to do*
빵	*bread*
사-	*buy* (verb stem)
사요	*buy* (stem plus polite ending -요)
나	*I / me*
-도	*too, also* (particle, attaches to nouns)

NEW EXPRESSIONS

Read the expressions that are used in the next dialogue. Note their meanings.

안녕하세요?	*Hello! / How are you?*
안녕하세요!	*Hello! / Fine.* (note: this phrase is both a question and a reply)
잘 지냈어요?	*How have you been doing (getting on)?*
잘 지냈어요.	*Fine, thanks (I've been getting on well).* (question and reply)
어디 가요?	*Where are you going?*
뭐 하러 … 가요?	*What are you going to . . . to do?*

Dialogue 1

어디 가요? **WHERE ARE YOU OFF TO?**

(name) -씨	(title used with people's names)
네	*yes*
지금	*now*
그럼	*then, in that case*
같이	*together*

 01.02 *Sangmin meets his friend Jaemin in the street and asks him where he is off to.*

1 How do the speakers say *hello* to one another?

2 How do they say *I am going*?

상민	재민씨! 안녕하세요?
재민	네. 안녕하세요! 잘 지냈어요?
상민	네, 잘 지냈어요. 어디가요?
재민	지금 시내에 가요.
상민	뭐 하러 시내에 가요?
재민	빵 사러 가요.
상민	나도 빵 사러 시내에 가요.
재민	그럼 같이 가요.
상민	네. 같이 가요.

3 Where is Jaemin going?

4 Why?

5 What do they agree at the end?

Language discovery 1

What do you notice about these names when written in Korean compared to when they are written in English?

김철수	*Cholsu Kim*
이민준	*Minjun Lee*
박장호	*Jangho Pak*
정민수	*Minsu Jung*

1 KOREAN NAMES

Korean names usually consist of three syllables. The first syllable is the surname (the most common Korean surnames being Kim, Lee and Pak), and this is usually followed by a two-syllable first name. There are odd exceptions: sometimes the first name will only contain one syllable. The two names in this dialogue, Jaemin and Sangmin, are both first names.

In Korean, the surname (when it is used) always comes first, the opposite of the English order. Therefore, Mr Pak Jaemin's surname is Pak, and his first name Jaemin. In this course we shall always use the Korean order (Pak Jaemin) rather than the English (Jaemin Pak). When you are writing Korean names in Korean script, remember also that Koreans put no space between the surname and the first name – they are treated almost like one word.

2 TALKING TO FRIENDS AND TALKING ABOUT THEM

When referring to someone you know well in a friendly situation, either to address them directly or to talk about them, it is quite acceptable to use their first name, just as in English. Following the name you should use the polite title -씨. You can refer to friends you know quite well and with whom you are on a similar social level as John -씨, Deborah -씨, Jaemin -씨, and so forth.

It is only when you are speaking to a very close friend that this -씨 can be dropped and you can just use their name (though if other people are present it is best to carry on using it). If you use -씨 you won't make any mistakes or offend anyone, whereas if you try dropping it, you could make a social mistake.

 Practise using the polite title -씨 with names of your own friends.

3 KOREAN VERBS

Korean sentences always end with a verb (a 'doing-word' like *walk*, *go*, *kick*, *steal*, etc). In English, the position of the verb is quite different: we would say, for example, *I go to the shops*, whereas a Korean will say *I shops-to go*. Main verbs always come at the end of the sentence, and getting used to this major difference in sentence structure takes a little while!

You may come across verbs which appear to occur in the middle of a sentence. Even these are, in a sense, at the end because they are used to end a clause. A clause is a part of a sentence which has its own verb and which could stand on its own as a sentence if it were changed a little bit.

For example, the sentence *If you come then I'll go* is made up of two clauses, both of which could stand on their own as sentences (*you come* and *I'll go*). Korean clauses and Korean sentences must always have a verb at the end.

You will notice that all the verbs have endings to them. The verbs at the end of the sentences all end in -요. This is a polite way of ending a sentence. The mid-sentence verbs in this lesson all end with -러. This is explained a little later on.

Korean verbs are made up of stems onto which endings can be added. Every verb has a stem; it is the most basic part of a Korean verb. Sometimes you might want to add as many as seven different endings at once onto a verb stem! In the vocabulary sections of this course we shall usually list verbs by their stem forms, and this is the form in which you should learn them. By the rules we teach you, you will learn how to make the other forms of the verb from these stems. In the first few lessons we shall remind you when we are teaching you the stem form. If we don't tell you a stem, it is because there is something unusual (irregular) about it, or because we are just going to learn one particular form of the verb in question for the time being.

Verbs are listed in a dictionary in what is known as the 'dictionary form'. This is simply the stem with the syllable -다 after it. You can use verbs that you learn from the dictionary simply by taking off this and using the stem as normal with the endings described in this course. There are some verbs which behave a bit oddly, however, and we will not go systematically through all the different kinds of verb stems until later on in the course, so you should hold fire a bit with the dictionary until that point.

The verbs in this lesson, 가- (*go*), 하- (*do*), 사- (*buy*), all occur with quite simple endings, and we will look at these now.

> **LANGUAGE TIP**
>
> Every Korean sentence has a verb at its end, and every verb has an ending on it. Sometimes other particles are inserted between a verb and its ending, but you should always think of a verb as consisting of these basic parts:
>
> Verb stem + (one or more optional particles +) Verb ending

4 POLITE SENTENCES WITH -요

The verb stems introduced so far all end in vowels, and to these you can add what is called the polite sentence ending, -요, to form a sentence. This polite sentence ending -요 is also known as a particle, and it is sometimes called the 'polite particle'. Note that the verb 하- is irregular, and the polite sentence form is 해요, not 하요 as you would have expected.

가요 is in itself a complete sentence (or clause) which means *I go, he goes, she goes, we go*, etc., depending on the context. There is no need to specify precisely who does the going in order to make a good Korean sentence. Thus, if you are talking about your mother, for example, and want to say that *she goes somewhere*, Korean only requires that you say 가요 – you don't need to use a word for *she*.

We ought to explain the term 'polite sentence ending' (or 'polite particle'). Korean has various styles or levels of speech which are used according to the social situation in which you are speaking. For example, when you are having a drink with close friends, you will use a very different speech style from that which you would use if you were addressing a meeting, or talking to somebody for the first time. The speech style is shown in Korean principally by the verb endings. Although we have formal and informal language in English, we do not have anything as systematic and widespread as the Korean system of verb endings to distinguish between formal, informal, and other styles of speech. These verb endings are crucial to every Korean sentence, since you cannot say a Korean sentence without selecting a speech style in which to say it. You have now begun to learn the most common, -요, which marks the polite style of speech. This can be used in most social situations, particularly if it is neither especially formal nor intimate. It is a 'middle-of-the-road' kind of style!

Verbs in the polite style may be statements, questions, suggestions or commands – this is expressed in the tone of voice that you use to say the sentence rather than being shown explicitly in the form of the verb. You have seen this several times already in the dialogue. The phrase 같이 가요 is first a suggestion, then when it is used a second time it is a statement. 잘 지냈어요 can be both a question, asking how someone is, or a statement, saying that you are fine. 안녕하세요 can also be both a question and a statement, depending on the way in which you say it.

 Add the polite sentence ending -요 to the following verb stems to complete the sentences:

a 가- (go)
b 하- (do)
c 사- (buy)

5 WHO ARE YOU TALKING ABOUT?

As we've already mentioned, Korean does not need you to specify the subject of the sentence, i.e. precisely who is doing the action the sentence describes. You can specify it if you want to for special emphasis, but as long as it is clear from the context, Korean does not require it. 어디 가요? therefore, means *Where are you going?* – but it is not necessary to say *you*, because the context makes it clear that the speaker is asking the hearer. If you look at the last seven sentences in the dialogue (from line 3), you'll see that only one uses a subject 나도 빵 사러 가요. The subject of that sentence 나도 is stated for emphasis.

6 WORD ORDER

We have seen that the word order of Korean sentences is very different from English. 잘 지냈어요? is a nice example, as it literally means *well have you been getting on?*, which is the opposite of what you would say in English. Usually the order is subject – object – verb. If we put this into very literal English this gives, *Peter the ball kicked, Mary the shops-to went.*

7 TO GO TO DO

The other verb ending introduced in this dialogue is -러 which means *in order to*. You add this onto a verb stem at the end of a clause, just as you added -요 to verb stems at the end of sentences. Note that, with verb stems which end in consonants (you haven't learned any yet, but will soon), you add the form -으러 (rather than just -러) to the verb stem.

The most complicated part here is sorting out the word order. Let's look at the English sentence *I'm going to the shops in order to buy bread.* Korean says this by putting the two clauses the other way round: *in order to buy bread I'm going to the shops.* However, that's not all! Remember that in addition, Korean puts its verbs at the end of clauses and sentences, and puts verb and clause endings after that. This gives us *I (bread buy-in order to) the shops-to go.* Notice the way one clause is embedded inside the other. Usually the subject of the sentence comes first (in this case, *I*), then the *in-order-to* clause, then the place where you're going, then the main verb:

| *I* (subject) | *go to the shops in-order-to buy bread* | (English) |
| *I* (optional) | *bread buy – in-order-to shops-to go* | (Korean) |

Therefore, the Korean sentence order is 나도 빵 사러 가요 (*I-too bread buy-in-order-to go*). The main verb of the sentence is the going, for example, 가요 or 시내에 가요. The other part of the sentence, the *in order to* . . . bit comes first, as in 빵 사러 가요, or 빵 사러 시내에 가요.

This is the correct order. Don't be tempted to try other orders – they will probably be wrong!

Note: This construction is only used with verbs of 'going' and 'coming'. It cannot be used with other verbs at the end of the sentence.

 # Vocabulary builder 2

ORDERING DRINKS AND SNACKS

 01.03 Listen to the words and try to pronounce them. Try to imitate the speaker.

아저씨	*waiter!* (when a middle-aged man)
소주	**soju**, *Korean distilled alcohol / vodka*
있-	(1) *exist, there is / are* (stem) (2) *have* (stem)
있어요	(as above, polite style)
맥주	*beer*
양주	*spirits, Western alcohol*
하나	*one*
-하고	*and*
주-	*give* (stem)
주세요	*please give* (polite request form)
안주	*snacks or side dishes for drinks*
-도	*also*
과일	*fruit*
오징어	*squid*
마른 안주	*dried snacks*
파전	*Korean-style pancake*

NEW EXPRESSIONS

Read the expressions that are used in the next dialogue. Note their meanings.

… 있어요?	*Do you have . . .?*
… 주세요	*Please give me . . .*
알겠어요	*fine / understood / right away*
감사합니다	*thank you*
여기 있어요.	*Here you are. / Here it is.*
맛있게 드세요.	*Have a good meal. / Enjoy your food.*
건배	*Cheers!*

 Dialogue 2

건배! CHEERS!

다	*all, everything*
그리고	*and (also)* (used to begin a sentence)
여기	*here*

01.04 *Sangmin goes to a bar with his friends and orders from the waiter.*

1 How does Sangmin say *Cheers*?

2 How do you ask someone to give you something? How many times does this happen in the dialogue?

상민	아저씨, 소주 있어요?
아저씨	네, 있어요. 소주, 맥주, 양주 다 있어요.
상민	그럼, 맥주 하나하고 소주 하나 주세요.
아저씨	네, 네. 알겠어요.
상민	그리고 안주도 주세요. 뭐 있어요?
아저씨	과일하고 오징어하고 마른안주하고 파전하고 … 다 있어요.
상민	그럼 과일하고 오징어 주세요.
(A little while later, the waiter brings the order . . .)	
아저씨	여기 있어요. 맛있게 드세요.
상민	감사합니다.
상민	*(to friends)* 건배!

3 What drinks does the waiter have?

4 How many drinks does Sangmin order?

5 What side dishes does he order?

Language discovery 2

Study the vocabulary to see how you ask *Is there (any) . . . ? / Do you have (any) . . . ?*. Can you find the places in the dialogue where this question is asked? How do you ask if there is any of the following?

a beer   **b** snacks   **c** fruit

> **LANGUAGE TIP**
> You can ask each of these questions with just two words in Korean. Notice where the verb goes – quite different to English!

10

1 THERE IS / THERE ARE

The verb 있어요 means *there is* or *there are*, depending on what you are talking about (*there is a book, there are some sheep*). The stem of this verb is 있-, and before the polite ending -요 can be added, the vowel 어- has to be inserted. This is because 있- ends with a consonant, whereas the verbs from the first dialogue all ended with vowels. As a reminder, stems ending in vowels usually make the polite form by adding -요. An exception is the verb 하-, which, as you will remember, becomes 해요 not 하요. Stems ending in consonants add the ending -어요 to form the polite style, unless the last vowel in the stem is an -아 or -오, in which case -아요 is added to make the polite style.

Polite style

vowel-stem	+ 요	
consonant-stem	+ 아요	if last vowel is -아 or -오 otherwise
consonant-stem	+ 어요	

The opposite of the verb 있- is 없- (*there isn't* or *there aren't*). From the rules given earlier, you can work out that its polite style form is 없어요.

This pair of verbs, as well as expressing existence and location, as in 저기 있어요 (*it's over there, it exists over there*), have another meaning of *have*. 있어요 can mean *I have / he has* (*one / some*), and 없어요 can mean *I don't have*. You can tell by the context which is the relevant meaning.

You will notice again that you can make a complete sentence just with a verb (like 있어요). You don't need to specify the subject (who has the object in question), and you don't even need to specify what it is that you are talking about, provided that the context makes it clear.

2 WAITERS AND SHOPKEEPERS

The word 아저씨 literally means *uncle*, but it is used as a general term to refer to a shopkeeper, waiter, or even a man in the street on occasions when formality is not called for. It can only be used for males. For females the term is 아줌마, which literally means *aunt*, but is used for any woman who is, say, over 35. The term 아가씨 should be used to refer to and attract the attention of young women.

3 KOREAN PARTICLES

In the introduction we talked about the way Korean adds little words called particles to the ends of words. You can see this clearly in the dialogues. We have shown the particles by inserting a hyphen between

the word and the particle, as in 나-도 (*me-too*), 시내-에 (*town centre-to =
to town*). Notice that the particle always comes after the noun that it
relates to. English often does the opposite of this. We would say *with me*
or *to school*, but Korean says *me-with* and *school-to*.

4 GIVING LISTS, AND SAYING *AND*

The Korean word for *and* is the particle -하고. Imagine that you want to
say one thing **and** another: *cigarettes and matches*. In Korean, the
particle -하고 attaches to the first noun of the pair, so that you would say:
cigarettes-하고 *matches*. The 하고 becomes a part of the word
cigarettes, since as a particle it has to be attached to a noun. If you want
to pause between the two words, you must pause after saying 하고, not
before, e.g. *cigarettes*-하고 (pause) *matches*. You must not say *cigarettes*
(pause) 하고 *matches*. This is because -하고 belongs to the noun it is
with; it is not a free or independent word like the English *and*.

If there are more than two items in a list, each word is followed by 하고,
with the exception of the last, e.g.:

cigarettes-하고   *matches*-하고   *ashtray*-하고   *lighter*

However, you can also add -하고 onto the last noun of the group if you
want to. This gives the sequence a vaguer ring – as though there might
be even more items in the list, but you are deciding to stop there (or can't
think of any more for the time being).

The particle -하고 can also mean *with*. Thus you can say 재민하고
시내에 가요 (*I'm going to town with Jaemin*). Once again, you can add
more names to the list, e.g. 재민하고 상민하고 시내에 가요. When you
are using -하고 to mean *with*, you can also use a slightly extended form
of the particle, -하고 같이, e.g.:

재민하고 같이 시내에 가요.

5 ASKING FOR THINGS

You have learned about Korean verb stems and the polite ending -요.
You will see that this dialogue contains the verb 주세요. The stem
here is 주-, and the usual polite style ending is -요. The bit in the middle,
however, you will learn about later. It is a form used to make polite
requests, but for now simply memorize the form 주세요 as a word
meaning *please give me*. You have also seen the same ending in the
phrase 맛있게 드세요. 맛있게 means *tastily*, and 드세요 comes from a
verb stem which means *imbibe* or *take in*. Therefore, the literal meaning is
please eat tastily.

6 ASKING FOR *ONE*

In the dialogue, an order is made for a beer and a **soju**. Notice how the number 하나 (*one*) comes after what is being ordered. To ask for *one beer* you say 맥주 하나 주세요. To ask for *one tea* you can say 차 하나 주세요.

Practice

You will need the following words for the exercises.

중국	*China*
일본	*Japan*
술집	*pub*
학교	*school*
밥	*rice (cooked rice)*
그 다음에	*after that . . .*
가게	*shop*
마시-	*drink* (verb stem)
앉-	*sit* (verb stem)
먹-	*eat* (verb stem)

As you are doing these exercises, don't be tempted to try to use any words we haven't given you. You shouldn't need any!

1 **Make up Korean sentences to say that there is or there are the following things. What other meaning could these sentences have?**

a

b

c

d

2 Imagine that the following Korean sentences are spoken to you. Make up an appropriate response in each case.

   a 어디 가요?   **d** 잘 지냈어요?
   b 여기 있어요.   **e** 뭐 마시러 술집에 가요?
   c 안녕하세요!   **f** 소주, 맥주, 양주 다 있어요.

3 Give the polite style form of the following verbs. Try making a short sentence out of each one.

   a 가-   **e** 없-
   b 있-   **f** 하-
   c 사-   **g** 앉- (*sit*)
   d 먹- (*eat*)

4 Get the attention of the waiter and ask him to give you the following things.

   a   **b**   **c**

5 Read the following notes made by a waiter for two orders. What is required at each table?

   a

   1 소주
   1 맥주
   마른 안주

   b

   오징어
   과일
   양주 – 위스키
   1 맥주

6 Make up two dialogues, based on the following scenarios.

   a You meet a friend who is going to the shop. Greet him and ask where he is going. Suggest that you go together. He agrees and suggests that after that you go to a bar for a beer.

   b You are in a bar where you meet a friend. Ask how he's been and order a beer and a **soju** for the two of you. Ask the waiter what snacks he has, make up an appropriate response and order some fruit.

⁇ Test yourself

1 Unjumble the following sentences. Don't forget to work out the meaning!

a 가요 – 일본에 – 지금

b 있어요 – 맥주 – 아저씨

c 사러 – 가게에 – 뭐 – 가요

d 주세요 – 오징어 – 양주하고

e 그리고 – 주세요 – 안주도

f 나도 – 가요 – 가게에

g 마른 – 다 – 밥 – 안주하고 – 있어요 – 맥주하고

2 Translate the following sentences into Korean.

a What are you going to buy at the shop?

b Hello Mr Kim! How are you?

c What are you doing after that?

d Are you going to the town centre now?

e Where are you going?

f We have beer, fruit and bread – all of them!

g Please also give me some rice.

h Here is your squid. Enjoy your meal!

i We don't have Western spirits. Then give me a beer, please.

j Some Korean pancake and a **soju**, please.

SELF CHECK

I CAN...
...say hello and greet people.
...talk about where I am going and why.
...ask questions.
...call for a waiter or waitress to order drinks and snacks.
...form basic Korean sentences that always end with a verb.
...make polite requests.

오래간만이에요! / 저 아니에요!

Long time, no see! / It's not me!

In this unit you will learn how to:
▶ *meet, greet and introduce people.*
▶ *find where you want to be.*
▶ *say that something is or isn't something else.*
▶ *give your sentences subjects and topics.*

CEFR (A1): *Can make an introduction and use basic greeting and leave-taking expressions; can recognize familiar words and basic phrases concerning self, family and concrete surroundings when people speak slowly and clearly.*

Meeting, greeting and addressing others

Koreans are very concerned about politeness, and this characteristic is especially noticeable when you meet people for the first time. It is wise to bow slightly when you 악수 (*shake hands*) with people, and be sure not to shake hands too hard. The Korean style is for the more senior person to do the shaking, while the other person allows their hands to be shaken. Kissing and hugging are not common forms of greeting or considered to be appropriate behaviour in public places.

Phrases such as 만나서 반갑습니다, which literally means *I've met you, so I'm pleased*, are very common. The form 처음 뵙겠습니다 is even more polite and literally means *I am seeing you for the first time*.

Generally speaking, Koreans do not address elders and superiors by name or with a pronoun such as *you*. Instead, they will use another title or term of address such as 선생님, literally meaning *teacher*. When addressing people of similar or younger 나이 (*age*), names are OK. To make it a little more polite, you can attach -씨 to their first name.

Which of the following people would you need to use a polite title to address?

a best friend
b supervisor at work

c younger sibling
d person you have just met

Vocabulary builder 1

MAKING INTRODUCTIONS

02.01 **Listen to the words and try to pronounce them. Try to imitate the speaker.**

요즘	*nowadays*	집	*house*	말씀	*words, speech*
사업	*business*	사람	*person*	많이	*much, many,*
-은	*(topic particle)*	집사람	*wife*		*a lot*
어때요?	*how is it?*	-이에요	*it is (equivalent*	저	*me*
우리	*we / our*		*to) (noun)*	-는	*(topic particle)*

NEW EXPRESSIONS

Read the expressions that are used in the next dialogue. Note their meanings.

오래간만이에요!	*Long time, no see!*
요즘 사업은 어때요?	*How's business these days?*
그저 그래요	*so-so*
말씀 많이 들었어요.	*I've heard a lot about you.*
(만나서) 반갑습니다!	*Pleased to meet you!*

Dialogue 1

오래간만이에요! **LONG TIME, NO SEE!**

김 선생님	*Mr Kim (선생님 also means teacher)*
그래요?	*really (?), is it / it is so (?) (question and reply)*
진짜	*really*

02.02 *Mr Kim meets an old friend, Mr Pak, and is introduced to Mr Pak's wife.*

1 How does Mr Pak say *This is my wife*?

박선생	김 선생님, 안녕하세요?
김선생	아! 박 선생님! 안녕하세요!
박선생	오래간만이에요!
김선생	네. 그래요. 진짜 오래간만이에요.
박선생	잘 지냈어요?
김선생	네. 잘 지냈어요. 요즘 사업은 어때요?
박선생	그저 그래요. *(pointing to his wife)* 우리 집사람이에요.
김선생	아! 그래요? 반갑습니다. 말씀 많이 들었어요.
부인	반갑습니다. 저는 장윤희예요.
김선생	저는 김진양이에요. 만나서 반갑습니다.

2 How is Mr Pak's business doing?

3 What does Mr Kim say about Mr Pak's wife? What is Mr Pak's wife called?

Language discovery 1

 Look at the following examples showing how different titles are used. Can you recognize any universal rules?

최 선생님   정 선생님
박 장호 선생님   철수씨
이 민준 선생님   정민수씨

1 KOREAN TITLES

When you want to address Korean men politely, you can use the title 선생님, which literally means *teacher*, but in practice means *Mr* or *Sir*. The title can be used on its own to speak to someone you don't know, with the surname (김 선생님, 박 선생님), or with the full name (박 재민 선생님). It is never used just with someone's first name, so you cannot say 진양 선생님 (nor, for that matter, can you say 김씨, which would be considered to be quite rude). Notice that, like the polite title -씨 used with first names, the title comes after the person's name, not before as in English.

The title 선생님 originally meant *the one who was born first*, and it therefore shows respect in addressing the person being spoken about as an elder. It is also the normal word for *a teacher*, and the context is the only way of telling whether it means that someone is a teacher, or whether they are simply being addressed as Mr.

Addressing women is a little more complex. Often women are addressed as being their husbands' wives. This means that Mrs Cho who is married to Mr Kim (Korean women keep their own surnames rather than taking their husbands') may be addressed as 김 선생님 부인 (*Kim-Mr-wife*). You could even say the English *Mrs Cho*, 미세스 조, and sometimes *Miss* is also used, 미스 박.

There are at least three words for *wife*. The first is the honorific term 부인, used when referring to someone else's wife. However, this term is never used to refer to your own wife. In Korean culture you are meant to downplay yourself, your family and your possessions, therefore to speak about your own wife you use the non-honorific word 집사람 (literally *house person*) or 아내. Note that when referring to relatives, and even your house, you say 우리 (*our*) rather than 내 or 제, meaning *my*. Thus, you would say 우리 집사람 (*our wife*), even though she is no one else's.

2 THE COPULA

When you want to say that something is something else (e.g. *Mr Kim is a Japanese teacher, this (thing) is a table, this office is the Korean department office*), you use a special verb form called the copula. Like other Korean verbs, it comes at the end of the sentence. However, it behaves a little differently from ordinary verbs. To say '*A is B*' (as in, *this is a Chinese book*), you would say:

A   B-이에요 (or B-예요.)   *this Chinese book-ieyo*

The form -이에요 is used when 'B' ends in a consonant, and -예요 is used when 'B' ends in a vowel:

선생님이에요   *is a teacher*

맥주예요   *is beer*

Please note that *is* in this sense means *is equivalent to*, *is identical with*; it does not mean *is located in* or *is a certain way* (e.g. *is green*, *is angry*). English does not make this distinction. Look at the following sentences:

This is a book.
The book is on the table.
The book is green.

All these use the English *is*, and yet only the first *is* means *is identical to*. The second *is* expresses location, the third describes the book. It is only for the first, when you are saying that *one thing is equivalent to* or *the same as something else* that the copula (이에요) is used in Korean. You must be very careful with this, as when you start to learn Korean it can be tempting to use the copula where you should not.

We have described the form A-B-이에요, but the simple form B-이에요 is just as common. This occurs several times in this lesson, and in all cases there is an implied A which is unspoken. Look at the following examples (we have put the implied A in brackets):

오래간만이에요   *(a matter of) long time no see – it is*

우리 집사람이에요   *(this person) my wife – is*

The context tells you what the subject of the sentence is, therefore you don't have to say it explicitly as you do in English.

> **LANGUAGE TIP**
> The term **copula** is just a fancy word for the verb *to be*, when you want to say that something is something else. In Korean, this takes the form:
> <something> <something else> (이)에요

 Complete the following sentences using either 이에요 or 예요. Work out whether the noun ends in a vowel or a consonant.

a 우리 집사람_____   **c** 오래간만_____
b 저는 장윤희_____   **d** 제 아내_____

3 어때요 AND 그래요

Korean has a group of words which mean *is (a certain way)*. 어때요 means *is how?*, as in:

선생님 어때요?　　　*What is the teacher like?, How is the teacher?*

사업은 어때요?　　　*What's business like?, How's business?*

그래요 means *is like that*. It can be used as a statement, e.g. 그래요 (*it is like that, that's right, it is (so)*). As a question, 그래요? means *Is it like that? Is that so? Really?*

4 TOPICS

Korean has a particle which can be attached to a noun or a phrase to emphasize that it is the topic of the sentence, that is to say, the thing which is being talked about. Sometimes we do this in English with an expression like *as for . . .* , for emphasis. We might say, for example, *As for my business, it's going pretty well at the moment*, or *As for me, I don't like cake*. Korean does this kind of thing very frequently with the topic particle -은/는. In the two sentences above, the nouns *my business* and *me* would both be followed by the topic particle in Korean to show that they are the topics of their sentences.

The particle has two forms, -는 when the noun you are making a topic ends in a vowel, and -은 when it ends in a consonant. Examples are 소주는 (*as for soju*), 재민씨는 (*as for Jaemin*), 선생님은 (*as for teacher*), 사업은 (*as for business*).

> **LANGUAGE TIP**
> Particles are little word fragments which carry important meaning and are always added to the end of words in Korean.

🔓 **Choose the appropriate topic particle for each of the following words.**

a 저＿＿＿＿＿
b 집사람＿＿＿＿＿
c 학교＿＿＿＿＿
d 술집＿＿＿＿＿

Vocabulary builder 2

FINDING WHERE YOU WANT TO BE

 02.03 Listen to the words and try to pronounce them. Try to imitate the speaker.

한국	*Korea(n)* (pronounced 항국)
말	*language*
한국말	*Korean language*
아니요	*no*
-이/가	(subject particle)
아니에요	*is not* (opposite of -(이)에요, negative copula)
일본	*Japan*
일본말	*Japanese language*
학과	*department (of college / university)*
사무실	*office*
어디	*where?*
저기	*(over) there*
무슨	*what, which*
일	*matter, business, work*
만나-	*meet (stem)*
왔어요	*came (past tense form)*

NEW EXPRESSIONS

Read the expressions that are used in the next dialogue. Note their meanings.

실례합니다.	*Excuse me, please.*
… 이세요?	*Are you . . . , please?* (i.e. the person I'm looking for)
죄송합니다.	*I'm sorry.*
… 어디예요?	*Where is . . . ?*
실례지만 …	*Excuse me, but . . .*
무슨 일이세요?	*What is it? How can I help you? What's the problem?*
… 만나러 왔어요	*I came to see . . .*

Dialogue 2

저 아니에요! IT'S NOT ME!

02.04 *Mr O is looking for the Korean teacher, Mr Kim. However, first he meets Mr Lee.*

1 Which two variations of the verb 실례하다 are presented in the dialogue?

오선생	실례합니다
이선생	네?
오선생	한국말 선생님이에요?
이선생	아니요. 저는 한국말 선생님이 아니에요. 저는 일본말 선생님이에요.
오선생	아, 죄송 합니다. 여기가 한국학과 사무실이 아니에요?
이선생	네. 한국학과가 아니에요. 여기는 일본학과예요.
오선생	그럼 한국학과 사무실이 어디예요?
이선생	저기 있어요.
(Mr O goes over to the Korean department.)	
오선생	실례지만, 여기가 한국학과 사무실이에요?
김선생	네. 무슨 일이세요?
오선생	한국말 선생님 만나러 왔어요.

2 Where are Mr O and Mr Lee having their conversation?

3 Why does Mr O go to the Korean department?

Language discovery 2

Study how different verb endings alter the meaning of the sentences. What do you think each verb ending means?

실례합니다.	*Excuse me.*
실례지만 여기가 한국학과 사무실이에요?	*Excuse me, but is this the Korean department?*
죄송합니다.	*I'm sorry.*
죄송하지만 한국학과 사무실이 어디예요?	*I'm sorry but where is the Korean department?*

1 MORE ON VERB ENDINGS

We have seen that Korean verbs take many different endings. This lesson contains the phrase 실례합니다 (*excuse me*), which is made from the verb stem 실례하-. The polite style form of this, as you would expect from the last lesson, is 실례해요, since 하- is irregular. The 합니다 form is what is known as the formal style, and usually when you are asking someone to excuse you, this is the form you will want to use. The formal and polite styles can be interchanged in many cases; but the formal is generally more suitable when speaking to someone older or higher in status than you. You will learn about how to make the formal style later.

This lesson also contains the form 실례지만. This is an abbreviation of 실례하지만, the -지만 ending meaning *but*. The complete expression means *I'm sorry, but* ... Don't worry about the -지만 ending for now; you will learn it thoroughly later. Simply remember 실례지만 as a set expression.

2 JOINING NOUNS TOGETHER

As you know, Korean attaches all kinds of particles on the end of nouns to give particular meanings. We have indicated particles by putting a dash between the noun and its particle. However, Korean also allows many nouns to be strung together in a sequence. Examples are 한국 + 말, which gives 한국말 (*Korean language*) and 한국학과 which means *Korean department*. We write some of these as one word (like 한국말), and flag the individual words and the compound form in the vocabulary.

Korean words can also be made by combining smaller nouns with particles. The term 선생님 is made up of 선생 and -님 (an honorific particle). But we can add 일본 to the front (일본 선생님). 일본 means *Japan*, so the full expression means *(esteemed) Japanese teacher*.

3 FINDING THE PERSON YOU WANT

The copula is Korean's special verb form which allows you to ask if something is something else. You could use it, therefore, to ask a person if they are Mr Kim, say, or Mr Pak. However, when you do this, it is normal to use a special form of the copula -이세요? This form is an honorific form – it shows politeness to the other person. For the moment simply learn it as a phrase: ··· 이세요? For example:

박 선생님이세요?	*Are you Mr Pak?*
한국말 선생님이세요?	*Are you the Korean teacher?*

4 SENTENCE SUBJECTS

In the previous dialogue you met the topic particle, and this dialogue introduces you to the subject particle, which is similar. The subject particle -이 attaches to the end of nouns which end in a consonant, and the subject particle -가 attaches to nouns which end in a vowel. This gives: 맥주가 (*beer*), 학교가 (*school*); 선생님이 (*teacher*), 과일이 (from 과일, *fruit*).

Naturally enough, the particle marks out the subject of the sentence. For example, in the sentence *The man kicked the dog*, 'the man' is the subject. In the sentence *The man is fat*, 'the man' is again the subject.

However, unfortunately, things are not quite so simple! In both of these sentences, the man could also be the topic, if the topic particle -는 were used instead of the subject particle. What is the difference between the subject and topic particles?

When something is mentioned for the first time, usually the subject particle is used. Later on, when the subject is repeated in the conversation, you can switch to use the topic particle instead.

The topic particle, you will recall, is particularly for emphasis like the English *as for*. It is particularly common when comparing two things, e.g. *as for me* (me-는), *I hate shopping. As for Mum* (Mum-는), *she just loves it*.

Do not worry too much about whether, in a given sentence, it is more correct to use the subject or the topic particle. Most sentences will be correct with either, although some will sound more natural to a Korean (and eventually to you) with one rather than the other. Gradually you will get the feel of which particle to use as your sense of the language develops. It is important that you do use one or the other in your sentences whenever you can, however. Do not just leave off particles, as it can tend to confuse Koreans when foreigners do so, even though they often leave them out themselves in casual speech.

> **ARTICLES**
> Remember, Korean has no word for *a* or *the*, that is, no definite or indefinite article. It's one respect in which Korean is easier than English, so make the most of it!

Complete the following sentences using the appropriate topic (T) or subject (S) particle.

a 여기_____(T) 우리 집사람이에요. 우리 집사람_____(T) 장윤희예요.

b 맥주와 소주_____(S) 있어요. 마른 안주_____(T) 없어요.

c 사무실_____(S) 어디예요? 여기_____(T) 일본학과 사무실이에요?

5 NEGATIVE COPULA

You have learned how to say *A is B* (*this thing-A is a book-B*). Now you must learn the negative copula, *A is not B*, as in *this thing is not a book, Mr Kim is not my teacher, this book is not a Chinese book*. The form is:

(A-subj/top) (B-subj) 아니에요

(subj = subject particle; top = topic particle; you can use either)

저는 선생님이 아니에요.   *I am not a teacher.*

(B-subj) 아니에요

한국학과가 아니에요.   *(This) is not the Korean department.*

Look at the examples in the dialogue very carefully to be sure that you have understood this pattern.

6 WHEN *YES* MEANS *NO*

Answering questions that require *yes* and *no* answers can be a bit tricky in Korean.

If the question is positive (*Do you like mushrooms?*) then you answer as you would in English (*Yes, I like them / No, I don't*).

However, if the question is negative (*Don't you like mushrooms?*), then the answer you give will be the opposite to what you would say in English, e.g.:

Don't you like mushrooms?

English	*Yes, I do like them.*	*No, I don't.*
Korean	*No, I do like them.*	*Yes, I don't.*

Aren't you going out tonight?

English	*Yes, I am going out.*	*No, I'm not.*
Korean	*No, I am going out.*	*Yes, I'm not.*

It goes without saying that you need to think very carefully when answering negative questions in Korean!

Imagine that you are asked the following negative questions. Follow the instructions and give the response in Korean.

a 장윤희씨 아니에요?
Say no, you aren't Yunhee Chang.

b 여기가 김선생님 사무실이 아니에요?
Say yes, it is Mr Kim's office.

c 이것은 오징어가 아니에요?
Say no, it isn't squid.

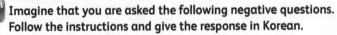

7 WHERE IS IT?

To ask where something is in Korean, you say: (B-subj) 어디예요?

However, confusingly, you can also say (B-subj) 어디 있어요?

When you answer a *where is . . . ?* question, you must always use the verb
있어요 e.g.:

학교가 거기	*The school over there is / exists.*
있어요.	*The school is over there.*

 Translate the following sentences into Korean.

a Where is the pub?
b Where is the office?

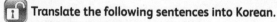 Practice

You will need the following words for the exercises.

건강	*health*
회사	*company* (i.e., the company, business)
가족	*family*
미국	*America(n)*
아들	*son*
학교	*school*
대학교	*university*
신문	*newspaper*
잡지	*magazine*
지금	*now*

1 The following Korean sentences have gaps where particles and word endings should be. Complete the sentences with the appropriate word endings into the gaps from the selection given. If there is a choice between A and B, make sure you use the correct form. Then work out the meanings of the sentences.

a 상민_____! 나_____ 시내_____ 가요. (에, 도, 씨)
b 뭐 하_____ 학교_____ 가_____? (요, 에, 러)
c 김 선생님_____ 어때요? (은/는)
d 여기_____ 사무실이에요?   (이/가)
e 아니에요. 여기_____ 사무실_____ 아니에요. (은/는, 이/가)

2 Say hello to the following people, and ask about how things are with them. For example, for the first one you would write the Korean equivalent of *Hello Mr O, how's the company?* (*As for the company, how is it?*).

a Mr O   the company
b Mrs Cho   business
c Mr Pak   the family
d Taegyu   school
e Miss Pak   her health

3 Look at the following drawings. Imagine that you are teaching a child the names of the objects and, pointing at each one in turn, you say *this thing* (이것은) *is* . . .

f Now make up five more sentences, saying that this thing is not what you see in the picture.

4 Make up five questions for the following five people. For the first two, ask if they are so-and-so. For the last three, ask negative questions (*you aren't so-and-so are you?*). For all five of your questions make up positive and negative answers. Make sure that you get the words for *yes* and *no* the right way round with the last three!

a an American person
b Mr Lee
c a Chinese teacher
d Mr Paek's son
e a school teacher

5 **Translate the following sentences into Korean. Remember that you should not be translating literally, but getting across the meaning with the words, phrases and constructions you have been learning.**

a I'm Pak Sangmin. Oh, really? Pleased to meet you.

b How is school nowadays?

c Excuse me, are you the Japanese teacher?

d Waiter! Do you have any squid? How is the squid? It's not bad.

e Isn't this the Korean department office? No, it isn't.

f I'm not Mrs Woo. Oh, really? I'm sorry.

g This is our Chinese teacher? Really? I've heard a lot about you.

h Is this the Japanese shop?

i I'm going to see the Korean teacher too.

j I came to meet Mr Pak's wife.

k Where is the Korean department?

l Where is the school office?

6 **Make up a short dialogue in which two old friends meet and ask each other how they are getting on. One of them has his son with him and introduces the son to the other person.**

7 **Kim Dukhoon is looking for the Chinese teacher in the Chinese department, but finds himself talking to the wrong person in the wrong place.**

Dukhoon approaches the teacher and says:

실례지만 여기가 중국학과 사무실이에요? 중국말 선생님 만나러 왔어요.

How might the teacher respond?

?⃞ Test yourself

1 Translate the following dialogue into English.

A 실례합니다. 박 선생님이세요?

B 아니에요. 저는 박 선생님이 아니에요. 박 선생님은 중국 선생님이세요. 여기는 중국학과 사무실이에요.

A 아! 죄송합니다. 실례지만 한국학과는 어디예요?

B 저기 있어요. 나도 지금 선생님 만나러 한국학과에 가요.

A 그럼, 같이 가요.

2 Complete the missing bits of the following dialogue with appropriate Korean sentences. Remember to check what comes after as well as what comes before, so that the whole conversation makes sense.

A 백 선생님, 오래간만이에요!

B

A 네, 네. 요즘 사업은 어때요?

B

A 지금 어디 가요?

B

A 사무실이 어디예요?

B *(over there)*

A 무슨 일이 있어요?

B

3 Yongmin has written a few sentences to introduce himself and a friend to a group of people he's never met before. Using the words given, complete the sentences so that they make sense.

선생님   안녕하세요   예요   이에요   우리

_____. 저는 최 용민_____. 저는 중국어 _____이에요. 그리고 이 분은 _____ 누나_____. 누나는 한국학과 선생님이에요.

SELF CHECK	
I CAN...	
⬤	...address people using the appropriate title.
⬤	...ask someone how they've been or how things are.
⬤	...introduce someone.
⬤	...use the copula to say something is or isn't something else.
⬤	...assign particles to the topic and subject noun of sentences.
⬤	...ask where something is.

2 오래간만이에요! / 저 아니에요! *Long time, no see! / It's not me!*   29

3

죄송합니다, 잘못 걸었어요! / 주문하시겠어요?

Sorry, wrong number! / Would you like to order?

In this unit you will learn how to:
▶ *make phone calls.*
▶ *make arrangements to meet people.*
▶ *discuss what you like and dislike.*
▶ *count (numbers and counting).*
▶ *make suggestions and say you can't do something.*

CEFR: *Can handle numbers, quantities, cost and time (A1); can make arrangements to meet, decide where to go and what to do (A2); can explain likes or dislikes (A2); can make and respond to suggestions (A2).*

Eating out in Korea

Eating out with a friend for 점심 (*lunch*) or 저녁 (*dinner*) is a common enough habit in Korea, just as it is in the West. You will actually find that Koreans tend to eat out a little more often than Westerners, and also that eating out can be done more cheaply in Korea.

When eating out with Koreans it is very rare to split the bill. In Korea it is normally one person who pays the bill – either the person who has done the inviting, or the most senior figure (in age or status). It is generally regarded as the senior person's job to pay for everyone else, and you must not offend Koreans by insisting on breaking their cultural tradition. After all, everyone ends up being the senior party at some time or other, so everything works out fairly in the end!

At Korean 식당 (*restaurants*), you will always be provided with 물 (*water*) and 반찬 (*side dishes*) as part of the service. In place of water, you may be given 보리차 (*barley tea*) instead. Note that side dishes are bottomless – don't be afraid to ask for more! Attracting the waiter's attention with a shout of 여기요! (*Over here!*) and showing him the empty dish usually does the trick, or you can ask 조금 더 주세요 (*Could you give me some more please*).

How can you attract the waiter's attention in a busy restaurant?

30

Vocabulary builder 1

SINO-KOREAN NUMBERS

 03.01 **Listen to the words and try to pronounce them. Try to imitate the speaker.**

공/영	*zero*	사	*four*	팔	*eight*
일	*one*	오	*five*	구	*nine*
이	*two*	육	*six*	십	*ten*
삼	*three*	칠	*seven*		

NEW EXPRESSIONS

Read the expressions that are used in the next dialogue. Note their meanings.

여보세요	*hello (on the phone)*
죄송하지만 …	*I'm sorry, but . . . / Excuse me, but . . .*
… 좀 바꿔주세요?	*Can I have / speak to . . . , please?*
여기 그런 사람 없어요.	*There's no one here by that name.*
(전화) 잘못 거셨어요.	*You've got the wrong number (you've misdialled).*
죄송합니다.	*I'm sorry. / I apologize. / Excuse me.*
잠깐 기다리세요.	*Please wait a moment.*
말씀 하세요.	*Please speak (I'm listening!).*
시간 있어요?	*Do you have (free) time?*
… -을 사고 싶어요.	*I want to buy . . .*
좋아요.	*Sound's good. / OK.*
… 앞에서 만납시다.	*Let's meet in front of . . .*
이따가 봅시다.	*We'll see each other later. / See you later.*

 # Dialogue 1

 죄송합니다, 잘못 걸었어요! **SORRY, WRONG NUMBER!**

전화	*telephone*
영국	*England, British*
대사관	*embassy*
-의	*belonging to (possessive particle)*
점심	*lunch*
-에	*at (a certain time)*
시간	*time, hour*
제가	*I (humble form, subject)*
열두시	*twelve o'clock*
호텔	*hotel*

Tony is trying to contact his old Korean friend, Mr Kim, but at first he dials the wrong number.

1 How does Tony ask for Mr Kim?

토니	여보세요? 죄송하지만 김선생님 좀 바꿔주세요.
박	여기 그런 사람 없어요.
토니	거기 삼팔구의(에) 이오공육 아니에요?
박	아니에요. 전화 잘못 거셨어요.
토니	죄송합니다.

(At last Tony gets through, has a brief chat to Mr Kim, and arranges to meet him for lunch.)

토니	여보세요? 죄송하지만, 김선생님 좀 바꿔주세요.
김선생 부인	잠깐 기다리세요.
김선생	네. 말씀하세요.
토니	아, 안녕하세요? 저는 영국대사관의 토니예요.
김선생	아, 안녕하세요. 오래간만이에요.
토니	오늘 점심에 시간 있어요?
김선생	네, 있어요.
토니	그럼, 제가 점심을 사고 싶어요.
김선생	네, 좋아요. 열두시에 롯데 호텔 앞에서 만납시다.
토니	좋아요. 그럼, 이따가 봅시다.

2 What number did Tony mean to call? How many Sino-Korean numbers are there in the phone number?

3 Who does Tony identify himself as?

4 What does Tony ask Mr Kim? Why?

5 When and where do they decide to meet?

Language discovery 1

What is the Korean word for each of the following numbers?

a 0   d 5   f 8
b 2   e 6   g 9
c 3

1 NUMBERS AND COUNTING

Korean has two completely different sets of numbers, which makes things very awkward for the language learner. There is a Korean set, often called pure Korean numerals, and another set which are of Chinese origin, usually called Sino-Korean numerals. Numbers are used for counting things, and which set you use in any situation depends on what it is that you want to count! To count hours, for example, you use the pure Korean numbers, but to count minutes, the Sino-Korean numbers must be used. You just have to learn which set of numbers are used with which objects. For example, if someone orders two portions of something and two dishes of something else, you simply have to know that the word *portion* takes the Sino-Korean numbers (so the word for *two* is 이), and that *dishes* takes the pure Korean numbers (so the word for *two* is 둘)! There is no shortcut, and we will tell you more about this as the course progresses. In this unit you will meet the Sino-Korean numbers only.

03.03 **Listen to the numbers and try to pronounce them. Try to imitate the speaker.**

십일	*11*	십육	*16*	이십일	*21*
십이	*12*	십칠	*17*	이십이	*22*
십삼	*13*	십팔	*18*	이십삼	*23* (etc.)
십사	*14*	십구	*19*	이십구	*29*
십오	*15*	이십	*20*	삼십	*30*

Once you have learned 1 to 10, everything is straightforward. Twenty is just 'two-ten', 30 'three-ten', etc.:

이십	*20*		백	*100*
삼십	*30*		천	*1,000*
사십	*40*	(etc.)	만	*10,000*
구십	*90*			

Here are a few more complicated examples for you to pick up the pattern:

구십팔	98	삼백팔십사	384
오십육	56	이천구백칠십	2,970
백십일	111	삼만오천육백이십오	35,625

 Now try reading these complicated numbers yourself. What numbers are they?

a 팔십사
b 사백칠십오
c 육만구천이백이십일

As you will have observed, there are a number of oddities in the pronunciation of numbers when they are put together, especially concerning the number six. Just remember that the number six can be pronounced in different ways, depending on the surrounding syllables.

Phone numbers are given in Korean by listing the digits in their Sino-Korean form. Seoul numbers have seven or eight digits, and speakers usually give the first three or four, then the sound -에, then the second four. In English, one might quote the area code, then say -에, then the telephone number:

삼오이-에 공팔칠삼	352–0873
구륙륙-에 삼사구일	966–3491
공일오삼오-에 오륙팔삼이륙	01535 568326

2 SENTENCES WITH *BUT*

You have previously seen that 실례지만, meaning *I'm sorry, but . . .* or *Excuse me, but . . .* is a form of 실례합니다. This unit takes another verb, 죄송합니다, and puts it in the -지만 form: 죄송하지만, to mean *I'm sorry, but . . .* As you will have guessed, -지만 is a verb ending which means *but*, and it can be attached to any verb base.

Here are a few other verb stems you have learned, each put into the -지만 form:

가-	go	가지만	goes, but . . .
하-	do	하지만	does, but . . .
사-	buy	사지만	buys, but . . .
있-	is / are, have	있지만	has, but . . .
마시-	drink	마시지만	drinks, but . . .
먹-	eat	먹지만	eats, but . . .
앉-	sit	앉지만	sits, but . . .

Notice the form with 있-, where the double ㅆ becomes pronounced as a ㄷ when -지만 is added. In Korean 한글 you still write the double ㅆ, but the word is pronounced 있지만>이찌만.

 What does the following sentence mean?

김 선생님은 맥주 잘 마시지만, 저는 양주 잘 마셔요.

> **LANGUAGE TIP**
>
> Many Korean verbs consist of two words, the second of which is 하-, which literally means *to do*. You've met this verb in expressions like 좋아해요, where the underlying verb is 좋아하-, and 안녕하세요, where the underlying verb is 안녕하-, and the expression means *to do well or peaceably*. The 하- stem is also present in the expression 미안하지만, meaning *I'm sorry, but . . .*

3 MAKING REQUESTS MORE POLITE

The word 좀 is flagged in the vocabulary as meaning *please*. It is not, however, of itself the direct equivalent of our English word *please*, because some of its uses are quite different. However, if you insert the word 좀 in a request immediately before the verb at the end of the sentence, it does have a similar effect to *please*. It is most frequently used when asking to be given something, that is, before the verb 주- (*give*). In this unit you meet it in the sentence: 김 선생님 좀 바꿔 주세요 (*Can I speak to Mr Kim, please?*). You might use it in a sentence such as 맥주 좀 주세요 (*Please give me some beer*). It softens the request, and consequently makes it more polite.

 Make the following requests more polite by adding in the word 좀.

a 물 주세요
b 책 읽어 주세요
c 라디오 켜 주세요

4 INTRODUCING HONORIFICS

In this unit you meet several verbs that end with -세요. The ones you have seen are: 하세요 (from 하-), 기다리세요 (from 기다리-), and 있으세요 (from 있-). These verbs are in what we call the polite honorific form which is shown by the ending -세요. All you have to do is add -세요 to a verb stem which ends in a vowel, and -으세요 to a verb stem which ends in a consonant, like this:

마시-	마시세요	있-	있으세요
하-	하세요	앉-	앉으세요
기다리-	기다리세요		

The most common use for this ending is as a polite request asking someone to do something, e.g. *please (do it)*, so that 기다리세요 means *please wait*. Notice that we've called the ending the polite honorific. You've met the polite ending -요 before, and this ending also has it, hence the name polite honorific. But it also has a -세- in it, which is the honorific bit. This serves to honour the person you are talking to, that is, the person you are requesting to do whatever it is. It is a form of respect, and it is this honorific part that makes the ending -(으)세요 into a polite request.

This is the most common use you will meet for the polite honorific. The other way in which it can be used is either to ask a question of somebody you particularly esteem, respect or wish to honour, or simply to make a statement about them.

For now make sure you are completely happy with the polite request meaning, but also be aware of the other uses in the back of your mind, since these honorifics are something that we shall return to later on.

 Decide whether the following statements are true or false. If false, give the true statement.

a 가세요 is an example of the polite honorific ending.

b 먹어요 is an example of the polite honorific ending.

5 SAYING WHAT YOU WANT TO DO

The form -고 싶어요 (the form 싶어요 coming from the stem 싶-) can be added onto any verb stem which describes an action, to produce the meaning *want to* (verb). Thus 나는 먹고 싶어요 means *I want to eat*. The -고 attaches straight to the verb stem, whether it ends in a consonant or a vowel, and there are no irregularities. Note that you can't put any other words between the -고 and the 싶어요 parts. Treat them as if they are inseparable, even though there is a space between them. Here are a couple of examples:

먹-	*eat*
저는 점심 먹고 싶어요.	*I want to eat lunch.*
만나-	*meet*
진양 만나고 싶어요.	*I want to meet Jinyang.*

6 MAKING SUGGESTIONS

A final verb-ending pattern to learn in this unit is -(으)ㅂ시다. -ㅂ시다 is added onto a verb stem ending in a vowel, and -읍시다 is added if the verb stem ends in a consonant. This pattern of using the vowel 으 to add to nouns or verb stems that end in consonants is one that you are becoming familiar with. The example you have seen is the ending (으)세요, but the topic particle 는/은 is similar. You will meet many more examples as you work through the course.

The meaning of 읍시다 is *let's do (such-and-such)*, and it is a relatively polite or formal form, as opposed to something you would say in a very informal or colloquial conversation. Note once again that you can only add this form onto a verb which describes an action, just as you saw with -고 싶어요. Thus you can say *let's go for a walk*, since that describes an action, but you can't say *let's be pretty* using -(으)ㅂ시다, since being pretty is a state and not an action. Here are a couple of examples of the form:

열두시에 같이 시내에 갑시다.	*Let's go to town together at 12.*
음료수 마십시다.	*Let's have a drink.*

Vocabulary builder 2

ORDERING AT A RESTAURANT

 03.04 **Listen to the words and try to pronounce them. Try to imitate the speaker.**

종업원	*waiter, assistant* (remember 아저씨 is the term to call him over)
앉-	*sit* (stem)
음료수	*drink*
우선	*first*
음식	*food*
좋아하-	*like* (stem)
아주	*very*
매운	*spicy* (adj)
거	*thing, object, fact* (abbreviation of 것)
못	*cannot*
-나	*or* (particle)
주문하-	*order* (stem)
-인분	*portion*
두	*two* (pure Korean number)
그릇	*dish / bowl*
물	*water*
아가씨	*waitress!* (lit: girl, unmarried woman)
김치	classic Korean side dish, marinated cabbage, spiced strongly with chillies
더	*more*

NEW EXPRESSIONS

Read the expressions that are used in the next dialogue. Note their meanings.

어서 오세요.	*Welcome!*
이 쪽으로 앉으세요.	*Please sit over here (over this side).*
고맙습니다.	*Thank you.*
음료수 하시겠어요?	*Would you like something to drink?*
주문하시겠어요?	*Would you like to order?*
… 드릴까요?	*Would you like . . . ? (lit: Shall I give you . . . ?)*

Dialogue 2

주문하시겠어요? **WOULD YOU LIKE TO ORDER?**

불고기	*bulgogi, Korean spiced marinated beef*
갈비	*marinated and fried spare ribs* (usually pork, cheaper than bulgogi)
냉면	*thin cold noodles*
물 냉면	*thin noodles in cold soup* (spicy and refreshing!)
비빔	*mixed*

03.05 *Tony and Mr Kim meet up and go to a restaurant for lunch. They order drinks, and then have a discussion about their culinary likes and dislikes.*

1 Which two dishes does Mr Kim suggest they eat? How does he say it?

종업원	어서 오세요. 이쪽으로 앉으세요.
김선생	고맙습니다.
종업원	음료수 하시겠어요?
김선생	우선 맥주 좀 주세요.
김선생	한국 음식 좋아하세요?
토니	네, 아주 좋아하지만, 매운 거 잘 못 먹어요.
김선생	그럼 불고기나 갈비를 먹읍시다.
토니	네, 좋아요. 그리고 저는 냉면도 먹고 싶어요.

(The waitress arrives to take their food order.)

종업원	주문하시겠어요?
토니	불고기 이인분하고 냉면 두 그릇 주세요.
종업원	물냉면 드릴까요? 비빔냉면 드릴까요?
토니	물냉면 주세요.

(A little while later the waitress arrives with the food.)

종업원	맛있게 드세요!

(During the meal, to the waitress:)

토니	아가씨, 물하고 김치 좀 더 주세요.

2 What does Tony think about Korean food?

3 Is Tony content with Mr Kim's suggestion?

4 What does Tony ask the waitress for at the very end of the dialogue?

Language discovery 2

 What is the Korean for the following sentences?

a Yes, that's good.

b Do you like Korean food?

1 좋아요 AND 좋아해요

There is an important difference between these two verbs. 좋아요 is a kind of verbal adjective which means *is good*. It may by implication mean that you like it, but the root meaning is that something is good. It is important to see the distinction, and here is an example to illustrate the difference. 김치 좋아요 means that *the kimchi is good*. You might conceivably recognize it as being good kimchi (as far as kimchi goes) without actually wanting to say that you like it. Even if you hate kimchi, you might still be able to discern between good and bad examples.

Contrariwise, 좋아해요 means *like*. 김치 좋아해요 means that you, or whoever else is being spoken about, actually likes the stuff. It might be the case that you like kimchi, even if it's not quite at its best. You can say you like something without commenting on its relative quality.

 Can you explain the difference between 김 선생님 좋아요 and 김 선생님 좋아해요?

2 OR

-(이)나 can be added after a noun to mean *or*, just like -하고 can be added after nouns to mean *and*. (noun) -(이)나 (noun), therefore, means (noun) *or* (noun). 갈비나 불고기 먹읍시다 means *let's eat kalbi or bulgogi*.

You can make this *either . . . or* idea sound even more vague by adding -(이)나 to both nouns. Then the translation would be something like *let's eat kalbi or bulgogi or something*. In a similar way you can have just one noun plus -(이)나 to make the sentence more vague so that it means (noun) *or something*. Take the sentence 갈비나 먹읍시다. This would mean that you are not all that bothered about what exactly you eat, you are just suggesting kalbi. Something else might be just as acceptable.

 Translate the following sentences that use -(이)나 into English.

a 학교나 대사관에 갑시다
b 소주나 맥주나 마십시다

3 WHEN YOU CAN'T DO IT

The little word 못 can be added to a sentence to give the meaning that something cannot be done: 시내에 못 가요 (*I can't go to the city centre*). Note that your inability to do something is being described – you can't physically do it, rather than that you are choosing not to do so, or that you won't. If you simply choose not to go to the city, if you aren't going out of choice, don't want to go or refuse to go, you can't use this construction. It expresses impossibility, tending to imply a situation is outside the speaker's control. Whether you want to go or not, you can't.

The word 못 goes as close to the verb as possible, right near the end of the clause immediately before the verb.

Watch out for the sound change that occurs at the end of 못 when the verb following begins with an ㅁ. 못 plus 만나- gives (몬만나요) (*I can't meet*).

 Add 못 to these sentences to change their meanings, then translate them into English.

a 책 읽어요
b 비빔 냉면 먹어요

4 MEASURING AND COUNTING

We will have a detailed section on measuring and counting later on, but for now, notice the two patterns in this lesson which will give you the key:

불고기	이	인분
냉면	두	그릇
(noun)	(number)	(measure)

This is important. First you state the substance you are measuring, then the number you want, then the unit that you are measuring it by (here portions and dishes).

Practice

V You will need the following words for the exercises.

식당	*restaurant*
백화점	*department store*
와인	*wine*
말하-	*speak, say*

1 **Make up a sentence for each of the following sets of information, saying that you want to do A and B. For example, for the first, your Korean sentence will say *I want to meet Mr Pak and Mrs Kim*.**

a	Mr Pak	Mrs Kim	meet
b	bread	fruit	buy
c	bulgogi	갈비	eat
d	English teacher	Japanese teacher	wait for
e	beer	whisky	drink
f	octopus	냉면	order

Now repeat the exercise, saying that you want to do either A or B.

2 **The following is an excerpt from a page in someone's telephone book. Put the names of each person and their number into Korean script.**

3 **Change the following sentences to say that they can't be done. For example, for the first you will write a Korean sentence saying that you can't go to the Japanese embassy.**

a I'm going to the Japanese embassy.
b 지금 점심 먹으러 식당에 가요.
c 재민씨, 상민씨 기다리세요?
d Sangmin eats spicy food.
e I am meeting Mrs Jang in front of the Chinese embassy.
f 백화점에 가요.

4 Put the following verbs into the polite honorific form (ending in -세요), and also into the *let's do* form. Then make up four sentences, two with each of the two verb forms (you can use any verbs you want to make the sentences).

a 가-   c 보-   e 기다리-   g 만나-
b 주문하-   d 앉-   f 사-

5 What is the difference between the following two pairs of sentences?

a 이 갈비가 아주 좋아요.
  이 갈비를 아주 좋아해요.
b 박 선생님의 아들 좋아요.
  박 선생님의 아들 좋아해요.

6 The following sentences should be translated into Korean. They are intended to practise suggestions and also how to say *but*.

a Let's speak in Chinese.
b Let's go to the department store.
c Let's drink some beer or wine.
d I want to go to America, but I can't.
e I like whisky but I can't drink it. (Implication: it isn't good for me or it makes me too drunk!)
f I want to telephone Mr Kim, but I misdialled.

7 What are the following numbers in English?

a 구십칠.   d 팔백육십일.
b 오십삼.   e 삼만사천 사백구십오.
c 이백칠.

8 You are arranging to meet your friend. She asks you where you should meet. Answer her, suggesting a place and a time.

Test yourself

1 Unjumble the following sentences.

a 하세요? – 음식 – 좋아 – 한국

b 힐튼 – -이에요 – 저는 – -의 – 상민 – 호텔

c 앞에서 – 학교 – 만납시다 – 열두시에

d 오늘 – 시간 – 점심 – 있으세요? – -에

e 물 – 주세요 – 우선 – 좀

f 먹어요 – 매운 – 잘 – 거 – 못

g 냉면 – 갈비 – 두 그릇 – 삼인분 – 주세요 – -하고

2 Translate the following sentences into English.

a 매운 거 좋아하지만 한국음식 잘 못 먹어요.

b 실례지만 영국 대사관이 어디 있어요?

c 이쪽으로 앉으세요. 음료수 하시겠어요?

d 시간이 있으세요? 그럼 이따가 만납시다.

e 김선생님? 잠깐 기다리세요.
죄송하지만 여기 그런 사람 없어요. 잘못 거셨어요.

f 거기 팔육삼의 공오사이에요?

SELF CHECK

	I CAN...
○	...make a phone call and ask to speak to someone specific on the phone.
○	...make arrangements to meet people.
○	...say I want to do something.
○	...discuss what I like and dislike.
○	...count using the Sino-Korean number system.
○	...say but.
○	...use honorific verb endings.
○	...make suggestions and say I can't do something.

모두 얼마예요? / 길 찾기

*How much is it altogether? /
Finding the way*

In this unit you will learn how to:
▶ *buy items in a shop.*
▶ *find your way around.*
▶ *say where something is and where some activity takes place.*
▶ *use classifiers when counting things.*

CEFR: *Can handle numbers, quantities and cost (A1); can give and receive information about quantities, numbers, prices, etc. (A2); can make simple purchases by stating what is wanted and asking the price (A2); can ask for and give directions referring to a map or plan (A2).*

South Korean currency

The currency in South Korea is the 원 (*won*). Korean money is comprised of 동전 (*coins*) of 10원, 50원, 100원 and 500원, and 지폐 (*bank notes*) of 1,000원, 5,000원, 10,000원 and 50,000원. Each of these has a picture of a well-known figure or item. For example, the 10원 동전 depicts 다보탑 (*Dabo pagoda*), which is located in 불국사 (*Bulguksa*) in 경주 (*Gyeongju*), and the 50원 동전 has sheathes of 쌀 (*rice*), representing ancient Korean agricultural society. The 100원 동전 has a portrait of 이순신, a great admiral from the 조선 (*Chosun*) dynasty, and the 500원 동전 has a 학 (*crane*). The 1,000원 and 5,000원 지폐 depict two renowned 조선 scholars, 퇴계이황 (Toegye YiHwang) and 율곡이이 (Yulgok Yiyi) respectively. The 10,000원 지폐 depicts 세종대왕 (*King Sejong*), who invented 한글 (*Hangul*), and finally the 50,000원 지폐 depicts 신사임당 (Shin Saimdang, mother of Yulgok Yiyi).

현금 (*cash*), as with the West, is a common method of payment in Korea. The use of 신용 카드 (*credit cards*) is also very widespread. There are one or two peculiarities, however, including the fact that Korea does not use cheques. The online system is highly developed and you can send money electronically very easily and securely. Cash machines are plentiful in the city and most now accept international cards. One thing to note is many of these machines will ask you for the amount you wish to withdraw in units of 만원 (*10,000 won*). For example, if you want to withdraw 200,000 won, you will need to select 20 만원 (*20 units of 10,000 won*).

On how many of Korea's coins and notes can you find portraits of famous figures?

Vocabulary builder 1

BUYING ITEMS IN A SHOP

 04.01 **Listen to the words and try to pronounce them. Try to imitate the speaker.**

둘	*two* (when you mean *the two of them, both*)
한	*one* (pure Korean, when used with a counter or measure word)
권	*volume* (measure word)
만	*10,000*
원	*won* (unit of Korean currency)
-씩	*each, per*
모두	*altogether, everything, everyone*
세	*three* (pure Korean)
가지	*kind, example* (counter for the noun 종류)
종류	*type, sort, kind*
제일	*the most*
싼	*cheap* (adjective)
싸-	*is cheap*
그러니까	*therefore, because of that*
비싼	*expensive* (adjective)
비싸-	*is expensive*
건	*thing, object* (abbreviation of 것 topic particle)
영수증	*receipt*

NEW EXPRESSIONS

Read the expressions that are used in the next dialogue. Note their meanings.

뭘 찾으세요?	*What are you looking for? Can I help you?*
(모두) 얼마예요?	*How much is it (altogether)?*
알겠습니다	*I understand; OK, right, fine* (formally)
착각했어요.	*I have made a mistake.*
안녕히 가세요	*goodbye* (to someone who is leaving)
안녕히 계세요	*goodbye* (to someone who is staying)

Dialogue 1

 모두 얼마예요? HOW MUCH IS IT ALTOGETHER?

사전	*dictionary*
한영	*Korean–English*
영한	*English–Korean*
한자	*Chinese characters*

 04.02 *Chris goes to a Korean bookshop to buy some dictionaries and unfortunately has a little trouble over the price.*

1 How does Chris ask to buy both the Korean–English and English–Korean dictionaries?

2 How much is the English–Korean dictionary? What is the exact expression used to express the price?

점원	뭘 찾으세요?
크리스	사전 있어요?
점원	네. 한영사전 드릴까요?
크리스	네, 한영사전하고 영한사전 둘 다 주세요.
점원	여기 있어요.
크리스	얼마예요?
점원	한 권에 만원씩, 모두 이만원이에요.
크리스	한자 사전도 있어요?
점원	한자 사전은 세 가지 종류가 있어요.
크리스	제일 싼 거 주세요.
점원	잠깐 기다리세요 … 여기 있어요.
크리스	고맙습니다. 모두 얼마예요?
점원	한자 사전 삼만원 … 그러니깐 모두 오만원이에요.
크리스	제일 싼 게 삼만원이에요? 그럼, 제일 비싼 건 얼마예요? 십만원이에요?
점원	아! 죄송합니다. 착각했어요. 모두 삼만원이에요. 영수증도 드릴까요?
크리스	네 주세요.
점원	알겠습니다. 여기 있어요. 안녕히 가세요!
크리스	안녕히 계세요.

3 How much is the total bill?

4 Does Chris get a receipt?

Language discovery 1

 Study the following sentences and identify what the underlined words signify.

a 한 권에 만원씩, 모두 이만원이에요.
b 한자 사전은 세 가지 종류가 있어요.
c 삼 만원이에요.

1 COUNTERS

In English, we sometimes use counters (counting words) to count objects. We might say, for example, two *cups* of coffee, or three *packets* of soup. Cups and packets are counters or measures by which we count and measure things like coffee and soup. On other occasions we do not use counters, for example, we say two books, three houses. However, in Korean, counters are frequently used when English does not use them. To say the two previous sentences, for example, a Korean might say:

| 책 두 권 | *book two volumes* | *two books* |
| 집 세 채 | *house three buildings* | *three houses* |

This is the usual pattern in Korean for counting things, or for talking about a certain number of something. Here are some common Korean counters which take the Sino-Korean numbers you have already learned:

분	*minute*	삼분	*three minutes*
초	*second*	이십초	*20 seconds*
일	*day*	삼십일	*30 days*
년	*year*	사년	*four years*
층	*floors*	삼층	*three floors*, (in building) *third floor*
원	*won (Korean money)*		
명	*person*		

Note that the word 명 can also be used with pure Korean numbers.

You can ask how many of something there are with the word 몇, for example: 몇 명? 몇 년? 몇 분?

This is not to say that Korean always uses counters. There are some words which do not take a special counter, that is to say, the word itself is the counter, as it is in English with books and houses. Thus, for counting days with 일 (*day*) you don't need to say 일삼일. In fact, that would be wrong. You simply say 삼일. If a counter is not used, therefore, the number comes before what you are counting, instead of after it.

2 PURE KOREAN NUMBERS

You now need to know the pure Korean numbers. We teach you up to 99. In fact, there are no pure Korean numbers above 99, so Sino-Korean numbers have to be used for 100 and over. For smaller numbers, however, it is important to know the pure Korean numbers and to use them when they are required, since otherwise you will be easily misunderstood (or not understood at all!) by Koreans.

 04.03 **Listen to the numbers and try to pronounce them. Try to imitate the speaker.**

하나	1	열하나	11
둘	2	열둘	12
셋	3	열셋	13
넷	4		
다섯	5		
여섯	6		
일곱	7		
여덟	8	스물	20
아홉	9	서른	30
열	10	마흔	40
		쉰	50
		예순	60
		일흔	70
		여든	80
		아흔	90

The following numbers change their forms when they are followed by a noun. You can get the changed forms by deleting the final sound (letter).

하나 → 한,   둘 → 두,   셋 → 세,   넷 → 네,   스물 → 스무

Most counters are used with pure Korean numbers, so with the exception of those you have already learned which take Sino-Korean numbers, you are safe to use pure Korean numbers. Here are some examples of common counters which are used with pure Korean numbers:

시	o'clock	마리	animal
시간	hours (duration)	권	volume (for books)
살	years of age	잔	cup (ful)
사람	person	상자	box
분	person (honorific)	병	bottle

Decide whether each of the following counters uses pure Korean or Sino-Korean numbers.

a Years of age, 살
b Minutes (time), 분

c Money, 원
d Bottles, 병

3 PRICES

This lesson introduces you to a construction for saying how much things cost, using the word 씩, which is difficult to translate, but gives the sentence the flavour of *so much each, so much apiece*, or *so much per such and such a quantity*. Study the following sentences to see how it is used:

한 권에 삼만원씩	*30,000 won per book (volume)*
사과 오천원씩	*apples 5,000 won each*
사과 한 상자에 오만원씩	*apples 50,000 won a box*

To make sentences out of these, all you have to do is add the copula:

사과가 오천원씩이에요.   *Apples are 5,000 won each.*

Translate the following sentences into English.

a 물이 한 병에 만오천원이에요
b 사전이 세 권에 육만원이에요

4 INTRODUCING ADJECTIVES

You have now met several Korean words that function in the way that adjectives do in English. In Korean they are usually called modifiers, but they work rather like adjectives. Remember that they always come before the noun they describe. Here are the ones you have met so far, with a couple of extras thrown in:

비싼	*expensive*
싼	*cheap*
그런	*such a, that (kind of)*
매운	*spicy*
좋은	*good*
나쁜	*bad*

You'll notice that they all end in -(으)ㄴ, and later on in the course you will learn how they can be formed from their associated verbs.

One very common construction in Korean is to find these words before the noun 것, which means *thing* (and sometimes also *fact* or *object*). This noun 것 itself needs a little explanation, as it commonly occurs in several different forms. On its own the word is pronounced (건), but written 것 (remember your pronunciation rules!). It is sometimes abbreviated to 거. With the topic particle its form is 것은 or, in casual speech, 건. With the subject particle its form is 것이, but it is often shortened to 게.

An example of the noun 것 with an adjective would be: 싼 게 or 싼 것이, which mean *the cheap thing*, or, more commonly, *the cheap one*. You might put these into sentences as follows:

저는 비싼 거 좋아해요.	*I like expensive things.*
그런 거 못 먹어요.	*I can't eat that (kind of) thing.*

> **LANGUAGE TIP**
> Adjectives are made from verbs, but have the ending -ㄴ or -은, if the verb ends in a consonant. 비싸요 means *it is expensive*; 비싼 is the adjective *expensive*.

5 SUPERLATIVES

You can easily make superlatives in Korean (e.g. *the most expensive*, *the most pretty*, *the best*, *the fastest*) by putting the word 제일 before the adjective / modifier:

제일 매운 음식	*the most spicy food, the spiciest food*
제일 비싼 거	*the most expensive (thing) (subject)*
제일 좋은 사람	*the best person*

 Modify the following to change the adjectives into superlatives.

a 맛있는 음식
b 시원한 물
c 싼 사전

6 LINKING WORDS

In continuous speech, Korean likes to show the way that sentences relate to each other by using linking words to begin consecutive sentences. In English we are encouraged not to begin sentences with *but*, *and*, and similar words, but Korean does this sort of thing a lot and it is good style. It makes your Korean sound natural. Here are the most common examples:

그러나	*but (whereas)*
그렇지만	*but*
그리고	*and*
그런데	*however, but*
그러니까	*therefore, that being so*
그럼	*so, therefore (more colloquial)*

> **LANGUAGE TIP**
> The three linking words that are really crucial are: 그렇지만 (*but*); 그런데 (*however, but*); and 그리고 (*and*).

7 SAYING GOODBYE

You will see from the dialogue that Korean has two ways for saying goodbye. 안녕히 가세요 is used to say *goodbye* to someone who is leaving (i.e. about to walk or go away) and 안녕히 계세요 is used to say *goodbye* to someone who is staying when the person saying it is going. Sometimes both speakers will be going, so in that case both would say 안녕히 가세요. It sounds a bit tricky at first, admittedly, but once you get used to the idea it's really quite simple. All you have to think about is who is leaving and who is staying. 안녕히 means *in peace*, so 안녕히 가세요 means *go in peace* (from 가-, *go*), and 안녕히 계세요 means *stay in peace* (made, surprisingly enough, from the honorific form of the verb 있-, *exist*, *stay*).

Getting the right word when you say *goodbye* is a good way of showing some authenticity as a Korean speaker.

 # Vocabulary builder 2

GIVING DIRECTIONS

 04.04 **Listen to the words and try to pronounce them. Try to imitate the speaker.**

이-	*this one* (noun), *this* (noun)
근처	*district, area, vicinity*
은행	*bank*
은행원	*bank clerk*
저-	*that one* (a long way away, old English *yon*)
그-	*that one* (nearer than 저)
우체국	*post office*
-에서	location particle (place in which something happens); *from*
왼	*left*
안	*not* (used to make verbs negative)
사거리	*crossroads*
오른	*right*
지점	*branch*
여기서	*from here* (abbreviation of 여기에서)
아니요	*no*
걸어서	*on foot*
분	*minute*
정도	*extent, about* (approximately)
걸리-	*takes* (time duration)

NEW EXPRESSIONS

Read the expressions that are used in the next dialogue. Note their meanings.

이 근처에 … 어디 있어요?	*Where is the . . . in this area?*
… 쪽으로 가면	*If you go in the direction of . . .*
… 쪽으로 가세요	*Go in the direction of . . .*
여기서 멀어요?	*Is it far from here?*
… 분 정도 걸려요	*It takes approximately . . . minutes*

Dialogue 2

 길 찾기 FINDING THE WAY

기업은행	*Trade Bank*
외환은행	*Exchange Bank*
창구	*window, cashier window*
돈	*money*
외환	*exchange*
종로	*Jongno (one of the main streets in Seoul, north of Han River)*
업무	*business, service*

04.05 *Mr Pak needs to find a bank to get some money changed, but he has a few problems finding what he is looking for.*

1 Where is the nearest bank? Which direction does the bank clerk tell Mr Pak to go from the post office?

박선생	실례합니다. 이 근처에 은행이 어디 있어요?
은행원 A	저 우체국에서 왼쪽으로 가면 기업은행이 있어요.
박선생	고맙습니다.
(At the counter in Trade Bank.)	
박선생	영국 돈을 한국 돈으로 좀 바꾸고 싶어요.
은행원 B	우리 은행은 외환 업무를 안해요. 외환은행으로 가세요.
박선생	외환은행이 어디 있어요?
은행원 B	종로 쪽으로 가세요. 종로 사거리에서 오른쪽으로 가면 한국 외환 은행 지점이 있어요.
박선생	여기서 멀어요?
은행원 B	아니요. 걸어서 오 분 정도 걸려요.

2 What did Mr Pak want to do at the bank? How does the bank clerk say they don't provide the service Mr Pak requires?

3 Where is the Exchange Bank located? How far away is it?

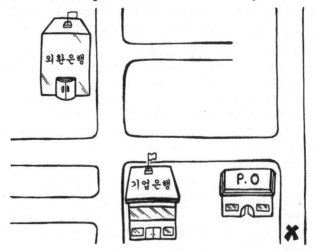

Language discovery 2

Look at the following phrases and their translations. What do you think the underlined Korean words mean?

왼쪽<u>으로</u> 가면 ...	*If you go left ...*
종로 쪽<u>으로</u> 가세요.	*Go towards Jongno.*

1 DIRECTIONS

The particle -(으)로 is used to indicate direction towards. It won't surprise you to learn that the form -으로 is added to nouns that end with consonants and -로 to nouns that end with a vowel. The meaning, then, is *towards*, *in the direction of*, and therefore it usually occurs with verbs of going and coming.

Another meaning is *into* (another shape or form), and the most important use for that is the one you meet in the dialogue, changing money from one currency into another one.

2 SAYING *FROM*, AND SAYING WHERE SOMETHING HAPPENS

The particle -에서 on the end of nouns means *from* (a place). It could be used in the following circumstances, for example:

From the bank (-에서) *to the post office* (-까지) *takes ten minutes.*

I've come from the embassy (에서): 대사관에서 왔어요.

There is another important (and slightly more complicated) use of -에서, in addition to this meaning. When you are describing where an activity is taking place, you mark the place noun with -에서. For example, if you want to say that you are doing your homework in the study, you put the particle -에서 onto the word for *study*. -에서 thus marks the place where an activity is happening. If you want to say that you are doing some drawing in your bedroom, you put the particle -에서 onto the word *bedroom*, since that is where the activity of drawing is taking place.

Note that -에서 is not used to say where something exists (that is, with 있어요 and 없어요). In those cases, you simply mark the place noun with -에. Neither is it used to say where you are going to (motion towards is marked by 에, e.g. 학교에 가요, as you have already learned). Observe the following examples carefully:

가게에 책 있어요/많아요.

There are books in the shop. / There are many books in the shop. (existence once again)

가게에서 책을 사요

I am buying a book in the shop. (the activity of buying)

식당에서 만납시다.

Let's meet in the restaurant. (the activity of meeting)

식당에 가요.

I'm going to the restaurant. (motion towards the restaurant, going or coming)

Thus, -에 is used with verbs of motion towards (coming and going), and to speak about the existence or non-existence of something in a particular place. -에서 is used to say where an activity is taking place, or to mean *from*.

Add the correct particles to complete the following sentences.

a 은행 앞 _____ 만납시다.   *Let's meet in front of the bank.*
b 대사관 _____ 가요.   *I'm going to the embassy.*
c 식당 _____ 사람이 많아요.   *There are lots of people at the restaurant.*
d 우체국_____ 왔어요.   *I've come from the post office.*

3 *IF* CLAUSES

The verb ending -(으)면 (-으면 after verb stems ending in consonants, otherwise -면) can be added to the stem of any verb to make an *if* clause. The half of the sentence that comes before the -면 is the part that is governed by the if. This is best illustrated by examples:

종로 쪽으로 가면 은행이 있어요.
If you go in the direction of Jongno, there is a bank.

선생님이 맥주 주문하면 나도 맥주 주문해요.
If you (sir) order a beer, I'll order one too.

김 선생님 찾으면 저쪽으로 가세요.
If you're looking for Mr Kim, go that way.

Translate the following sentences into English.

a 사거리에서 왼쪽으로 가면 은행이 있어요

b 이 쪽으로 가면 오 분 걸려요

4 THE OBJECT PARTICLE

The direct object of a sentence is the bit of the sentence that gets something done to it by the subject or the actor in the sentence. This is best understood by examples. In the following sentences the objects are underlined:

I want to drink a beer. (what you, the subject, want to drink, the object, a beer)

He's playing cricket. (what he, the subject, wants to play, the object, cricket)

Don't watch television all the time! (what you, the implied subject, want to watch, the object, TV)

Korean often marks the objects in its sentences by adding the object particle to the noun which is the object of the sentence. The object particle is -를 after a vowel, and -을 after a consonant. Here are examples:

책을 삽시다.
Let's buy a book.

돈을 바꾸고 싶어요.
I want to change some money.

(NB 한국돈을 영국돈으로 바꾸고 싶어요)
I want to change Korean money into British money.

맥주 두 가지 종류를 사요?
Are you going to buy two (different) kinds of beer?

Please note that the verbs 있어요 and 없어요 always take subjects, and not objects, so you will not find them in conjunction with nouns that have the object particle. This means that you will always see sentences of the form 나는 책이 있어요; you would never see a sentence like *나는 책을 있어요, since 있어요 and 없어요 always take subjects. The same thing applies to verbs of quantity like 많-, since that verb and others like it are stating how much of something exists. They are thus similar to the verbs 있어요 and 없어요.

5 SAYING YOU'RE NOT DOING SOMETHING

Now it's time to learn how to say you do not, are not doing or are not going to do something (usually by choice). In other words, it is your decision, not circumstances beyond your control, which mean you are not doing whatever it is.

You use the little word 안 immediately before the verb, like this:

나는 맥주 안 마셔요.
I'm not drinking beer / I don't drink beer (it's your choice).

재민은 시내에 안 가요.
Jaemin's not going into town (he doesn't want to, chooses not to, etc.).

Compare: 재민은 시내에 못 가요 (*he can't, he has something else on*, etc.). Sometimes, however, the word 안 simply means *not*:

음식이 안 좋아요.
The food is not good (it's the food's fault – 못 would be inappropriate).

6 VERB STEMS ENDING IN - ㅣ

We have met several verb stems that end in - ㅣ, including 마시-, 걸리-, and 기다리-. These verbs change slightly when you add the polite particle -요. The last ㅣ changes to ㅕ, to give you the polite style forms: 마셔요, 걸려요 and 기다려요.

Practice

V You will need the following words for the exercises.

잔	*cup*
읽-	*read*
표	*ticket*
병	*bottle*
다른	*another*, different modifier/adjective

1 Complete the following sentences using the words below.

사전	은행원	여기서	종류가	다른
비싼	모두	-지만	가면	이에요
우체국	그런	싫어요	드릴까요	오른
있어요	가세요	저는	오십분	사업
의	은행			

a 우리 은행은 _____ 업무를 안 해요. _____ 은행에
_____.

Our bank does not do that (kind of business). Please go to another bank.

b 이쪽으로 _____ 식당이 있어요.

If you go this way there is a restaurant.

c 실례 _____ 한영 _____ 있어요?

Excuse me, but do you have a Korean–English dictionary?

d _____ 멀어요? 걸어서 _____ 걸려요.

Is it far from here? On foot it takes 50 minutes.

e _____ 한국 외환은행 _____ _____ 이에요.

I'm a bank clerk from the Korea Exchange Bank.

f 저 _____ 에서_____ 쪽으로 가면 외환 _____ 이
있어요.

If you go right at the post office there is an exchange bank.

g 맥주 두 가지 _____ 있어요.

We have two kinds of beer.

h _____ 팔만원이에요. 영수증 _____?

Altogether it's 80,000 won. Would you like a receipt?

i 오래간만 _____. 요즘 _____ 은 어때요?

Long time no see! How's business nowadays?

j 제일 _____ 술 마시고 _____.

I want to drink the most expensive alcohol.

2 Think up appropriate Korean questions to go with the following answers.

  a 죄송하지만, 여기는 그런 사람이 없어요.

  b I'm sorry, I don't have time.

  c 아니요. 잘못 거셨어요.

  d Pleased to meet you. I've heard a lot about you!

  e 잠깐 기다리세요. 여기 있어요.

  f No, I don't like Korean food.

  g I don't particularly want to drink beer right now.

3 Here are a number of items, and the price per item. Make up a sentence which says in Korean what the cost per item is and then say what the total cost is. For example, if you see a picture of six glasses, and the cost per glass is 500 won, you would write something like 한 잔에 오 백원 씩이에요. 그러니까 모두 삼천원이에요.

4 The following sentences have no particles in them. Put them in!

  a 여기_____ 왼쪽_____ 가면 상업 은행 지점_____ 있어요.

  b 시간_____ 있으면 열시_____ 호텔 앞_____ 만납시다.

  c 중국 돈_____ 영국 돈_____ 좀 바꾸고 싶어요.

  d 우리 은행_____ 외환 업무_____ 안 해요.

  e 저_____ 매운 음식_____ 못 먹어요. 갈비_____ 먹고 싶어요.

  f 여기_____ 그런 사람_____ 없어요.

  g 그런 것_____ 못 마시면, 물_____ 마십시다.

h 영한사전 두 가지 종류_____ 있어요.
i 한 권_____ 이만원_____, 그러니까 모두 삼만원이에요.

5 Practise counting the following things out loud.

    a 3 books, 8 books, 22 books
    b 1 day, 3 days, 67 days
    c 1 person, 7 people, 34 people
    d 3 octopus, 9 octopus, 14 octopus
    e 2 bottles, 10 bottles
    f 9 dogs, 1 dog (dog = 개)
    g 1,000 won, 10,000 won

6 Make up five Korean sentences based around the following verbs. Each of your sentences should put the verb in the negative, with the word 안.

    a 주문하-
    b 걸리-
    c 드세요
    d 기다리-
    e 읽-

    Which of your sentences would still make sense if you replaced 안 with 못? What would be the difference in meaning?

7 Make up a dialogue between a shopkeeper and a child going shopping. Here is the shopping list (NB *milk* = 우유; *bottle* = 병).

SHOPPING LIST

2 bottles milk	Meat
Bread	10 beers
Kimch'i	Apples

❓ Test yourself

1 **In the following English sentences, which nouns are direct objects and would thus be marked with -를/을 if they were to be translated into Korean? Note that some sentences may have more than one object, and some may not have any.**

   a I want to watch a film tonight.
   b What are you going to do when you see him?
   c How many cars does your family have?
   d He just said a bad word.
   e Can I eat some bread? No, but there are some crackers.

2 **Translate the following sentences into Korean.**

   a Excuse me, is there a restaurant in this area?
   b I can't eat naengmyon. I can't eat kalbi either.
   c How much is it? One plate is 2,000 won, so it's 6,000 won altogether.
   d Go left here. If you go five minutes, you'll see (= there is) Jongno crossroads. Go left. The bank is on your right.
   e How much is the cheapest one?
   f It takes about 10 minutes on foot.
   g There's no branch of the Korea Exchange Bank in this area.
   h I want to change some money. I have about 50,000 won.
   i In Korea there are 10 kinds of kimchi. In England there are none.
   j Would you like a Korean language dictionary?
   k What type would you like?
   l Please give me the cheapest.
   m Is Mr Kim a bad man?
   n You're going to the post office? OK, goodbye!

SELF CHECK

I CAN...

- ...ask and say how much something is.
- ...buy items in a shop.
- ...say goodbye.
- ...use both pure and Sino-Korean number systems with appropriate counters.
- ...use negation.
- ...make if clauses.
- ...ask the way somewhere.
- ...describe where something is and where some activity takes place.

5 동대문 시장 가는 버스 있어요? / 이 사과가 싱싱해 보이지 않네요!

Is there a bus going to Dongdaemun market? / This apple doesn't look too good!

In this unit you will learn how to:

▶ *catch buses in Korea and make sure you have got to the right place.*
▶ *shop for food at the market.*
▶ *express surprise or exclamation.*
▶ *make comparisons.*
▶ *join two sentences together to make one.*

CEFR: *Can get simple information about travel, public transport and give directions (A2); can use simple descriptive language to make brief statements about and compare objects (A2); can cope with less routine situations in shops (B1); can make a complaint (B1).*

🔲 Markets

전통 시장 (*traditional markets*) are one of the most visited 관광지 (*tourist attractions*) in Korea. Seoul has several famous and fascinating 시장 (*markets*), in particular 동대문 (*Dongdaemun*) and 남대문 (*Namdaemun*) are its two biggest and most popular. 남대문 is more compact, perhaps more pleasant to look around and has more tourists. It is a well-established market boasting 600 years of history and over 1,700 products. 동대문 sprawls right on all the way down 청계천 (*Cheonggyecheon, Cheonggye stream*), and is the centre of Korea's wholesale and retail fashion industries. It depends a bit on what you want to buy as to which is best, but both are well worth a visit! Both are also night markets so the best time to go is between one and six in the morning.

As with any 시장, there is plenty of bargaining to be done at Korean markets. The best advice is to go shopping with a Korean or someone who has been in Korea a long time and who knows how to get a good deal. Some shopkeepers already give the lowest 가격 (*price*), and you must be aware that it is not fair to expect such dealers to cut their prices. Others will give quite an inflated price when they see you are a 외국인 (*foreigner*) or 관광객 (*tourist*). In general, however, Korea is a much safer place for not getting ripped off than perhaps some other Asian countries. As a rule, the places where there are fewer foreigners are more likely to offer the best deals (and less likely to be accessible to non-Korean speakers!).

 What are the two famous markets in South Korea? Say their names in Korean.

Vocabulary builder 1

GETTING THE BUS

 05.01 Listen to the words and try to pronounce them. Try to imitate the speaker.

가는	*going to, bound for*
버스	*bus*
-아니라서	*since it is not / since I am not*
다른	*another, different*
-에게	*to*
정류장	*bus stop*
서-	*stop (stem), stand*
번	*number*
타-	*take (transport), travel on (transport)*
-보다	*more than*
많다	*is many / is a lot (ㅎ is not pronounced; polite style: 많아요)*
재미있-	*is interesting, is fun*
정말	*really*
바로	*directly*
길	*road, route*
건너편	*opposite side*
요금	*fee, fare*

빨리	*quickly*
저기	*over there, over yonder*
거기	*over there (nearer than 저기)*
오-	*come (stem) (polite style: 와요)*
비가 오-	*rains, is raining (polite style: 비가 와요)*

NEW EXPRESSIONS

… 가는 버스 있어요?	*Is there a bus going to . . . ?*
(잘) 모르겠어요.	*I don't know (at all).*
안 파는 게 없어요.	*There's nothing which is not sold. (You can buy everything.)*
뭐가 있느냐고요?	*You're asking what there is? (You mean you don't know?) (based on 있-, there is, exists)*
제 생각에는	*in my opinion*

Dialogue 1

동대문 시장 가는 버스 있어요? IS THERE A BUS GOING TO DONGDAEMUN MARKET?

파는 게	*item for sale, items sold*
안 파는 게	*something which is not sold, not available*
물건	*goods*
원숭이	*monkey*
팔아요	*sell (polite style form, stem is irregular)*
촌사람	*country bumpkin, yokel*
필요없-	*is not necessary, is not needed, has no need of*
필요있-	*is necessary, is needed*

Mr Kim is a stranger in Seoul who wants to find his way to Dongdaemun market. He ends up being persuaded to go to Namdaemun market instead.

1 Mr Lee is unable to help Mr Kim find his way. What is the reason he gives for this and how does he phrase it in Korean?

김선생	실례지만 여기 동대문 시장 가는 버스가 있어요?
이선생	저도 서울 사람이 아니라서 잘 모르겠어요.

(To Mrs O, another passer-by.)

김선생	이 정류장에 동대문 시장 가는 버스가 서요?
오선생	아니요. 이 정류장에는 동대문 시장 가는 버스가 없어요. 이십 번 버스를 타면 남대문 시장에 가요.
김선생	남대문 시장이요? 남대문 시장에는 뭐가 있어요?
오선생	뭐가 있느냐고요? 남대문 시장에는 안 파는 게 없어요.
김선생	동대문 시장보다 물건이 더 많아요?
오선생	제 생각에는, 남대문 시장이 동대문 시장보다 물건도 더 많고 재미 있어요. 그렇지만 남대문 시장에서 원숭이는 안 팔아요. 동대문 시장에서는 팔지만 …
김선생	정말이에요? 그런데 저는 원숭이는 필요 없어요.
오선생	그럼 이십번 버스를 타세요.
김선생	어디서 타요?
오선생	바로 길 건너편 정류장에서 타세요.
김선생	버스 요금이 얼마예요?
오선생	정말 촌사람이시군요! 천백원이에요.
김선생	고맙습니다.
오선생	빨리 가세요. 저기 버스가 와요.

2 To which market does the number 20 bus go? How does Mrs O say, If you take the number 20 bus . . . ?

3 What is the choice like at Namdaemun? Is it more interesting?

4 What can't you get at Namdaemun?

5 Where should you catch the bus? How much is the bus fare?

Language discovery 1

 The phrase 서울 사람이 아니라서, as used in the dialogue, means since I'm not from Seoul. Study the following additional examples and identify the word that means since.

이 책은 사전이 아니라서 ⋯	*Since this book isn't a dictionary . . .*
이것은 사과라서 ⋯	*Since this is a book . . .*
이 은행은 외환은행이라서 ⋯	*Since this bank is an Exchange Bank . . .*

1 -이라서, -아니라서

아니라서 from the phrase 서울 사람이 아니라서 is related to the negative copula 아니에요 and you will see that both forms include the part 아니-. 아니라서 is a different form of 아니에요, and it means *since (it) is not a (noun)*. The -라서 bit means *because* or *since*. The sentence in the dialogue therefore means *since I am not a Seoul person . . . , since I'm not from Seoul . . .*

To say the opposite of this, that is, *since something is something else*, you use the form -이라서 instead of 아니라서. Thus, you could say *since I'm a Korean* with the words: 한국 사람이라서 . . .

Here are examples of both constructions, and you should also study the example in the dialogue:

한국 사람이 아니라서 한국말 잘 못해요.
Since I'm not a Korean I can't speak Korean very well.

영국 사람이라서 술 잘 마셔요.
Since I'm an English person I'm a good drinker.

2 PARTICLE ORDER

You've now learned several important particles: the subject particle -이/가 and the topic particle -는/은, which are used to indicate either the subject of your sentence, or what it is you're talking about. The object particle -를/을 is used to indicate the object of the sentence (the thing that gets something done to it). All of these particles are optional, though you'll sound more authentic if you can use them.

You will have noticed that sometimes Korean allows you to put more than one particle onto the end of a word, as in the example 남대문 시장에는 뭐가 있어요? This makes a topic out of the phrase at Namdaemun market. You have to be careful that the particles are put into the correct order, however. For example, you can say 한국에도 있어요 (*they have it* *in Korea, too*), but *한국도에 있어요 is wrong. You can learn the correct orders by observing the example sentences in this course. There are some rules, however, which you will find useful.

Many particles cannot occur together because their meanings would be contradictory (the same noun cannot be both subject and object, for example), so it is best to stick to only using combinations that you have seen.

However, the particles -도 and -은/는 (*too, also* and topic) can be added after most other particles (but not the subject or object particles), both giving extra emphasis to the noun and particle to which they are added. Possible examples are -에서는, -에서도 and so on. You might like to study the following two examples which illustrate the use of combined particles:

김 선생님은 한국에도 일본에도 가요.
Mr Kim goes both to Korea and to Japan.

서울에는 식당 많아요.
In Seoul (topic) *there are many restaurants.*

Put the particles in the correct order to complete the following sentences.

a 학교_____ (도/에) 갑시다.
   Let's go to the school too.
b 영국_____ (에서/는) 차 마셔요.
   In England they drink tea.
c 서울_____ (에/는) 시장이 많아요.
   In Seoul there are a lot of markets.

3 CHECKING ON SOMETHING

The particle -요 (or -이요 after consonants) can be added to any noun to check what has been said, to clarify something or to show surprise. In the dialogue one speaker asks which bus goes to Namdaemun market, and the other says 남대문 시장이요? This translates as *Namdaemun market? You said Namdaemun market, right? You want Namdaemun market?* or something similar. If a shopkeeper told you that an apple cost 10,000 won (a ridiculously high price), you might say 만원이요? (*10,000 won? You must be joking!*). Depending on the intonation it can express surprise or incredulity or can simply be used to check whether what you heard was correct.

4 COMPARING THINGS

You can compare one thing with another quite simply in Korean. Let's take an example sentence. To say *English beer is better than Korean beer*, the pattern is as follows (first with the English words to show how the construction works, then with Korean):

English beer (subject or topic) *Korean beer* -보다 *is more good*.
영국 맥주는 한국 맥주보다 더 좋아요.

You can even omit the word 더 if you want to. Here is another example in which something is claimed to be more tasty (tastier) than something else:

제 생각에는 한국 음식이 중국 음식보다 (더) 맛이 있어요.
In my opinion, Korean food is tastier than Chinese food.

The particle -보다 is added to the second noun of two that you want to compare. **A B**-보다 커요, *A is taller than B*.

 Translate the following sentences into Korean using the particle -보다.

a The market is more interesting than school.
b Kalbi is more expensive than bulgogi.

5 MANY AND FEW, BIG AND SMALL

Korean uses the word 많아요 to say that *there are many of something*. It uses another word 크- to say that *something is big* (polite style 커요). The stem for the verb 많아요 is 많-. The ㅎ is still there in Korean writing in the polite form 많아요, but is silent in pronunciation.

To say *something is small* you use the verb 작-, polite form 작아요; to say *there is or are few of something* use the verb 적-, polite form 적어요. Here are some examples:

영국에는 영국 사람이 많아요.
In England there are many English people.

영국에는 한국 사람이 적어요.
In England there are few Koreans.

이 책은 크고 저 책은 작아요.
This book is big and that one is small.

6 JOINING SENTENCES TOGETHER

You have learned the word 그리고 which can be used to begin a second sentence with the meaning *and . . .* Take the example sentences:

한국 음식 좋아요. 그리고 일본 음식도 좋아요.
Korean food is good. And Japanese food is good too.

These two sentences can be joined into one by taking the verb stem of the first (좋- from 좋아요), and adding the ending -고 to it:

한국 음식 좋고 일본 음식도 좋아요.

NB ㅎ + ㄱ = ㅋ, therefore 좋고 is pronounced (조코).

This verb ending -고 is common in Korean, and it can be used with all verbs. Here is another example:

김 선생님은 책을 읽고 장 선생님은 텔레비 봐요.
Mr Kim reads books and Mr Chang watches TV.

> **LANGUAGE TIP**
> The particle -고 is one of the most useful and simple ways of joining two sentences together.

 Combine each of the following pairs of sentences into one sentence using the particle -고 instead of 그리고.

a 오늘은 남대문 가요. 그리고 내일은 동대문 가요.
b 20번 버스를 타요. 그리고 은행 앞에서 내려요.
c 점심에는 비빔밥을 먹어요. 그리고 보리차를 마셔요.

7 EXCLAMATIONS

The verb ending -군요 can be added to verb stems in order to express surprise or mild exclamation. Look at the example in the dialogue, where you will find it with the copula. It is particularly common with the copula, often in the honorific form -이시군요, and it is this form that you have met:

김 선생님이시군요! 반갑습니다
Ah, so you're Mr Kim (surprise, surprise!)! Pleased to meet you!

You do not need to use this form yourself, but you need to be able to recognize it if a Korean uses it. Here is an example of its use with the normal (non-honorific) copula:

김 선생님 아들이군요! 지금 어디 가요?
So you're Mr Kim's son! Where are you going now?

Vocabulary builder 2

 05.03 **Listen to the words and try to pronounce them. Try to imitate the speaker.**

사과	apple
상자	box
-에	each, per
너무	too (much)
깎아주-	cut the price (for someone's benefit)
가져가-	take
그래도	however, nevertheless, but still
데	place
가보-	go and see, visit (a place)
아침	morning
-부터	from
재수	luck
싱싱하-	is fresh
어떤	certain, some (as a question word = which?)
-나	approximately, about (derived from the meaning or you have learned)
-만	only
옆	next door
내-	pay

NEW EXPRESSIONS

Read the expressions that are used in the next dialogue. Note their meanings.

좀 깎아주세요.	Please cut the price a bit for me.
(오늘 아침부터) 재수 없네.	I've had no luck (from the morning). I'm unlucky.
싱싱해 보이지 않네요.	They don't look fresh.
썩었어요.	It's gone bad, it's gone off.
깎아드릴게요.	I'll cut the price for you.
뭐라고요?	What did you say?

 Dialogue 2

이 사과가 싱싱해 보이지 않네요! **THIS APPLE DOESN'T LOOK TOO GOOD!**

05.04 A Korean girl, Minja, goes to the market to buy some boxes of apples. She has some trouble, but eventually manages to strike a good deal.

1 How much are the boxes of apples at the first grocer? What expression is used to describe the price per box?

민자	여기 사과 얼마예요?
점원 A	한 상자에 삼만 원이에요.
민자	너무 비싸네요. 좀 깎아주세요.
점원 A	그럼 한 상자에 이만 팔천 원에 가져 가세요.
민자	그래도 비싸요.
점원 A	그럼 다른 데 가보세요. *(to himself)* 오늘 아침부터 재수없네!

(Minja goes to another grocer.)

민자	이 사과가 싱싱해 보이지 않네요. 어떤 건 좀 썩었어요.
점원 B	그래요? 그럼 좀 깎아드릴게요.
민자	얼마나요?
점원 B	한 상자에 삼만 천 원만 주세요.
민자	뭐라고요?! 옆 가게보다 더 비싸네요.
점원 B	좋아요. 그럼 이만 칠천 원만 주세요.
민자	좀 더 깎아주세요.
점원 B	좋아요. 한 상자에 이만 오천 원 내세요.
민자	고맙습니다. 세 상자 주세요.

2 What's wrong with the apples at the second grocer?

3 How much does Minja end up paying for each box of apples? How many boxes does she buy?

Language discovery 2

 Look at the following sentences and their translations. What do you think the particle for *only* is?

한 상자에 삼만 천원만 주세요. *Give me only 31,000 won per box.*
그럼 이만 칠천 원만 주세요. *Then only give me 27,000 won.*

1 ONLY

The particle -만 means *only*, so that 삼만원만 means *only 30,000 won*, and 책만 주세요 means *please give me the book only* or *please just give me the book*. 나만 왔어요 means *only I have come*. -만 can be added to any noun in this way.

2 MORE SURPRISES

The verb ending -네요 can be added to any verb stem, and it indicates surprise, although usually of a milder form than -군요. This is perhaps a more useful pattern to learn to use for yourself. Look carefully at the examples from the dialogues:

비가 오네요
Oh no, it's raining!

애기가 책을 읽네요
Wow, the baby is reading a book!

그럼, 그 사람은 한국 사람이네요
So he's the Korean person, then! Or, so that person is a Korean, then!
(depending on the intonation)

3 MONTHS OF THE YEAR

The months of the year in Korean are as follows (note carefully June and October, in which the number loses the last letter).

 05.05 **Listen to the months and try to pronounce them. Try to imitate the speaker.**

일월	*January*	칠월	*July*
이월	*February*	팔월	*August*
삼월	*March*	구월	*September*
사월	*April*	시월	*October*
오월	*May*	십일월	*November*
유월	*June*	십이월	*December*

4 *TO* AND *FROM* (WITH PEOPLE)

When you want to say *to* a person (write *to* a person, speak *to* a person, give *to* a person), you use the particle -한테 or the particle -에게. The particle -께 can be used when the person is honorific. For example:

어머니에게/께 편지 써요.
I'm writing a letter to Mum.

재민한테 주고 싶어요.
I want to give it to Jaemin.

아버지에게/께 이야기해요.
I'm speaking to Father.

친구한테 보내요.
I'm sending it to a friend.

From a person is said with the particle -한테서 or -에게서:

친구한테서 돈 받아요.
I receive money from my friend.

월요일날에 어머니에게서 편지 받아요.
I receive a letter from my mum on Mondays.

아버지한테서 전화 왔어요.
I got a phone call from Dad (a call came).

 Complete the Korean translations of the sentences using the correct particle for *to* or *from*. If there is more than one possibility, give both.

a I received a text from my younger sister.
여동생 _____ 문자 받았어요.

b I give a present to my teacher.
선생님 _____ 선물 드려요.

c I receive a present from my teacher.
선생님 _____ 선물 받아요.

d I made a call to my friend.
친구 _____ 전화 했어요.

ⓘ Practice

1 Read through the dialogue again and answer the following questions in Korean. Make sure to use full sentences in your answers.

김선생	이 정류장에 동대문 시장 가는 버스가 서요?
오선생	아니요. 이 정류장에는 동대문 시장 가는 버스가 없어요. 이십 번 버스를 타면 남대문 시장에 가요.
김선생	남대문 시장이요? 남대문 시장에는 뭐가 있어요?
오선생	뭐가 있느냐고요? 남대문 시장에는 안 파는 게 없어요.
김선생	동대문 시장보다 물건이 더 많아요?
오선생	제 생각에는, 남대문 시장이 동대문 시장보다 물건도 더 많고 재미 있어요. 그렇지만 남대문 시장에서 원숭이는 안 팔아요. 동대문 시장에서는 팔지만 …
김선생	정말이에요? 그런데 저는 원숭이는 필요 없어요.
오선생	그럼 이십번 버스를 타세요.
김선생	어디서 타요?
오선생	바로 길 건너편 정류장에서 타세요.
김선생	고맙습니다.

a 동대문 시장이 남대문 시장보다 더 재미있어요?
b 동대문 시장에서 뭘 안 팔아요?
c 이십 번 버스를 타면 어디 가요?
d 남대문 시장에는 물건이 많아요?
e 이십 번 버스를 어디서 타요?

2 Make up answers or appropriate responses to the following questions.

a 동대문 시장에 가고 싶어요. 같이 가요
b 오늘 아침에 뭘 하세요?
c 이 과일이 안 싱싱해요
d 버스 요금이 얼마예요?
e 한국 좋아해요? 한국말 재미있어요?

74

3 Imagine that you suddenly recognize or are surprised by seeing the following people or things. This exercise is intended to practise the -군요 form with the copula. Don't forget to use the honorific form of the copula when appropriate.

  a Mr Kim's dog
  b Mr O's wife
  c a Japanese book
  d the Korea Exchange Bank
  e your friend, Hyongjun
  f the Chinese teacher

4 Make up sentences comparing the following sets of information. For the first set you would make up a sentence to say that Korean food is more tasty than Japanese food.

a Korean food	Japanese food	tasty
b Here	there	more of them
c Train	bus	faster (빨라요)
d Mr Kim	Mr Pak	more luck
e Namdaemun	Dongdaemun	more expensive

5 Which of the following particle sequences are acceptable and which are not?

  a 시간에는 (시간 = time)
  b 음식을은
  c 어머니에게도
  d 길에서는
  e 버스에가
  f 국이를 (국 = soup)
  g 아침부터를
  h 밤부터는

6 Translate the following sentences and put them into the -네요 mild surprise form.

  a My, these dictionaries are expensive!
  b Taegyu is coming!
  c What are you doing? (surprise!)
  d This newspaper's really interesting.

7 Write a dialogue between a Korean in Paris who wants to get a bus to the Louvre and a Japanese, who the Korean mistakenly thinks is a Korean. Fortunately, the Japanese can also speak Korean so, after explaining that he is Japanese, not Korean, he tells him that the Louvre is nearby (not far). He doesn't need to take a bus and it only takes seven minutes to walk.

8 어느 버스가 학교에 가는 버스에요? 십팔번 버스가 어디 가요?

? Test yourself

1 Translate the following sentences into English.

a 여기 비싸네요. 옆 가게에 가봅시다.

b 여기서 팔지만 다른 데에 가면 더 싸요.

c 서울 시내에 가는 버스를 어디서 타요?

d 오늘 아침부터 재수없네요!

e 일본은 한국보다 더 비싸요. 그래도 한국도 비싸요.

f 제 생각보다 한국에 영국 사람이 많아요.

g 깎아드릴게요. 한 상자에 만 삼천원에 가져 가세요.

h 주문하시겠어요?

i 여기가 한국 아니라서 김치를 파는 데 적어요.

j 원숭이 있느냐구요? 동대문 시장에 가보세요.

2 Join the following pairs of sentences using the -고 clause ending.

a 이 사람이 박 선생님이에요. 저 사람이 강 선생님이에요.

b 어머니는 책 읽어요. 아버지는 텔레비를 봐요.

c 고기 못 먹어요. 사과도 못 먹어요.

d 십일 번 버스가 남대문 시장에 가요. 이십 번 버스는 동대문 시장에 가요.

e 상준도 버스 타요. 명택도 버스타요.

SELF CHECK

I CAN...

- ...ask if a bus goes to my desired destination.
- ...shop for food at the market and ask for discounts.
- ...comment on items, for example say something is expensive or cheap.
- ...make comparisons using the word -보다.
- ...join two sentences to make one using the particle -고.
- ...count the months.

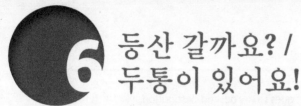

6

등산 갈까요? /
두통이 있어요!

*Shall we go mountain climbing? /
I've got a headache!*

In this unit you will learn how to:
▶ *talk about short-term plans.*
▶ *suggest and discuss activities.*
▶ *say that you are ill and get sympathy.*
▶ *use the probable future tense (what you expect to do or what is
most probable).*
▶ *make suggestions and tell others what you are thinking
of doing.*

CEFR: *Can make and respond to suggestions (A2); can briefly give reasons
and explanations for opinions and plans, and actions. (B1); can present
clear, detailed descriptions on a wide range of subjects related to a field
of interest (e.g. describe an illness or health condition in detail) (B2).*

Hobbies and pastimes

운동 (*sports*) are a very popular 취미 (*pastime*) in Korea. In addition to
the traditional martial arts 태권도 (*taekwondo*) and 씨름 (*folk wrestling*),
all modern sports are widely enjoyed. The most popular spectator sports
are the American imports: 야구 (*baseball*) and 농구 (*basketball*). 축구
(*football*) is also hugely popular and international 축구 경기 (*football
games*) are passionately supported. Korea has good facilities for 골프
(*golf*), with plentiful courses and driving ranges. The cold winters and
mountains make Korea a good choice for 스키 (*skiing*), too, with several
resorts located within a short drive of the capital 서울 (*Seoul*).

The mountains are also popular destinations for 등산 (*mountain
climbing*). On a sunny 주말 (*weekend*) in 봄 (*spring*) or 가을 (*autumn*),
expect popular mountain climbing destinations to be extremely busy!
Many choose to climb the mountains every morning to collect water from
the 약수터 (*mineral springs*); others may climb the mountains to visit 절
(*temples*) or simply to do a bit of exercise.

Other 취미 include the 노래방 (*karaoke*), and Koreans also love to
drink – they sometimes even break into song as they do so! As for games,

Koreans enjoy 고스톱 (*go-stop*), a game played with small cards with flower designs, originally from Japan, 바둑 (*baduk*), which is rather like draughts, and 장기 (*janggi*), which is similar to chess. In recent years, the popularity of 컴퓨터 게임 (*computer games*) and 인터넷 게임 (*internet games*) has also soared unbelievably.

Which sports are popular in Korea, and what are their Korean names?

Vocabulary builder 1

MAKING PLANS

 06.01 **Listen to the words and try to pronounce them. Try to imitate the speaker.**

날씨	*weather*
내일	*tomorrow*
별일	*a special matter, something particular*
등산	*mountain climbing*
쇼핑(하-)	*shopping (do / go shopping)*
-기로 했어요	*decided to*
일요일 (일요일날)	*Sunday (Sunday, longer form)*
언제	*when*
산	*mountain*
많지 않아서	*since there aren't many*
했어요	*did (past tense form of 하- do)*
어느	*which one*
편하-	*is comfortable, is convenient*
입구	*entrance*

NEW EXPRESSIONS

Read the expressions that are used in the next dialogue. Note their meanings.

내일 뭐 할 거예요?	*What are you going to do tomorrow?*
별일 없으면 …	*If you don't have anything special on . . .*
등산이나 갈까요?	*Shall we go mountain climbing or something?*
불국사에 갈까 해요.	*I'm thinking about going to Bulguksa.*
안 되겠네요.	*It won't be any good, then (unfortunately).*
아마 괜찮을 거예요.	*It will probably turn out (be) OK.*
입구에서 만날까요?	*Shall we meet by the entrance?*

Dialogue 1

등산 갈까요? SHALL WE GO MOUNTAIN CLIMBING?

대학	university
동창	colleague (fellow student in this case)
불국사	Bulguksa (Korean Buddhist temple, the largest in Korea)
도봉산	Tobongsan (mountain in Seoul)

06.02 *Mr Kim wants to take Tony mountain climbing, but with Tony's busy schedule they have some difficulty finding a convenient date.*

1 How does Tony say *I have decided to go shopping*? Where is he going to go?

김선생	요즘 날씨가 아주 좋아요.
토니	네. 한국은 영국보다 날씨가 좋아요.
김선생	내일 뭐 할 거예요? 별일 없으면 등산이나 갈까요?
토니	가고 싶지만 내일은 집사람하고 동대문 시장에서 쇼핑하기로 했어요.
김선생	그럼 다음 일요일은 어때요?
토니	다음 일요일에는 대학 동창들하고 불국사에 갈까 해요.
김선생	그럼 다음 일요일도 안 되겠네요. 언제가 좋을까요?
토니	그 다음 일요일은 아마 괜찮을 거예요.
김선생	좋아요. 그럼 그 다음 일요일에 갑시다.
토니	저도 등산을 좋아해요. 그런데 영국에는 산이 많지 않아서 등산을 많이 못 했어요. 그런데 어느 산에 갈까요?
김선생	도봉산이 편할 거예요.
토니	그럼 도봉산 입구에서 만날까요?

2 What is Tony considering doing next Sunday? How does he say *I'm thinking about going*?

3 When do Mr Kim and Tony eventually decide to go mountain climbing?

4 What does Tony think of mountain climbing?

Language discovery 1

 Look at the following sentences and their translations. What verb ending is used to indicate the future tense in Korean?

내일 뭐 할 거예요?
What will you do tomorrow?

그 다음 일요일은 아마 괜찮을 거예요.
The following Sunday will probably be OK.

도봉산이 편할 거예요.
Tobongsan will be convenient.

1 PROBABLE FUTURE

The most common way to give a sentence a future meaning in Korean is to add -(으)ㄹ 거예요 to the stem of the main verb. As you would expect, you add -ㄹ거예요 if the stem ends in a vowel, and -을 거예요 if the stem ends in a consonant. Thus 만나- becomes 만날 거예요 (*I will meet*), and 앉- becomes 앉을 거예요 (*I will sit*).

We have called the form the probable future, because there are other ways of expressing the future tense in Korean – there is a definite future, for example, which you might use if there is scarcely any doubt that you will do something, or if you want to stress your intention to do it. The probable future is the most common, and is used in most everyday situations when you want to say that you are going to do something:

내일 중국 대사관에 갈 거예요.
I will (probably) go to the Chinese embassy tomorrow.

내년에 차를 살 거예요.
I'm going to buy a car next year. (내년, *next year*)

The same form has another meaning, in addition to the future. It can also mean something like is probably (verb)*ing*.

비가 올 거예요.
It is probably raining.

> **LANGUAGE TIP**
> Among the several different ways of expressing the future tense in Korean, the -(으)ㄹ 거예요 form is one of the simplest and most common – so make sure you master it.

2 MAKING DECISIONS

To say that you have decided to do something, simply add -기로 했어요 onto the verb stem of the verb you have decided to do. To say that you have decided to eat with Mr Kim, for example, you would say: 김 선생님하고 점심을 먹기로 했어요:

대학 동창하고 등산하기로 했어요.
I've decided to go mountain climbing with my friend(s) from university.

내일 친구를 만나기로 했어요.
I've decided to meet my friend tomorrow.

 Change the following sentences from the future tense into statements saying *I've decided to* ... Follow the example.

Example: 아리랑 식당에서 점심 먹을 거예요 → 아리랑 식당에서 점심 먹기로 했어요

a 동창하고 학교 갈 거예요
b 여기에 앉을 거예요
c 신문 읽을 거예요

3 THINKING ABOUT IT

Sometimes when you still haven't made definite plans, you want to say that you are thinking about doing something. You might say, for example, *I am thinking about going away for the weekend*. Korean provides an easy way of allowing you to do this. Simply add the ending -ㄹ까 해요 to a verb stem ending in a vowel, or -을까 해요 to a verb stem ending in a consonant. That's all there is to it. To take one example, suppose you were thinking of going to 설악산 on Sunday, you simply say, 일요일에 설악산에 갈까 해요. Can you work out the meaning of the following example? 점심에 비빔밥을 먹을까 해요.

 Translate the following sentences into Korean.

a I'm thinking about going to the embassy.
b I'm thinking about drinking soju.

4 SHALL WE?

To say to someone *shall we do something or other?*, you add a verb ending very like the one you have just learned. Add -ㄹ까요? to a verb stem ending in a vowel, and -을까요? to a verb stem ending in a consonant. To say to someone *shall we sit here?* you would therefore say 여기 앉을까요?, and to say *shall we have a beer?* you would say 맥주 마실까요?

Translate the following sentences into English.

a 농구할까요?
b 갈비 먹을까요?
c 친구에게 편지 보낼까요?

5 DAYS OF THE WEEK

The following are the days of the week in Korean.

06.03 **Listen to the days of the week and try to pronounce them. Try to imitate the speaker.**

월요일	*Monday*	금요일	*Friday*
화요일	*Tuesday*	토요일	*Saturday*
수요일	*Wednesday*	일요일	*Sunday*
목요일	*Thursday*		

> **TIME**
> The months use one of the normal numbering systems, but the days of the week have their own terms.

Vocabulary builder 2

EXPLAINING YOUR SYMPTOMS

06.04 **Listen to the words and try to pronounce them. Try to imitate the speaker.**

또	*again; moreover, also, furthermore*	더워서	*because it is hot*
항상	*always*	같-	*seems like*
아프-	*hurts (stem) (polite style:* 아파요*)*	배	*stomach*
		약	*medicine*
두통	*headache*	약국	*chemist's, drugstore*
머리	*head*	힘	*strength, energy*
걱정	*worry, concern*	다리	*leg*
걱정하-	*be worried*	전신	*the whole body*
		아픈	*hurting, painful* (adjective)

NEW EXPRESSIONS

Read the expressions that are used in the next dialogue. Note their meanings.

글쎄요	*I dunno, I'm not sure, Who knows?*
저는 몸이 좀 좋지 않아요.	*I don't feel very well.*
그렇지 않아요	*of course not*
꾀병을 부리지요!	*You're making it up!* (feigning an illness)
걱정하지 마세요!	*Don't worry!* (colloquial form:* 걱정 마세요*)*
그럴 거예요	*It will probably be like that.*

아닌 것 같아요	I don't think so; it doesn't seem like it
전신이 다 아프군요!	Your whole body must be hurting!
시끄러워요!	Shut up!, Be quiet! (lit: it's noisy)
놀리지 마세요	don't joke, don't kid me, don't tease
약을 먹어야겠어요.	I'll have to take some medicine.

Dialogue 2

두통이 있어요! **I'VE GOT A HEADACHE!**

게다가	on top of that	농담	joke (noun)
사실	fact (the fact is …)	농담하-	jokes (verb)

06.05 *Yongtae is sick – everything seems to be hurting – and his friend Jaehoon isn't very sympathetic. When Yongtae wants his friend Jaehoon to get him some medicine, Jaehoon has another suggestion. But Yongtae is not impressed.*

1 **How is Yongtae feeling? What does he say that has a similar meaning to 몸이 안 좋아요?**

> 재훈 저 시내에 가는데 같이 갈까요?
> 용태 글쎄요 . . . 저는 몸이 좀 좋지 않아요.
> 재훈 또 몸이 좋지 않아요? 용태씨는 항상 꾀병을 부리지요!
> 용태 아니요. 그렇지 않아요. 오늘은 정말 아파요.
> 재훈 오늘은 어디가 아파요?
> 용태 두통이 있어요. 머리가 좀 아파요.
> 재훈 그게 다예요? 걱정하지 마세요. 아마 날씨가 더워서 그럴 거예요.
> 용태 아닌 것 같아요. 배도 아파요.
> 재훈 많이 아파요?
> 용태 그래요. 많이 아파요.
> 재훈 그럼 약을 사러 약국에 갑시다.
> 용태 저는 못 가요. 힘이 없어요. 게다가 다리도 좀 아파요.
> 재훈 다리도요? 전신이 다 아프군요. 안 아픈 데가 있어요?
> 용태 시끄러워요! 놀리지 마세요. 약을 먹어야겠어요.
> 재훈 여기 만병통치약 술이 있어요! 사실 약보다 술이 더 좋아요.
> 용태 농담하지 마세요. 술 못 마셔요. 정말 병원에 가야겠어요.

2 **What does Yongtae think he should do? How does he say *I will have to go*?**

3 **What is the cure-all suggested by Jaehoon?**

Language discovery 2

 Look at the following sentences and their translations. Can you work out how to say you will have to do something in Korean?

약을 먹어야겠어요.	*I'll have to take some medicine.*
병원에 가야겠어요.	*I'll have to go to the hospital.*

1 WHAT YOU WILL HAVE TO DO

To form the construction to say that you will have to do something, take off the -요 of the polite style form of the verb and add -야겠어요. Take the verb 먹- as an example. The polite style is 먹어요, so taking off the -요 and adding the -야겠어요 ending, we have 먹어야겠어요. This can then be used in a sentence: 지금 먹어야겠어요 (*I am going to have to eat now (I'm obliged to))*.

2 VERB STEMS ENDING IN ㅣ

You have now seen a few verbs whose stems end in ㅣ, for example: 움직이- (*move*), 놀리- (*tease*), 마시- (*drink*), 기다리- (*wait*) and 걸리- (*lasts, takes (time)*). All these verbs change the last ㅣ to ㅕ and add 요 in order to form the present polite style. This gives the polite style forms 움직여요, 놀려요, 마셔요, 기다려요, 걸려요.

 Give the present polite form of the following verbs. The verb stems are given.

a 가르치-

b 그리-

c 피-

3 TO HURT

The verb stem 아프- (*hurt*) belongs to another group of verbs all ending in -으. These delete the ㅡ and add instead ㅏ or ㅓ, followed by 요 to form the polite style. Thus 아프- in the polite style is 아파요.

How do you know whether the last vowel before the 요 will be an ㅏ or an ㅓ? Simply remember this rule: if the preceding vowel is an ㅏ (as in 아프-) or ㅗ (as in 고프-), then the ㅡ becomes ㅏ, otherwise it is ㅓ.

Using the rules you've just learned for verb stems ending in -으, give the present polite form of the following verbs.

a 바쁘-

b 쓰-

4 DON'T DO IT!

When you want to tell someone not to do something, take the stem of the verb you want to tell them not to do and add -지 마세요 to it. Thus, 맥주를 마시지 마세요 means *please don't drink beer*. Two examples that are quite common are 걱정하지 마세요 and 놀리지 마세요. The first means *don't worry!*, and the second means *don't tease me!*

What other useful examples can you think of? How would you say *please don't wait here* and *don't do the shopping*?

5 LONG NEGATIVES

You have learned how to make negative sentences in Korean with 못 and 안, by putting them immediately in front of the verb. There is another way also, which is known as the long negative. There is no particularly significant difference between the two, though there are some circumstances in which you are more likely to find the long form than the shorter one you have learned already. To spell out these distinctions would be rather long winded and would also make the difference seem more important than it really is. The best advice is to imitate Korean speakers whenever you can. You will then pick up a feel for which to use. Generally, short negatives are better in short, simple sentences; long negatives should be used in more complex sentences.

Here is how to make the long negative. Instead of adding something before the verb you wish to negate, take the stem of that verb and add -지 않아요 or -지 못해요, depending on whether you want to give the sense of the Korean word 안 (*won't* or *isn't going to*) or 못 (*can't*).

Therefore, 못 가요 in the long negative form would be 가지 못해요, and 안 먹어요 in the long negative form would be 먹지 않아요. Here is an example of each:

아버지는 농담하지 않아요.
Dad doesn't tell jokes.

윤 선생님은 등산을 좋아하지만, 윤 선생님 부인은 등산을 하지 못해요.
Mr Yun likes mountain climbing, but his wife can't do it.

Translate the following sentences into English.

a 저는 김치를 못 먹어요
b 저는 김치를 안 먹어요
c 저는 김치를 먹지 못해요
d 저는 김치를 먹지 않아요

6 LINKING TWO CLAUSES WITH -는데: CIRCUMSTANTIAL MEANING

This sounds rather forbidding, but it isn't really all that difficult! Korean has a very common way of linking two clauses together to show that the first one is not all that you have got to say and that there is more coming in the second clause which relates to it. For example, look at this next sentence: 저 시내에 가는데. That is the end of the first clause. The meaning is straightforward enough, *I'm going into town*, but the -는데 added on to the end of 가- indicates that the speaker still has more to say which relates to what he has just said. It is a clue to the listener not to reply yet, but to wait until the rest has been said. The statement is not complete; there is more to come. In this case, the second clause is 같이 갈까요? (*shall we go together?*). Koreans use this pattern all the time to show that they have something more to say about what has just been said (in this case an invitation), and from now on you will meet the -는데 pattern frequently.

The formation of the pattern is easy: take any verb which expresses an action (that is, not an adjectival verb) and add -는데 to the stem. Note that you can also use -는데 with the verbs 있- and 없-, giving you the forms 있는데 and 없는데.

Verbs which describe things (e.g. *is green, is hot, is foolish*, etc.) take the form -(으)ㄴ데 instead (-은데 after consonant stems, -ㄴ데 after vowels). The copula also takes this form, -ㄴ데:

저는 박재민인데 김 선생님 만나러 왔어요.
I'm Pak Jaemin (and I've got more to say): I've come to meet Mr Kim.

You have not learned the past tense yet, but you might like to keep in the back of your mind the fact that -는데 is added to the past stem of all verbs, whether they describe an action or are adjectival. In other words, it doesn't make the distinction that the present tense does.

 Translate the following sentences into English.

a 학교에 사전이 있는데 또 사러 왔어요.
b 저는 내일 시간 있는데 재민씨가 바빠요.

7 DESCRIPTIVE VERBS AND PROCESSIVE VERBS

Korean has two basic kinds of verbs – descriptive and processive. Processive verbs describe a process, the doing of something, an action. Thus, 먹- (*eat*), 앉- (*sit*), 가- (*go*), 하- (*do*), 만나- (*meet*) are all processive verbs. Descriptive verbs describe something, so 좋- (*is good*) is an example, because it describes something as good. 좋아하- (*like*), by contrast, is processive, because it describes the process or action of the speaker liking something. Descriptive verbs function like adjectives in English. They are adjectival verbs.

We tell you all this because some verb endings will only work with one of the two kinds of verbs. What we have just said about -는데, for example, could have been said much more compactly by saying that -는데 can only be added to processive verbs, and that -(으)ㄴ데 is added to descriptive verbs and the copula. In the future we shall be making use of these two terms when we describe verb endings.

The two verbs 있- and 없- can be either processive or descriptive depending on their use, and we will tell you about whether or not they can be used with particular verb endings as we go along.

There is one other verb, the copula, which is in a class of its own. We will tell you about this also on a case-by-case basis, as we did with -는데.

 Practice

1 **The following dialogue concerns a boy who wants to go mountain climbing with Jisoo, a reluctant girl who keeps making up reasons why she can't go with him. Substitute your own answers into the missing parts, giving reasons why she can't go. (NB 안녕 is a way of saying hello to a close friend, or someone younger than you.)**

Boy	지수, 안녕! 내일 시간이 있어요?
Girl	(*State another plan*)
Boy	그럼 일요일에 별일 없으면 같이 등산 갈까요?
Girl	(*Too busy doing something else*)
Boy	다음 일요일은 어때요?
Girl	(*Another plan*)
Boy	언제 시간이 있어요, 그럼? 나를 안 좋아해요?
Girl	(*Doesn't like mountain climbing*)
Boy	그럼, 안 되겠네요.

2 Compose a simple conversation between two friends, one who has a headache and the other who thinks she doesn't have any medicine and suddenly realizes that she does.

3 Here are some situations in which you might use one of the following idiomatic expressions. See if you can match them up. In some cases, more than one expression will fit, so be sure to find all the possibilities and then choose the most likely.

a Your friend is making fun of you.
b You want to go out tonight with your friend, but she can't make it.
c You're in awful pain, and every part of your body seems to hurt.
d Someone has just said something really stupid.
e You're trying to concentrate, but someone is making too much noise.
f You've made a mistake.
g Your junior colleague has just said something you disagree with.
h Your boss has just said something you disagree with.
i Your mother is panicking about your health.
j You didn't hear properly what your younger brother just said.

착각했어요	전신이 다 아프군요
놀리지 마세요	그렇지 않아요
시끄러워요	아닌 것 같아요
걱정하지 마세요	재수 없네요
뭐라구요?	안되겠네요

4 This exercise is designed to help you practise the -는데 pattern. For each question we give you one of two clauses in which the first one always ends in -는데. Your task is to make up an appropriate clause which fits with the one we have given you to make a complete sentence.

   a 버스가 오는데
   b -(느) ㄴ데 안 가요.
   c 이 옷이 비싼데 (옷: clothes)
   d 영국 대사관에 가는데
   e 그 사람 좋은데

5 Put the following sentences into the long negative form.

   a 고기를 좋아해요.   **d** 이 사과가 싱싱해요.
   b 지금 못 가요.   **e** 버스 못 타요.
   c 주문해요.

6 Sangmin is in bed sick, with the following symptoms. Can you describe them?

? Test yourself

1 Here is an exercise about putting verbs into different forms. We give you some sentences with the verb stem and you make full sentences, putting the verb into the correct form.

   Future

   a 양주 마시면 내일 머리가 아프-
   b 이따가 점심을 먹-
   c 한국 사람 만나면 한자 사전 필요없-

Decided

d 병원에 가-

e 원숭이를 사-

f 오늘은 음식을 안 먹-

Thinking of

g 저는 'Star Wars' 보-

h 오늘 아침 쇼핑하-

i 일요일에 불국사에 가-

Shall we

j 언제 등산 가-?

k 김 선생님을 어디서 만나-?

l 우체국 앞에서 버스를 타-?

2 **Choose the best word from those given here to fit in the gaps in the sentences. More than one might be possible, so choose the best option.**

그렇지만	게다가	그런데
그런	글쎄요	그리고

a 힘이 하나도 없어요.   전신이 다 아파요.

b 같이 쇼핑 갈까요?   다른 데에 가기로 했는데요.

c 상민씨는 농담 많이 해요.   재미 없어요.

d 불국사에 가기로 했어요.   못 가요.

e 박 선생님 학교에 가세요.   김 선생님도 가세요.

SELF CHECK

	I CAN. . .
○	...ask what someone is going to do tomorrow.
○	...talk about short term plans.
○	...use the future tense.
○	...say I'm thinking of doing something.
○	...suggest and discuss different activities.
○	...express your aches and pains, and say I'm not feeling very well.
○	...tell someone I'm not going to do something.

7 복습
Review

Introduction

This unit is designed to give you the opportunity to soak up all the things you have learned already and to give you more practice both with practical language use, and with the grammar patterns. In addition, the unit has another important section which you must work through carefully – it describes all the common types of Korean verb stems and the way in which the endings are put on them. It is very important to master this, as you need to be comfortable putting different verb endings onto the different types of verb stem in order to progress quickly with your Korean studies. You should use this section to work through the grammar points, as you normally would, but you will also probably want to keep coming back to it for reference.

The unit is a further opportunity for you to revise both the practical topics we've gone through so far (finding your way, ordering food, and so on), and to check you are happy with all the major grammar points. If you find there are some topics which you are not so comfortable with, make sure you go back to the relevant lesson and cover them again.

Topic revision

Here is a list of the topics you have covered so far. Make sure that you know the basic words and phrases that you would need for each of them.

1 **meeting, identifying and introducing people**
2 **finding out what other people are up to: where they are going and why**
3 **buying drinks and going out for entertainment**
4 **making simple phone calls and arranging to meet people**
5 **discussing food and ordering food and drink in a restaurant**
6 **shopping and money**
7 **finding your way around**
8 **catching the right bus**
9 **planning your free time**
10 **feeling ill**

Korean verbs

You have been learning the stems of Korean verbs and you have learned about the way in which endings are put onto these stems to give particular meanings. You have learned about vowel stems to which the particle -요 is added to give the polite style; you have learned about consonant stems to which you add either -어요 or -아요 to give the polite style. However, each of these two types of verb stem – consonant and vowel – can be broken down into further categories (one of these you have seen already – stems that end in – ㅣ). Each of these sub-categories has certain peculiarities which affect the way in which verb endings are added. We are now going to take you through each of the main types of verb stem in Korean, to show you how the endings are added. Some of this will be revision, but much will be new. Many of the verb stems we teach you are also new, and these may occur in the exercises from now on. They are all common verbs, and you should learn them.

CONSONANT STEMS

Most stems which end in consonants take the polite style endings -어요 or -아요, depending on whether or not the last vowel of the stem was an ㅗ or an ㅏ. Verb endings like -고 and -지만 attach straight to the consonant base. Endings like -(으)ㄹ까요 and -(으)ㅂ시다 attach the longer form (with the 으) to the verb stem. Here are some examples:

먹-	eat	먹어요	먹지만	먹을까요
앉-	sit	앉아요	앉지만	앉을까요
받-	receive	받아요	받지만	받을까요
좋-	is good	좋아요	좋지만	좋을까요
읽-	read	읽어요	읽지만	읽을까요

Certain Korean verb stems which end in ㄷ change the ㄷ to a ㄹ before endings that begin with a vowel. The only very common verb that does this is:

| 듣- | listen, hear | 들어요 | 듣지만 | 들을까요 |

Some verbs whose stem ends in ㅂ change the ㅂ to a 우 before adding the polite ending -어요. The ㅂ remains in endings which begin with consonants (-고 and -지만), but changes to the letter 우 before endings with two forms like -(으)ㄹ까요 and -(으)ㅂ시다. The shorter form (without the -으) is then added:

덥-	is hot	더워요	덥고	더울까요
어렵-	is difficult	어려워요	어렵고	어려울까요
춥-	is cold	추워요	춥고	추울까요
가깝-	is near	가까워요	가깝고	가까울까요
맵-	is spicy	매워요	맵고	매울까요

Perhaps the most confusing category is the last, the ㄹ- irregular verbs. These all end in ㄹ, but the ㄹ disappears before all endings that have two forms: -(으)ㅂ시다, -(으)ㄹ까요 and so on, that is, the last column of our table. The shorter endings (without the -으) are then added.

살-	live	살아요	살고	살까요
놀-	play	놀아요	놀고	놀까요
알-	know	알아요	알고	알까요
팔-	sell	팔아요	팔고	팔까요
멀-	is far	멀어요	멀고	멀까요

VOWEL STEMS

You will find that all the vowel bases are regular in the final two columns. The only difficulty is in the formation of the polite style.

Most vowel bases add the ending -요 directly to the stem to form the polite style. Endings like -고 and -지만 are added straight to the stem; endings with two forms (-을까요 and -ㄹ까요; -읍시다 and -ㅂ시다) add the shorter form straight to the stem since the stem ends in a vowel (note 하- has an irregular polite style form):

가-	go	가요	가고	갈까요
자-	sleep	자요	자고	잘까요
떠나-	leave	떠나요	떠나고	떠날까요
일어나-	get up	일어나요	일어나고	일어날까요
구경하	view, sightsee	구경해요	구경하고	구경할까요
공부하-	study	공부해요	공부하고	공부할까요

The verbs 오- (come) and 보- (look or watch) are regular apart from their polite forms 와요 and 봐요. The stem 되- (become, is all right) also has an irregular polite style 돼요.

Stems that end in -이 change the 이 to 여 before the polite style 요 is added. Everything else is as you would expect. Do remember, however, that some verb ending patterns are based on the polite style minus the -요 ending. For example, there is an ending -서 which attaches to the polite style minus the 요. In this case, the stem 마시- would be 마셔서, since it is based on the polite style 마셔요 minus the 요, plus 서:

| 마시- | drink | 마셔요 | 마시고 | 마실까요 |
| 가르치- | teach | 가르쳐요 | 가르치고 | 가르칠까요 |

Stems that end in the vowel 으 delete this 으 before adding the polite style ending as you would for a consonant base (either -어요 or -아요):

쓰-	use; write	써요	쓰고	쓸까요
아프-	hurt	아파요	아프고	아플까요
바쁘-	is busy	바빠요	바쁘고	바쁠까요

Note, however, that verb stems which end in 르 not only delete the 으, but add another ㄹ before the polite style ending -어요 or -아요. Everything else is regular:

빠르-	is fast	빨라요	빠르고	빠를까요
모르-	not know	몰라요	모르고	모를까요
부르-	sing, call	불러요	부르고	부를까요

Bases that end in 우 change the 우 to 워 before the polite style -요 is added. 주- may generally not be shortened like this, however, and has the polite form 주어요 or 줘요:

배우-	learn	배워요	배우고	배울까요
피우-	smoke	피워요	피우고	피울까요
주-	give	주어요 (or 줘요)	주고	줄까요

🔓 Practice

1 **Translate the following sentences into English. Most of them should look familiar, as they are based closely on sentences you have met in the dialogues of previous units.**

   a 그럼, 같이 가요.
   b 오늘 점심에 시간이 있어요?
   c 진짜 오래간만이에요.
   d 저는 일본말 선생님이 아니에요.
   e 죄송합니다. 착각했어요.
   f 다음 월요일은 아마 괜찮을 거에요.
   g 저도 서울 사람이 아니라서 잘 모르겠어요.
   h 전신이 다 아프군요. 안 아픈 데가 있어요?
   i 영국 돈을 중국 돈으로 바꾸고 싶어요.
   j 그리고 저는 냉면도 먹고 싶어요.
   k 마른 안주하고 파전 주세요.
   l 한 상자에 이만원에 가져 가세요.

2 Telling the time in Korean is easy. To ask what time it is, you say 몇 시예요? Literally this means *how many hours is it?* To ask at what time something happens you would say either 몇 시에 학교에 가요? or 언제 학교에 가요?

The hours are counted by the pure Korean numbers, and the minutes by Sino-Korean numbers. *9 o'clock* is 아홉시; *2 o'clock* is 두시; *3.35* is 세시 삼십오분; *12.02* is 열두시 이분. You can say *at* a certain time with the particle -에. Thus, *at 2.40* is 두시 사십분에 and so on. You can say *half past* with the word 반. *Half past one* is 한시 반.

Answer the question 몇 시예요? for each of the following.

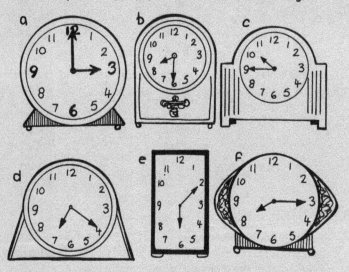

3 Give the polite style, the -고 form and the -읍시다 form of the following verbs.

a 하-
b 닫- (shut)
c 팔-
d 바쁘-
e 움직이- (move)

Check your answers carefully with the information about verbs that we have given you.

4 You are planning a trip away with your friend. Make up responses to his questions.

a 어디 갈까요?
b 뭐 하러 거기 가요?
c 언제 갈까요?
d 몇 시에 만날까요?
e 어디서 만날까요?

5 You go to a restaurant with your two friends. One of you wants to eat 불고기, another 갈비, and the third 냉면. Write a dialogue which includes the following questions from the waiter and your answers to them. (You decide to have a beer each.)

Can I help you?
Can you eat spicy food? (literally, do you eat well spicy food?)
Would you like anything to drink?
물도 드릴까요?

6 Make up five short dialogues based on the following information. The dialogue pattern is like this:

a *Where are you going?*
b *(answer)*

a *What are you going to buy / do / drink / eat there?*
b *(answer)*

Here is the information you need for the answers:

a 가게   오징어
b 학교   야구
c 식당   불고기
d 집   차
e 시장   과일

7 Here is a typical day for Mr Pak. Answer the questions that follow.

7.30	get up
9.00	shopping
10.00	meet Mr Lee's wife at Hilton Hotel
1.00	lunch at Chinese restaurant
2.00	doctor's appointment
6.00	home for meal
7.30	cinema
11.00	bed

a 박선생님은 몇 시에 일어나요?
b 10시에는 뭐 해요?
c 점심 때는 뭘 먹어요?
d 밤에는 어디 가요?
e 몇시에 자요?

8 Read the following questions and answer each one negatively with a full sentence (*no, I'm not* or *no, I don't*). Try to use the long negative pattern for one or two of the questions. Then make up another sentence saying what you do instead.

a 축구 좋아해요?
b 매운 거 잘 먹어요?
c 텔레비젼을 많이 봐요?
d 노래를 잘 불러요?
e 중국말 배워요?

9 Look at the following street plan and answer the questions with full Korean sentences.

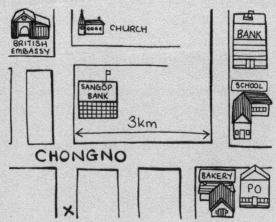

98

a 교회에서 영국 대사관은 멀어요?
b 이 근처에 한국 외환은행이 있어요?
c 학교가 어디예요?
d 학교가 가까워요?
e 우체국은 대사관보다 더 멀어요?
f 학교에 가면 시간 많이 걸려요?
g 우체국이 어디예요?

교회	church
학교	school
제과	bakery

10 Jaemin has gone shopping. Have a look at his shopping list. How would he ask the shopkeeper for the things on the list? What might he say if the apples are too expensive? How would he ask the total cost?

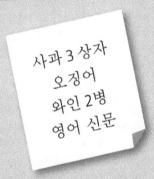

사과 3 상자
오징어
와인 2병
영어 신문

11 **English to Korean translation.**

a I'm going to school to study English too.
b Let's meet outside the shop. See you later!
c Enjoy your meal.
d I'll really have to go to hospital.
e Just pay 15,000 won, then.
f It takes about 15 minutes.
g How's business these days?
h Give me the cheapest one, please.
i The weather is good nowadays.
j I came to meet Mr Pak from the Korean embassy.
k I can't eat spicy things.
l Does the bus for the post office stop at this stop?

8

방금 나갔어요 / 어제 어디 갔었어요?

She's just gone out / Where did you go last night?

In this unit you will learn how to:
▶ *give information about where people have gone and why.*
▶ *give information about what happened in the past.*
▶ *use several important verb and clause endings.*
▶ *say because.*
▶ *ask for something to be done for your benefit.*

CEFR: *Can describe plans, arrangements, habits and routines, past activities and personal experiences (A2); can connect phrases in a simple way to describe experiences and events (B1).*

Dating culture in Korea

Koreans prefer to date someone who is, from the start, a potential match, rather than meet somebody by chance and risk any awkward situations or mismatches. As a result, Koreans often date through social circles or matchmaking companies to find potential partners.

Blind dates are extremely common and there are generally three different types of blind dates. The first is a one-on-one blind date known as a 소개팅. 소개 means *introduction* and 팅 is taken from the English word *meeting*. These are normally set up by a mutual 친구 (*friend*). The second type is a group blind date, where a group of male friends will meet up with a group of female friends to hang out and have a good time. These are known as 미팅 (*meetings*) and are most popular among young 대학생 (*university students*). The third and final type is a 선, normally a very serious 데이트 (*date*) arranged by the 부모님 (*parents*) through close 친척 (*family relatives*) or matchmakers. A 선 is more formal than a 소개팅, and both parties tend to have expectations of marriage right from the start.

What is the English word that the Korean names for one-on-one blind dates and group blind dates are based upon?

Vocabulary builder 1

PHONING TO CHANGE PLANS

08.01 Listen to the words and try to pronounce them. Try to imitate the speaker.

바꾸-	*change*
방금	*just now*
나가-	*go out*
혹시	*maybe, perhaps, possibly*
오늘	*today*
남자 친구	*boyfriend*
영화	*film*
저녁	*evening, supper*
데이트하-	*to date*
밤	*night*
늦게	*late*
돌아오-	*come back, return*
약속	*appointment*
취소하-	*cancel*
-려고	*with the intention of*
전화하-	*to telephone*
바쁜	*busy*
생기-	*to occur, happen, take place*
전하-	*communicate*

NEW EXPRESSIONS

Read the expressions that are used in the next dialogue. Note their meanings.

어디 갔는지 아세요?	*Do you know where (she) has gone?*
아마 알고 있을 거예요	*will perhaps know*
이상하네!	*(It is) strange!*
저런	*Oh dear!, Oh no!*
취소하려고 전화했거든요	*(because) I called with the intention of cancelling (the appointment) you see*
잘 됐네요	*it's turned out well, it's all for the better*
… 한테 전할 말이 있어요?	*Do you have a message for …?*

Dialogue 1

방금 나갔어요 **SHE'S JUST GONE OUT**

조금 전	*a little while ago*
조금	*a little, a bit*
전	*before*
전에	*previously*
-까지	*until*

08.02 *Jaemok rings up his girlfriend Chongmin to cancel a date with her, only to find that she'd already gone out for the evening with someone else!*

1 What does Mr Yun say when he picks up the phone?

윤선생	여보세요?
재목	여보세요. 정민씨 좀 바꿔주세요.
윤선생	네. 잠깐만 기다리세요.
(A little while later.)	
윤선생	미안합니다. 조금 전까지 있었는데, 방금 나갔어요.
재목	혹시 어디 갔는지 아세요?
윤선생	잘 모르겠어요.
	잠깐만 기다려 보세요. 우리 집사람이 아마 알고 있을 거예요.
부인	정민씨 오늘 남자 친구랑 영화 보러 나갔어요.
재목	그래요? 이상하네. 오늘 저녁에 나하고 만나기로 했는데.
부인	저런, 정민씨는 다른 남자랑 데이트 하러 갔는데 … 아마 밤 늦게까지 안 들어올거예요.
재목	그럼 잘 됐네요. 오늘 저녁 약속을 취소하려고 전화했거든요. 오늘 저한테 바쁜 일이 생겼어요.
부인	아, 그래요. 잘 됐네요. 정민씨한데 전할 말이 있으세요?
재목	아니요, 없어요. 안녕히 계세요.

2 How does Mr Yun say *My wife will probably know*?

3 Who does Jaemok speak to on the phone?

4 Where has Chongmin gone? Who is she with?

5 When does Mrs Yun say Chongmin will return?

Language discovery 1

 How are the following sentences said in Korean? Which ending is used to express probability?

a My wife will probably know.
b She probably won't return until late at night.

1 PROBABILITIES

You will remember that we said in the last unit that the probable future form -을 거예요 can also be used simply to mean *probably*. You have an example in this dialogue in the phrase 아마 알고 있을 거예요 (*my wife will probably know, perhaps my wife will know*). Notice that this isn't a proper future tense; it is just a way of expressing probability.

2 CONTINUOUS STATES

In English we have a present continuous tense, used in sentences like *I am going, he is sitting*. This continuous tense is indicated by the ending *-ing*. In English we use the continuous tense fairly frequently, whereas in Korean the continuous form is used only for special emphasis, to stress that something is going on continuously. This means that when in English you meet a verb form that ends in *-ing*, you must not automatically assume that you should translate it by a Korean continuous form; in most cases you should probably not do so.

Let's take an example to illustrate this. In English it is quite common to say a sentence like *I'm going home*. This uses the continuous tense. It would be very unusual to translate this by the Korean continuous tense, and you would only do so if you particularly wanted to stress the process or the ongoing action of your going home. You would be far more likely to use the normal Korean present tense form 나는 집에 가요.

There are certain circumstances in which the Korean continuous form is used, however, and you should note these. It is often used with the verb *to know*. The phrase 알고 있어요 literally means *I am knowing*, and the Korean emphasis is *I am in a state of knowing that*, and sometimes has the force *I already know that (you didn't need to tell me)*.

Other common uses are to stress what you are in the process of doing right now. Thus, as answers to the question 뭘 해요? (*what are you doing?*), you might say:

책 읽어요
책 읽고 있어요

They both mean *I'm reading a book*, but the second one stresses that you are in the process of reading the book even as you speak, that is what you are busy with and in the middle of doing.

Generally you should only use the present continuous tense when you are sure that you want to stress that particular meaning of continuous action.

To make the form, take the verb stem and add -고 있-, for example, in the polite style, -고 있어요. You will not normally find negatives in the continuous pattern; you would simply use a normal verb form, for example 안 읽어요 (*I'm not reading*).

 Translate the following sentences into English. Give all possibilities.

a 비빔밥 먹어요
b 비빔밥 먹고 있어요
c 비빔밥 안 먹어요
d 비빔밥 안 먹고 있어요

3 HAVING A GO AT . . .

You have already learned the verb 가보-, which we told you meant *go and see*. It is not really one verb at all, however, but a compound of the verb 가- (*go*) and the verb 보- (*see*). You can make other compound verbs by adding the verb 보- to another verb. You must take the other verb in the polite style -요 form, knock off the -요, and then add on the verb 보-. Here are some examples:

stem	polite	minus -요	plus 보-	meaning
가-	가요	가-	가보-	*go and see*
먹-	먹어요	먹어-	먹어보-	*eat and see have a go at eating*
기다리-	기다려요	기다려-	기다려보-	*wait and see try waiting*

The two most common uses for this pattern are as follows:

▶ It is often used in the polite honorific style to mean *please have a go at (verb) and see, please try out (verb)ing*. For example, 기다려보세요 in this lesson means *please wait and see, please try waiting, please have a go at waiting*.

▶ In the past tense it means *have you tried (verb)ing?, have you had a go at (verb)ing?*, e.g. 테니스를 해봤어요? (*have you ever played tennis? have you ever tried playing tennis?*).

4 THE PAST TENSE

The past tense in Korean is used very similarly to the past tense in English to say what someone did or was doing in the past. You just need to learn how to form it and, fortunately, that is fairly easy too. Take the verb *you want* in the polite style (e.g. 먹어요, 알아요, 기다려요, 앉아요), take the -요 off the end and add -ㅆ. What you now have is the past stem (previously you have been learning the present stem of verbs). This past stem can then be made into a verb form in the normal way, by adding, for example, the polite style ending -어요:

stem	polite	minus -요	plus -ㅆ	polite past
먹-	먹어요	먹어	먹었-	먹었어요
알-	알아요	알아	알았-	알았어요
기다리-	기다려요	기다려	기다렸-	기다렸어요
앉-	앉아요	앉아	앉았-	앉았어요

Remember that you can put all sorts of endings on the past base, just as you can on the normal verb bases that you have learned previously. Sometimes the forms you make will look a bit odd because of the rules of sound change – the -ㅆ might disappear into another sound, but it will still be there in Korean writing. For example, with the past base 먹었- you could make: 먹었어요, 먹었구나 (먹었 + -구나), 먹었고 (먹었 + 고), 먹었네요 (먹었 + 네요), etc.

Remember that the forms 했는데 and 갔는데 are also past tense forms in which the -ㅆ of the past tense has become ㄴ by the rules of sound change. These two forms are thus the past bases 했- and 갔- with the imminent elaboration -는데 added to them. This past tense -는데 form is very common in Korean.

To make honorific past forms, take the present verb base, and add -셨- to give you the honorific past base (if the stem ends in a vowel), or -으셨- (if the stem ends in a consonant). This can then be made into, for example, 앉으셨어요 (you (honorific) sat down), from the honorific past base 앉으셨-.

It looks difficult at first, but with practice you should soon crack it. Everything is regular, you just have to remember the right rules and apply them.

Give the polite past form for each of the following verbs. The stem and polite present form are given to help you.

	verb	stem	polite present	polite past
a	*to change*	바꾸-	바꿔요	
b	*to go out*	나가-	나가요	
c	*to telephone / call*	전화하-	전화해요	
d	*to come back / return*	돌아오-	돌아와요	

5 WITH THE INTENTION OF . . .

As you already know, sentences such as 빵 사러 시내에 가요 (*I'm going to the city centre to buy bread*) use constructions that add -러 to the verb in the first clause, to mean *in order to*. This construction can only be used with the two verbs *go* and *come* at the end of the sentence, however. This lesson introduces you to a way to say a similar thing, *in order to, with the intention of*, which can now be used with other verbs as well. You simply add -려고 to the stem of the verb of the first clause (-으려고 if the stem ends in a consonant). Here is a reminder of the example of the construction which you saw in the dialogue: 취소하려고 전화했어요 *I'm calling* (literally, *I have called*) *with the intention of cancelling* (*in order to cancel*).

Here are some more examples:

영어 배우려고 영어 책 샀어요.
(I) bought an English language book with the intention of learning English.

책 읽으려고 도서관에 가요.
(I) am going to the library in order to read books.

결혼하려고 돈을 벌었어요.
I earned some money with the intention of getting married

영어	*English language*	결혼하-	*get married*
한국어	*Korean language*	벌-	*earn*
-어	*language*		

Translate the following sentences into Korean using this -(으)려고 construction. Be careful which verb you choose to attach the ending to.

a I went to the restaurant in order to eat kalbi.
b I get the bus in order to go to school.

6 -거든요

The verb ending -거든요 is a common form in colloquial speech, although it is a bit difficult to pin down precisely what it means in English.

The pattern is used when you are adding an explanation to something that you have already said. In the dialogue Jaemok says *it's turned out well then*, and then he goes on to say another sentence which ends in -거든요. This sentence explains why he has just said that it turned out well – because he was ringing to cancel the date in any case. In a way, therefore, -거든요 means something like *it's because . . . , you see*, when you add an explanation to something. But you must have already said something else which the -거든요 phrase is an explanation of!

The ending -거든요 is added simply to the verb stem, either a present or a past stem, although the past is probably a bit more common.

If you are able to use it correctly, Koreans will be very impressed as it really does make your speech sound colloquial.

7 SAYING *AND THEN* AND *BECAUSE*

Along with the past tense, this grammar note is probably the most crucial part of this unit. It introduces you to a form which is used all the time in spoken and written Korean.

First, we will look at how to form it, and afterwards at what it means. It is used to end the first clause of a two-clause construction, and you take off the -요 of the polite-style present of the verb and add -서. For example:

stem	polite	minus -요	-서 form
먹-	먹어요	먹어	먹어서
마시-	마셔요	마셔	마셔서

The -서 pattern has two meanings. In both cases, imagine a sentence of the form (clause A) -서 (clause B).

▶ It can mean *after having done A, then B*, or *A and then B*, where there is a close sequential link between the two clauses (usually a link of time: *after A, then B*). An example would be: 학교에 가서 공부할 거에요, which could be translated as *I'll go to school and then study* or *After going to school, I will study*.

Here are some more examples:

친구를 만나서 술집에 가요.
I meet (my) friend and then (we) go to the pub.

한국에 가서 한국 친구를 만났어요.
I went to Korea, and then I met a Korean friend.

▶ It can mean *because A, then B*, and this is perhaps the meaning which you will use (and meet) most frequently. A good example would be:

비가 와서 학교에 못 가요.
It's raining, so I can't go to school. / I can't go to school because it's raining.

 Here are some more examples. Try translating them into English.

a 오늘 바쁜 일이 생겨서 약속을 못 지켜요

b 머리가 아파서 술을 못 마셔요

Vocabulary builder 2

 08.03 **Listen to the words and try to pronounce them. Try to imitate the speaker.**

요즘	nowadays, these days	우연히	by chance, coincidentally
바쁘-	is busy	다시	again
여자 친구	girlfriend	때	time
이름	name	-부터	from
대학교	university	자주	often, frequently
졸업하-	graduate (verb stem)	시작하-	begin, start
일하-	work (verb stem)	거의	nearly, almost
소개하-	to introduce	매일	everyday
처음	at first	노래방	karaoke
마음	mind, heart	내 (제)	my (my, humble form)
달	month	탁구치-	play table tennis
후	after	솔직히	frankly, honestly
파티	party		

NEW EXPRESSIONS

Read the expressions that are used in the next dialogue. Note their meanings.

요즘 재미가 어떠세요?	How are you doing? How are things these days?
그런 줄 알았어요.	I thought so.
어떻게 만났어요?	How did you meet?
마음에 들지 않아요.	I don't like (her). (마음에 안들어요)
… 마음에 들-	(I) like . . .
그런 편이에요	(we) tend to be so / do so (it's usually like that, etc.)
기억이 안나요	I don't remember
아마 어딘가 갔을 거예요	I expect (we) went somewhere or other; maybe . . .
솔직히 말해 보세요!	Tell me the truth!

108

Dialogue 2

어제 어디 갔었어요? **WHERE DID YOU GO LAST NIGHT?**

🎧 08.04 *Yongtae has a new girlfriend, and his friend Taegyu appears rather inquisitive.*

1 How does Yongtae say he met his girlfriend Chongmin? What form of the verb 소개하다 does he use?

용태 태규씨 안녕하세요?

태규 안녕하세요.
    요즘 재미가 어떠세요?

용태 요즘 바빠요.
    여자 친구가 생겨서 더 바빠요.

태규 그런 줄 알았어요.
    여자 친구 이름이 뭐예요?

용태 김정민이에요.
    작년에 서울대학교를 졸업하고 지금은 현대자동차에서 일하고
    있어요.

태규 어떻게 만났어요?

용태 친구가 소개해 주었어요.
    처음에는 그렇게 마음에 들지 않았는데, 한달 후에 파티에서
    우연히 다시 만났어요. 그때부터 자주 만나기 시작했어요.

태규 지금은 거의 매일 만나서 데이트 하지요?

용태 그런 편이에요.

태규 어제 밤에도 내가 전화했는데 없었어요.
    어제 밤에 어디 갔었어요?

용태 어제 밤이요? 기억이 안 나요. 아마 어딘가 갔을 거예요.

태규 기억이 안 나요? 그렇게 술을 많이 마셨어요?

용태 누가 술을 마셔요? 태규씨가 오히려 매일 술만 마시잖아요?

태규 어쨌든 어제 어디 갔었어요?

용태 노래방에 갔었어요. 내 여자 친구는 노래방을 아주 좋아해요.

태규 노래방에서 나와서 어디 갔었어요?

용태 탁구를 좀 쳤어요.

태규 그게 다예요? 솔직히 말해보세요.

용태 정말이에요. 아무 일도 없었어요.

2 How does Taegyu ask Yongtae where he went last night?

3 Where does Chongmin work?

4 What did Yongtae and Chongmin do together yesterday?

Language discovery 2

 Look at the following sentence and its translation. What construction is added to the verb *to meet* to imply he started to meet her from then on?

그때부터 자주 만나기 시작했어요.
He started to meet her from then on.

1 BEGINNING TO DO THINGS

You can say that someone is beginning to do something in Korean by adding -기 시작하- to a processive verb stem (a verb of doing). Here are two good examples:

학교에서 일본말을 공부하기 시작해요.
(We) are beginning to study Japanese at school.

요즘 어떤 영국 사람이 한국말을 배우기 시작했어요.
Nowadays some English people have begun to learn the Korean language.

 Use the -기 시작하- construction to translate the following sentences into Korean.

a I have begun to drink coffee.
b Taegyu is beginning to go to school.

2 FOR MY BENEFIT

You have learned how to ask people to do things by using polite requests ending in -세요. The construction you are about to learn enables you to make such requests even more polite, and to stress that they are for your benefit. Suppose you want to say *please do it for me, please do it (for my benefit)*. Previously you would have said 하세요. Instead, take the polite style of the verb (해요), knock off the -요 (해-), and add the verb stem 주- (give) and then add the verb ending you want. Usually you will still want to use the polite request ending, so you would make the form 해 주세요(해 + 주 + 세요) (*please do it for me*). The literal meaning of the construction is *please do it and give* and you can see how the verbs make this meaning when they are put together, and imply that you are asking for something to be done for your benefit. This is quite a common pattern.

 Translate the following sentences into Korean. Use the extra vocabulary given.

a Please buy me lunch today.
b Please lend me this umbrella.

우산	*umbrella*
빌려주	*-lend* (verb stem)
빌려주어요 (빌려줘요)	*lend* (polite form)

3 SENTENCE ENDINGS WITH -지요

You can end sentences with the form -지요 added to any stem. As you can see, it is a bit like the polite style (since it ends in -요). It means something like *I suppose, you know, I guess,* etc., and it gives your sentences a bit more flavour than the polite style. However, the exact meaning of -지요 corresponds to a number of English meanings, depending on whether they occur in statements, yes–no questions, or suggestions. It is used when the speaker wants to draw the hearer in to what is being said. The following examples illustrate some of the ways it can be used:

한국 사람이지요?
I suppose you are Korean, aren't you?

점심 벌써 먹었지요?
You've eaten lunch already, haven't you?

지금 점심 먹지요.
Let's have lunch now (I suggest we have lunch now).

술을 좋아하지요?
I guess you like alcohol, don't you?

4 THE DOUBLE PAST

Korean has what is known as a double past construction, which is a past tense of a verb formed in the normal way, with an additional -었- added. Thus, 먹었었- would be the double past base of 먹-.

The precise meaning of the form is a bit more difficult to define and is beyond the scope of this course. It emphasizes the remoteness of a past event and shows that an event occurred and was completed in the distant past. What you do need to know about it, however, concerns its use with the two verbs 가- and 오-, *go* and *come*. Compare the following two sentences:

어제 밤 여기 왔어요.	*I came here yesterday.*
어제 밤 여기 왔었어요.	*I came here yesterday.*

The implication of the first of these might well be that you are still here, you came and you remain. However, the implication of the second is that the action is over, that is, that you came, and that you went again and that it all took place in the past. The same would be true of 갔어요 and 갔었어요.

This rule is something of a simplification, but it will explain most of the occurrences of the double past that you are likely to need to know about for the time being. Take a close look at the example in the dialogue to see that emphasis: *we came to this restaurant last night* (and, by implication, we left again afterwards). The act of our coming (and going) all took place last night.

> **LANGUAGE TIP**
> You'll recognize the double past by its two uses of a 었 (e.g. 먹었었어요). It tends to locate an action in the distant past, and imply the experience in the distant past.

🔓 Practice

1 **Make the following into polite requests in Korean (asking someone to do something for your benefit).**

   a 하세요.
   b Please go shopping for me.
   c 점심 사세요.
   d Can you phone Mr Kim for me?
   e Please buy me some medicine.
   f 시작하세요.

2 **Reconstruct the following sentences to add a second sentence along the lines suggested in the brackets to explain what has just been said in the first sentence. This is practice for the -거든요 pattern.**

   a 오늘 학교에 못 가요   (head aches)
   b 일요일날에 시내에 못 가요   (another appointment)
   c 오늘밤 탁구 못 쳐요   (arm (팔) has begun to hurt)
   d 노래방에 가요? 나는 안 가요 (don't like karaoke)
   e 재민씨 못 가요? 그럼 잘 됐네요 (I can't go either)

3 **Read the following page from someone's diary and then answer the questions.**

6월 (June)	6월 (June)
월 6　토니와 점심 약속	월 13　不
화 7	화 14　대구 출장
수 8　회의	수 15
목 9　회의	목 16　↓
금 10　김 선생 생일 파티	금 17　휴가 시작
토 11　대학 동창회	토 18　집 청소
일 12　집사람하고 쇼핑	일 19　도봉산 등산

휴가　　　　　　　　　*holiday*
출장　　　　　　　　　*business trip*
동창회　　　　　　　　*alumni meeting*

오늘은 6 월 7 일 화요일이에요.

a 이번 토요일에 무슨 약속이 있어요?
b 언제가 김선생의 생일이에요?
c 이번 일요일에 무엇을 하려고 해요?
d 다음 일요일에는 어디가려고 해요?
e 언제부터 휴가예요?
f 어제는 누구하고 점심을 먹었어요?

4 **Translate the following (using verb compounds with 보- for the English to Korean examples).**

a 탕 먹어보세요! (탕: spicy soup)
b You should visit Bulguksa one time (lit: Please visit . . . !)
c 바쁘지만 가보세요.
d 탁구를 못 쳐봤어요? 그럼 한번 해보세요.
e Jaemin hasn't come yet? Please (try) waiting a little longer.

5 Use the following pairs of information to make up Korean sentences, each with two clauses linked by -서. The first three have the sense of *because A, B*, the last three are sequential: *and then*.

   a busy matter has come up   can't go
   b no food in house   go to restaurant
   c business is not good   no money
   d let's go outside   and wait
   e go to Sangmin's   what shall we do?
   f go to city   buy some fruit

6 Ask your friend if they have tried doing the following things. Make up appropriate answers.

⁇ Test yourself

1 Put the following sentences into the past tense.

  a 학교에 가요.
  b 맥주 많이 마셔요.
  c 약속을 못 지켜요.
  d 친구를 만나요.
  e 영화를 보고 싶어요.
  f 도봉산에 갈까 해요.

2 Complete the following paragraph using the appropriate words.

했어요	그렇지만	하려고	아침에
지켰어요	기로 했어요	생겨서	그러니까

오늘 _____ 친구를 만나 _____. _____ 바쁜 일이
_____ 못 만났어요. _____ 취소 _____ 전화 _____.
약속 못 _____.

3 Translate the following sentences into Korean.

  a I'm ringing to cancel my appointment. Something came up (you see).
  b Sangmin has just gone out to play table tennis.
  c At first I didn't particularly like kimchi, but I got used to it. (get used to: 익숙해지-)
  d When did you graduate?
  e We met by chance in a bar.
  f That's strange! Chris has come back already.
  g What did you do last night? Tell me the truth.

SELF CHECK

I CAN...
...ask where someone has gone.
...give information about where people have gone and why.
...use the past tense.
...use sentences describing the continuous state.
...ask for something to be done for my benefit.
...connect sentences to mean one thing happened because of another, or after another.
...recognize the difference between 왔어요 and 왔었어요, or between 갔어요 and 갔었어요.

작년에 사드렸잖아요! / 미안합니다, 정말로 몰랐어요!

We bought him that last year! / I'm sorry, I really didn't know!

In this unit you will learn how to:
▶ *disagree and apologize.*
▶ *buy presents.*
▶ *say you can and can't do something.*
▶ *use honorifics.*

CEFR: *Can agree and disagree (A2); can make and respond to suggestions and apologies (A2); can express and respond to feelings such as surprise (B1); can recognize and appreciate register shifts (C1).*

Gift giving in Korea

Gift giving is very common in Korea. 선물 (*presents*) are offered and received with two hands to show both gratitude and respect. Whenever a person receives a 선물, it is customary for the recipient to reciprocate the gesture and give another 선물 of similar value in return at a later date. Therefore, when you give a 선물, avoid choosing something too expensive, especially if you know the other person can't reciprocate.

When you are invited to someone's house it is common to bring a small 선물, especially if you are visiting for the first time. In such situations Koreans often give food or drink, with 과일 (*fruit*) being particularly popular. Business gifts are also common within Korean society and are often presented at the first meeting. The most expensive 선물 should be given to the person of highest rank and so on. Such 선물 can be criticized as being 뇌물 (*bribes*) in the West, but the intent of a 선물 at the first business meeting is to set the foundations for an amicable relationship and gifts are often reciprocal. For family occasions and celebrations, such as a 결혼식 (*wedding*) or 생일 (*birthday*), the best 선물 to give is 돈 (*money*). Contrary to in the West, 현금 (*cash*) is totally acceptable (it doesn't lack sincerity!) and is at times preferred.

In which of the following situations would a 과일 바구니 (*basket of fruit*) be an appropriate gift?

a housewarming party   **b** wedding   **c** business meeting

Vocabulary builder 1

CHOOSING PRESENTS

 09.01 **Listen to the words and try to pronounce them. Try to imitate the speaker.**

생신/생일	*birthday* (honorific / normal form)
무엇	*what* (full form of 뭐)
결정하-	*decide*
정하-	*decide*
도와주-	*to help*
이번	*this time*
잠바	*jacket (jumper)*
벌	*(counter for clothes)*
갖고 계시-	*have, possess* (honorific; polite style: 갖고 계세요.)
더이상	*any more*
필요 없어요	*is not needed*
필요하-	*is needed* (필요있- also exists but is less common)
셔츠	*shirt*
독서	*reading*
싫어하-	*to dislike*
대신	*instead, on behalf of*
생각	*idea*
우산	*umbrella*
양말	*socks*
전기 면도기	*electric shaver*
면도(를) 하-	*shave*
의견	*suggestion, opinion*
혼자	*alone, on one's own*

NEW EXPRESSIONS

Read the expressions that are used in the next dialogue. Note their meanings.

당신이 정할 수 없어요?	*Can't you decide?*
-는 어떨까요?	*How about . . . ?, What do you think about . . . ?*
그것 보라고!	*You see?!*
당신은 내 의견을 좋아하지 않잖아요	*You don't like my suggestions, you see!*
처음 말한대로	*as (I) first said, like (I) said at first*

Dialogue 1

작년에 사드렸잖아요! WE BOUGHT HIM THAT LAST YEAR!

V

남편	husband
할아버지	grandfather
당신	you (often used between husband and wife)
할머니	grandmother
그건	that thing (topic)
재작년	the year before last year

09.02 *A husband and wife are deciding what to buy Grandfather for his birthday. However, the task is not as easy as it sounds!*

1 How does the wife say they'd better decide what to buy Grandfather?

부인	내일이 할아버지 생신이에요.
남편	뭐? 벌써?
부인	그래요. 무엇을 사드릴까 결정해야겠어요.
남편	당신이 정할 수 없어요? 나는 바빠요.
부인	항상 내가 결정하잖아요. 이번에는 좀 도와주세요.
남편	좋아요. 잠바를 사드릴까요?
부인	잠바는 벌써 열 벌이나 갖고 계세요. 잠바는 더 이상 필요 없어요.
남편	그러면 셔츠는 어떨까요?
부인	셔츠도 더 이상 필요 없어요.
남편	그럼, 책은요?
부인	할아버지는 독서를 싫어하시잖아요?
남편	할머니는 독서를 좋아하시니까 대신 읽으시면 되잖아요.
부인	농담하지 마세요. 좀 더 좋은 생각을 말해보세요.
남편	우산은 어떨까요?
부인	할아버지는 비 올 때 나가지 않으시잖아요.
남편	그럼 양말은?
부인	작년에 사드렸잖아요.
남편	그럼 새 전기 면도기는 어떨까요?
부인	그건 재작년에 사드렸잖아요. 그리고 할아버지는 면도를 잘 안 하세요.
남편	그것 보라구! 당신은 내 의견을 좋아하지 않잖아요. 내가 처음 말한대로 당신 혼자 결정하면 되잖아요.

2 Why doesn't the wife agree to buying a jacket?

3 What did they give Grandfather for his birthday last year and the year before last?

Language discovery 1

Match the following sentences that use compound verbs to the correct translation.

a 좀 도와주세요   **1** Please help me.

b 잠바를 사드릴까요?   **2** Shall we buy him a jacket?

1 DOING SOMETHING FOR SOMEONE ELSE

When asking someone to do something for your benefit you combine verbs with the verb 주- *give*, as in 사 주세요 *please buy it for me*. Now we are going to expand on this to look at how to talk about doing things for other people's benefit, for the benefit of someone else. Once more you can make a compound verb which means literally *buy and give*, but which in practice means *buy for him, buy for his benefit*.

There are two ways of doing this, and it depends on whether the person for whose benefit you are doing something is esteemed (honorific) or not. When speaking about someone of honorific status, for example one's grandfather, instead of making the compound with the verb 주- as you would expect, Korean uses a special verb 드리- which means *give (to someone honorific)*. Compare the following two sentences: the first one means that you will have to decide what to buy for someone honorific, the second means you will have to decide what to buy for someone of your own or lower status (for example, your child):

무엇을 사드릴까 결정해야겠어요

무엇을 사줄까 결정해야겠어요

As you can see, Korean has two different verbs for *give*, depending on who you are giving to.

Here are some more examples using the two verbs for *give*:

할아버지에게 책을 읽어 드렸어요.
(I) read a book for my grandfather.

친구에게 책을 읽어 주었어요.
(I) read a book for my friend.

김 선생님을 기다려 드렸어요.
I waited for Mr Kim.

친구를 기다려 　주었어요.
I waited for my friend.

2 WONDERING, WORRYING AND DECIDING

In English we make quite a few constructions with the word *whether*,
e.g. *I'm wondering whether, I'm worrying whether* (or, *that*), *I'm trying to
decide whether* . . . Korean makes these kind of sentences by adding -ㄹ까
or -을까 to the base of the verb. This is the same ending as -(으)ㄹ까요?
(*shall we?*) without the -요; you met it also in -(으)ㄹ까 해요 (*I'm
thinking of*). The -(으)ㄹ까 pattern is used in the following construction:
김 선생님 갈까. This would form part of a sentence and it means
whether Mr Kim will go. It could be used with any of the following verbs:
걱정하- *worry*, 궁금하- *wonder*, 결정하- *decide*. Here are a couple of
example sentences:

여자 친구가 약속을 지킬까 궁금해요.
I wonder whether my girlfriend will keep the appointment.

운전수가 술을 많이 마실까 걱정했어요.
I was worried that the driver would drink a lot.

This basic -(으)ㄹ까 pattern is also found in a few common variations.

Sometimes -을까 is followed in colloquial speech by another word, 말까,
to mean *whether or not*, as in the following example:

갈까 말까 걱정해요.
I'm worrying whether to go or not.

This form with 말까 can only be used with verbs in which a person is
wondering whether or not they themselves will do something. You could
not use 말까 in a sentence to mean *I'm wondering whether it will rain or
not*, since there is no decision to be taken about whether or not to
actually do something.

Often when Koreans are saying that they are worried that something
might happen, they use a slightly longer form of the pattern: -을까봐:

비가 올까봐 걱정해요.
I'm worried that it might rain.

여자 친구가 나를 버릴까봐 걱정해요.
I am worried that my girlfriend might dump me.

 버리-   *throw away*

The other form is simply a contraction of this longer version.

Translate the following sentences into English.

늦-   *be late*
고민하-   *to*

a 학교 늦을까봐 걱정했어요.
b 여동생이 숙제를 할까 말까 궁금해요.
c 무엇을 먹을까 빨리 결정하세요.

3 THINGS YOU'LL HAVE TO DO

This unit should remind you of the way to say that you are going to have to do something (often the context concerns something that you'd really rather not have to do). The pattern is -야겠어요, and it is added onto any processive verb base. The form literally means something like *only if I do such and such will it do*; -야 is a particle which means *only if*.

내일까지 이 일을 끝내야겠어요.
I'll have to finish the work by tomorrow.

내년에는 꼭 결혼해야겠어요.
I'll have to marry next year.

끝내-   *finish (verb stem, to finish something)*
꼭   *without fail, definitely*

 Translate the following sentences into Korean using the -야겠어요 ending.

a I'll have to eat bibimbap tomorrow.
b I'll have to go to Dongdaemun market in the evening.

4 YOU CAN AND YOU CAN'T

Korean has a very common way of saying that you can or can't do something (in the sense of being able to carry it out, rather than knowing how to). Take a processive verb stem (a verb of doing), add the ending -ㄹ 수 if the stem ends in a vowel and -을 수 if it ends in a consonant, and then add either 있어요, to say you can do the verb, or 없어요, to say that you can't. For example:

먹을 수 있어요   *I can eat it*
먹을 수 없어요   *I can't eat it*
갈 수 있어요   *I can go*
갈 수 없어요   *I can't go*

It's as simple as that! But you must practise it until you can do it fast.

Translate the following sentences into English.

a 오늘 집에 돌아올 수 없어요.
b 저 한자를 읽을 수 있어요?

5 RETORTING

Sometimes people say things which are really stupid and Korean provides a nice (and not too rude) way of pointing that out and implying (just gently) that the person should have known better.

Look again at the following dialogue extract.

남편	그럼, 책은요?
부인	할아버지는 독서를 싫어하시잖아요?
남편	할머니는 독서를 좋아하시니까 대신 읽으시면 되잖아요.
부인	농담하지 마세요.
	좀 더 좋은 생각을 말해보세요.
남편	우산은 어떨까요?
부인	할아버지는 비 올 때 나가지 않으시잖아요.
남편	그럼 양말은?
부인	작년에 사드렸잖아요.
남편	그럼 새 전기 면도기는 어떨까요?
부인	그건 재작년에 사드렸잖아요.

The man keeps suggesting what to buy for Grandfather for his birthday and the wife thinks his suggestions are a bit silly. For example, he suggests buying something they bought last year. The implication is that the man should know what they bought for Grandfather last year, so he shouldn't have been so stupid as to suggest buying it again. Therefore the wife says:

작년에 샀잖아요! (from 샀-, past base of 사-)
We bought that last year!

Note the implication: you should know we bought him that last year, stupid! What did you go and suggest it again for?

One of the very common uses of the pattern is to give an answer when someone asks you something obvious, to which they should really know the answer. Suppose someone met you and you were dressed all in black and they asked you why. You could say 'because I'm going to a funeral!' and you would put -잖아요 onto the stem of the main verb of the sentence. Suppose you are going to get married and someone asked you why. You might respond:

사랑하잖아요!
It's because I love them, stupid!

 사랑하-   *love*

It's a very useful pattern, and one that makes your Korean sound natural and colourful.

The ending -잖아요 attaches to a present or a past base, and to honorific bases (note the sound change ㅆ to ㄷ when -잖아요 is added to past bases).

 Find other examples of this -잖아요 ending in the dialogue extract. Translate them into English.

6 HAVING ONE RIGHT THERE

You know how to say that someone has something by using the verb 있어요. Korean has another verb form, which stresses a bit more the act of possessing: 갖고 있- and 갖고 계시- (the second one is the honorific form and is usually found in the polite honorific form 갖고 계세요).

Often it has the force 'I have one right here', 'I have one with me now'. Imagine a situation in which someone wants a lighter. Someone else in the room has one and as he fumbles in his pockets, he might well say, 나는 갖고 있어요. This stresses that he has one with him right there.

This is a form you need to be able to recognize rather than to actually use frequently yourself.

Vocabulary builder 2

TRAFFIC OFFENCES

 09.03 **Listen to the words and try to pronounce them. Try to imitate the speaker.**

경찰	*policeman*
운전수	*driver*
면허증	*(driving) licence*
보여주-	*to show*
주차한	*parked*
주차하-	*to park*
똑	*exactly, precisely* (often used with 같-)
같은	*same*
같-	*be the same, be similar*
방향	*direction*
빨간	*red*
색	*colour*
일방통행	*one way*
일방통행로	*one-way street*
표지	*sign, signpost*
큰	*big*
실수	*mistake*
실수하-	*make a mistake*
들어오-	*to enter*
위험하-	*be dangerous*
벌금	*fine, penalty*
표지판	*signpost*
조심하-	*be careful, be cautious*

NEW EXPRESSIONS

Read the expressions that are used in the next dialogue. Note their meanings.

왜요? 무슨 문제가 있어요?	*Why? What's the problem?*
뭘 말이에요?	*What are you talking about?*
정말 몰라서 그러세요?	*Do you really not know (what you're doing)?*
그래서요?	*So what?*
정말 몰랐어요.	*I really didn't know / realize.*
한 번만 봐주세요!	*Please let me off just this once!*
수고하세요!	*Work hard!* (said to someone doing their job)

Dialogue 2

미안합니다, 정말로 몰랐어요! **I'M SORRY, I REALLY DIDN'T KNOW!**

09.04 A policeman catches a driver going the wrong way up a one-way street.

1 **What do you notice about the way the policeman and driver speak to each other? Which style of speech do they use? Why do you think this is the case?**

경찰	실례합니다. 면허증 좀 보여주세요.
운전수	왜요? 무슨 문제가 있나요?
경찰	정말 몰라서 그러세요?
운전수	뭘 말이에요?
경찰	여기 주차한 차들을 한 번 보세요. 차를 다 똑같은 방향으로 주차했잖아요.
운전수	그래서요?
경찰	그러면 저 빨간 색 일방 통행 표지를 못 봤어요?
운전수	아! 일방통행로군요. 미안합니다. 정말로 몰랐어요.
경찰	큰 실수를 하셨어요. 일방통행로에 잘못 들어오면 아주 위험하고 벌금도 많아요.
운전수	정말 표지판을 못 봤어요. 한 번만 봐주세요.
경찰	다음부터 조심하세요. 벌금은 오만원입니다.
운전수	고맙습니다. 수고하세요.

2 **What traffic offence has the driver committed? What are the consequences for such an offence?**

3 **What reason does the driver give for having committed the traffic offence?**

Language discovery 2

 Look again at the following dialogue extract. Identify the honorific forms of the following verbs.

경찰	큰 실수를 하셨어요.
	일방통행로에 잘못 들어오면 아주 위험하고 벌금도 많아요.
운전수	정말 표지판을 못 봤어요.
	한 번만 봐주세요.
경찰	다음부터 조심하세요.
	벌금은 오만원입니다.
운전수	고맙습니다. 수고하세요.

a 했어요
b 봐줘요
c 조심해요

1 HONORIFIC FORMS

It's now time that we talked a bit more systematically about honorific verbs. You have already learned that honorifics are used in Korean to show respect to the person you are talking about and in the present tense this is often done by using the form which you have learned as the 'polite request form' -(으)세요. In actual fact this form is not only used to make requests, it is also used to make statements or to ask questions about anyone to whom you wish to show respect. It is very common in Korean, and you will use it whenever you meet and talk to new people of equivalent or senior status (to ask them questions, for example).

Actually, the form -(으)세요 is an abbreviation of the honorific particle (으)시, plus the vowel -어(-오ˇ), plus the polite particle -요. This contracts to give the form you know -(으)세요.

Just as there are present and past stems, so also there are honorific stems. The honorific present stem is the usual stem plus the honorific particle -(으)시. The honorific past stem is the usual stem plus -(으)셨-:

stem	hon stem	hon past stem
앉-	앉으시-	앉으셨-
읽-	읽으시-	읽으셨-
가-	가시-	가셨-
오-	오시-	오셨-

You can add verb endings to the present honorific stem, as you would a normal verb with a stem ending in -이-. Everything about the honorific stems is regular apart from the present polite style which contracts to -(으)세요, as you have already learned:

할아버지는 은행에 가시고 할머니는 우체국에 가세요.
Grandfather is going to the bank and Grandmother is going to the post office.

김 선생님 운전하실 수 있어요?
Can Mr Kim drive?

김 선생님 운전할 수 있으세요?
Can Mr Kim drive? (identical)

벌써 가셨구나! (from 가셨-, past honorific base of 가-)
He's already gone (surprise, surprise)!

탁구를 치셨어요.
He played table tennis.

 Translate the following sentences into English.
a 거기 앉으세요.
b 어디 가세요?
c 언제 오셨어요?
d 시장에서 뭐 사셨어요?

2 QUESTIONS WITH -나요

The particle -나 is often used as a way of asking questions and when you use it in the polite style, you should also add the polite particle -요 to give -나요. (Without the -요 it is an informal question which you could only use between friends or to ask a question of someone younger or of lower status than you.)

It is added onto the stem of any verb (either the present stem or the past stem). Here are a couple of examples:

주문했나요?	*Have you ordered? (했- past base of 하-)*
신문 거기 있나요?	*Is the newspaper over there? (from 있-)*
어디 가나?	*Where are you going?*
점심 먹었나?	*Did you have lunch? (먹었- past base of 먹-)*

3 INTRODUCING MODIFIERS: MAKING VERBS INTO NOUNS

You now need to learn about something called modifiers, which are a kind of verb. First, we will show you how to make them, and then we will worry about what they mean. In this unit we shall just look at one of their uses and then later we shall look at the other uses.

How you make the modifier form of a verb depends on whether it is a processive or a descriptive verb.

Processive verbs

For processive verbs, add -는 to the verb stem. Thus the modifier form of 가- is 가는, the modifier form of 먹- is 먹는, and so on. You will find that when you add -는 to verb stems that end in consonants, sound changes will take place. For 먹-, therefore, the Hangul letters will literally read 먹는, but the pronunciation (according to the rules of sound change you learned before) will be [멍는].

To make a past tense modifier form for processive verbs you add -(으)ㄴ to the stem, so that the past tense modifier forms of 먹- and 가- are 먹은 and 간. You cannot do this with the verbs 있- and 없-. These verbs behave like processive verbs, so that the modifier forms are 있는 and 없는 in the present tense – they do not have past tense modifier forms.

Descriptive verbs

For descriptive verbs, simply add -ㄴ if the stem ends in a vowel, and -은 if it ends in a consonant. As you can see, this is identical to the past tense modifier form for processive verbs. There is no past tense modifier form for the descriptive verbs.

Try to memorize these rules.

We will now look at just one meaning of the modifier form of verbs. Sometimes you want to talk about the act of doing things (doing verbs), as though they were nouns. In English, for example, we say things like *I like swimming* which means I like the act of swimming, and of course 'swimming' comes originally from the verb 'swim'.

Korean is able to express *the act of* (verb)*ing* by using a modifier form, plus the noun 것, often abbreviated to 거. Here are examples:

가는 것	*the act of going*
영화 보는 거	*the act of seeing a film*
여기 앉는 거 (from 앉-)	*the act of sitting here*

You can then simply add verbs like 좋아요/좋아해요/싫어해요/안 좋아해요 afterwards to say what you think about those particular activities.

Match the following examples to the correct translation.

편지   *letter*
쓰-   *write*

a 영화 보는 거 좋아해요?   **1** Do you like seeing films?
b 여기 있는 거 좀 보세요.   **2** It's dangerous to drink and drive.
c 편지 쓰는 거 싫어해요.   **3** I hate writing letters.
d 술 마시고 운전하는 거   **4** Please look at what is here.
   위험해요.

Practice

1 Say that you are worried about the following things.

  a That teacher will come (to a party).
  b That there won't be enough food.
  c That Mr Kim might not come.
  d That your girlfriend might not like you any more.
  e That it might rain.

2 Here are some situations. Make up Korean sentences to say what you will have to do because of them, using -야겠어요.

  a Your head hurts.
  b You can't meet your boyfriend tonight.
  c You need to use a dictionary, but you don't have one.
  d You go out and realize you've forgotten something. (You'll have to go back.)
  e You want to know what's going on at the theatre. (You'll have to look at the newspaper.)

3 You're trying to decide about the following things. Say so in Korean, using a similar pattern to the one you were using in Question 1.

  a What to buy.
  b What to wear. (wear: 입-)
  c Where to sit.
  d What to order.
  e Where to go at the weekend.

4 Translate the following sentences into Korean, using the pattern
-(으)ㄹ 수 있어요/없어요 that you have learned in this lesson.

   a Can I come too?
   b Is this edible?
   c Can you meet me tomorrow?
   d I can't speak Japanese.
   e I don't have any money, so I can't buy it.
   f I can't park here.

5 Make up retorts to the following Korean statements using the
   -잖아요 pattern.

   a 왜 안 샀어요?   (I bought it yesterday, didn't I!)
   b 이 사람이 남자 친구예요?   (No, I'm already married, stupid!)
   c 면도 안 하세요?   (I already did it!)
   d 이 책을 읽어보세요.   (I hate reading, stupid!)
   e 이 사람이 누구세요?   (It's my wife! You only met her
                              yesterday!)

6 Imagine you are talking to your sister and discussing with
   her what to buy your brother for a birthday present. You make
   the following suggestions of what to buy, but she manages
   to find a reason against it until the very last suggestion.
   Give your suggestions and the answers she makes, trying to
   make the dialogue as interesting as you can. (NB jeans,
   청바지; CD, 씨디)

? Test yourself

1 Make the following passage honorific where appropriate. We have told you that normally you only need one honorific verb in a sentence, but for the purposes of this exercise use as many honorifics as you can. Look out for sentences that should not have them, however!

김 선생님은 대학교 선생님이에요. 런던 대학교에서 한국말을 가르치고 일본말도 가르쳐요. 매일 아침 공원에 가서 산책해요. 개하고 같이 가요. 공원은 아주 좋아요. 김 선생님 의 개는 고기를 잘 먹어요. 작년부터 부인도 가끔 산책하기 시작했어요. 부인도 가면 둘이 식당에 가서 커피 한잔 마셔요.

2 Translate the following sentences into English.

a 오늘 전화 드려야겠어요.

b 이 식당에서는 술을 마실 수 없어요.

c 커피 드셨나요? 커피 사드릴까요?

d 같이 영화 볼 수 있어요? 저는 영화 보는 거 정말 좋아해요.

e 점심에 무엇을 먹을까 결정해야겠어요.

SELF CHECK

I CAN...
...disagree and apologize.
...suggest ideas for buying presents.
...say you can and can't do something.
...use honorific verb forms.
...use modifiers.

10 그걸 어떻게 하셨어요? / 두통

What did you do with it? / Nasty headaches

In this unit you will learn how to:

▶ *describe things that you have lost and say when and where you lost them.*

▶ *buy medicine from a Korean 약국 or chemist.*

▶ *use 'when' clauses.*

▶ *say it seems as though something or other will happen.*

CEFR: *Can describe past activities and personal experiences (A2); can tell a story or describe something in a simple list of points (A2); can understand clearly written, or spoken, straightforward instructions (B1).*

Chemists

Most 약국 (*chemists*) – often just signposted as 약 (*medicine*) – open from 9 a.m. until late evening, often 9 p.m. Despite these long opening hours, getting 약 at night is very difficult. Even in Seoul, an 응급실 (*A & E department*) may be the only option. Expect the range and strength of 약 that 약사 (*pharmacists*) are allowed to dispense to be superior to what you can get at home.

Korea has no GP system. Patients choose a specialist clinic based on their ailment and go straight there. For most everyday illnesses you would go to the 내과 (*internal medicine clinic*). For cuts and sprains and so on, you would go to the 외과 (*external medical clinic*). Other clinics people often attend include the 이비인후과 (*ear, nose and throat specialist*), 피부과 (*dermatologist*) and 산부인과 (*gynaecologist*).

As well as Western 약, oriental medicines are also commonly dispensed at the 약국. Oriental medical clinics, known as 한의원, are also widespread, and offer various 한약 (*herbal remedies*) and traditional treatments such as 침술 (*acupuncture*).

Where would you go if you broke your ankle in Korea?

Vocabulary builder 1

DESCRIBING A LOST BAG

 10.01 **Listen to the words and try to pronounce them. Try to imitate the speaker.**

가방	*a briefcase, a bag*	사실	*in fact*
놓-	*put down, leave*	카드	*a card (e.g. credit card)*
찾아보-	*have a look, look for*		
찾-	*search*	물어보-	*ask*
이렇게/그렇게	*like this / like that*	잃어버리-	*lose*
		한 (number/time) 쯤	*about, around, approximately*
생기-	*look (like)*	때	*time (when)*
검정	*black*	생각나-	*remember, it comes to mind*
가죽	*leather*		
만들-	*make* (ㄹ- irregular verb like 팔-, 놀-, etc.)	청소하-	*clean up*
		경찰서	*police station*
서류	*document*	보내-	*send*
중요하-	*be important*	보관하-	*keep*
들어 있-	*be contained, be included*		

NEW EXPRESSIONS

Read the expressions that are used in the next dialogue. Note their meanings.

없는 것 같은데요.	*It doesn't look as though there is anything / are any.*
무슨 일입니까?	*How can I help you?, What's the problem?*
어떻게 생겼어요?	*What does it look like?*
(… -한테) 한번 물어볼게요.	*I'll just ask (such and such a person).*
그걸 어떻게 하셨어요?	*What did you do with it?*
… -이/가 어딘지 좀 가르쳐주세요.	*Please tell me where (such and such) is.*
좌회전한 다음에	*after doing a left turn*
우회전한 다음에	*after doing a right turn*

🔊 Dialogue 1

그걸 어떻게 하셨어요? **WHAT DID YOU DO WITH IT?**

손님	*customer*	영업	*business*
사장(님)	*manager* (honorific form)	끝나-	*finish* (as in *it finishes*)
식사하-	*have meal*	째	*number* (time)
나오-	*come out*	골목	*alley, small road*
저희	(humble form of 우리,	예	*yes* (same as 네)
	our, my)	저 …	*er . . . , hmm . . .*

10.02 A customer returns to the restaurant after realizing they left their bag there the previous night.

1 How does the restaurant employee say *I don't think we have anything*?

손님	저 실례합니다. 저는 어제 친구들이랑 여기 왔었는데요, 가방을 놓고 갔어요.
종업원	제가 가서 한번 찾아보지요. 가방이 어떻게 생겼어요?
손님	네, 아주 크고, 검정색이고, 가죽으로 만들었어요.
종업원	저기 서류 가방이 있는데, 저거예요?
손님	아니요, 서류 가방이 아니에요.
A little while later.	
종업원	없는 것 같은데요. 뭐 중요한 게 들어 있나요?
손님	예, 사실 아주 중요한 서류하고 책하고 은행카드가 들어 있어요.
종업원	저런! 잠깐 기다려보세요. 사장님한테 한번 물어볼게요.
The manager comes.	
사장	안녕하세요? 무슨 일입니까?
손님	제 가방을 잃어버렸어요. 어제 여기서 식사하고 놓고 나왔어요.
사장	몇 시에 저희 식당에서 나가셨나요?
손님	한 열한 시 쯤이에요.
사장	영업 끝날 때쯤 … 아, 예, 생각나요. 오늘 아침 청소할 때 가방이 하나 있었어요.
손님	그걸 어떻게 하셨어요?
사장	경찰서에 보냈어요. 그 사람들이 보관하고 있을 거예요.
손님	경찰서가 어디인지 좀 가르쳐주시겠어요?
사장	식당에서 나가서 좌회전한 다음에 오른쪽으로 세 번째 골목에 있어요.
손님	정말 감사합니다. 안녕히 계세요.

2 How does the manager say *when we were finishing up . . . ?*

3 What time did the customer leave the restaurant?

4 Where is the bag now? How do you get there from the restaurant?

Language discovery 1

 Look at the following two sets of sentences. What is the particle that creates the plural form of a noun in Korean?

어제 친구들이랑 여기 왔었는데요.
I came here with my friends yesterday.

어제 친구랑 여기 왔었는데요.
I came here with my friend yesterday.

1 MAKING PLURALS

A Korean noun can be either singular or plural, depending on the context. In other words, Korean does not have one word for *dog* and another word for *dogs*; it has just one word 개 which can mean either. It is very rare that there is any ambiguity or confusion because of this, however.

There is a plural particle which can be used to show explicitly that a word is plural – it is -들. You can then add subject, object, topic (-이, -을, -은) or other particles, such as -도 or -하고, onto the plural form. Thus you could have any of the following forms: -들도, -들은, -들이, -들을, -들하고, -들한테, and so on.

2 ENDING SENTENCES WITH -는데요

The clause ending -는데 indicates that you have something more to say, that you are going to elaborate on what you have just said. You can also end a sentence with -는데 by adding the polite particle -요 after it. The use is very like that for -는데, except that saying -는데요 allows you to make more of a pause than using -는데. Often -는데요 is used to explain who you are, where you have come from, or what you want to do. The following sentence would go on to give more specific information, either about what the person you are speaking to should do about it or what you would like to happen (on the basis of having explained who you are, for example!). This all sounds a bit confusing in writing, and it is perhaps best to explain by example. In the following sentences, the first could be ended in Korean with -는데요. Notice how the second sentence often makes an explicit request, or homes in to ask something:

I'm from the BBC. (는데요)	I'd like to do an interview.
I'd like to buy a bicycle. (는데요)	Can you show me your range?
I'm the brother of your friend. (는데요)	Pleased to meet you! May I have a seat?

Since -는데요 is a colloquial expression, you will sometimes find it used in other ways which do not seem to fit exactly into the system we have described here. However, for using the form yourself, if you remember the rules we have given you, you won't go wrong.

Note also that -는데요 and the related -는데 are added to the present stem of processive verbs, and on to the past stem of both processive and descriptive verbs. The form (으)ㄴ데요 and the related (으)ㄴ데 are only used for the present tense of descriptive verbs. Taking a processive verb and a descriptive verb in both past and present tenses, then, we would get the following forms:

	하- (processive)	좋- (descriptive)
present	하는데요	좋은데요
past	했는데요	좋았는데요

Remember that in the past examples the first of the two ㄴ sounds (before the hyphen) represents the double ㅆ of the past base which has become pronounced as an ㄴ through the pronunciation rules described previously.

3 IT SEEMS LIKE

You can say that *it seems like something is happening* in Korean by using modifier forms of verbs plus 것 같아요. 같- is a verb which means *is like*, so 비가 오는 것 같아요 means literally *the act of raining it is like*, or, in effect, *it seems like it's raining*. Remember that the modifier forms are different depending on whether the main verb is processive or descriptive.

Here are some examples:

선생님이 티비를 보시는 것 같아요.
It seems like the teacher is watching TV.

민호가 빵을 먹는 것 같아요.
It seems like Minho is eating bread.

영국은 날씨가 나쁜 것 같아요.
It seems like the weather is bad in England.

이 집이 좋은 것 같아요.
This house seems to be nice.

Translate the following examples into English.

a 영국은 날씨가 나쁜 것 같아요.
b 이 집이 좋은 것 같아요.

4 WHEN SOMETHING HAPPENS

The form -(으)ㄹ is added to the stem of verbs, for example, in the endings -(으)ㄹ까(요), -(으)ㄹ까 해요 and -(으)ㄹ거에요. In actual fact this -(으)ㄹ is the future modifier. It is a modifier just like -는 and -(으)ㄴ, but it has a future meaning. This means that you can use the pattern you have just learned (modifer + 것 같아요) to say it seems like something will happen:

비가 올 것 같아요.   *It seems like it will rain.*

갈 것 같아요.   *It seems as though s/he will go.*

Put the following sentences into the future modifier form.

a 민호가 빵을 먹는 것 같아요.
b 선생님이 TV를 보시는 것 같아요.

An even more important use of -(으)ㄹ is when it is followed by the noun 때 which means *time*. The whole construction (verb stem)-(으)ㄹ 때 means *when (verb) happens*. Have a look at the examples:

학교에 갈 때   *when I go to school*

비가 올 때   *when it rains*

어머니 돌아올 때   *when Mum gets back*

Here are some examples in sentences. Match the sentences to the correct translation.

a 방에서 나올 때 방을 청소하세요.

1 When you come out of the room, please clean it up.

b 한국말을 가르칠 때 학생들이 많았어요?

2 When you eat, drink some water too.

c 밥 먹을때 물도 같이 마셔요.

3 Were there many students when you taught Korean?

Vocabulary builder 2

BUYING MEDICINE FROM THE CHEMIST

 10.03 **Listen to the words and try to pronounce them. Try to imitate the speaker.**

약사	*pharmacist, chemist*
심하-	*is serious*
언제	*when*
원인	*reason, cause*
눈	*an eye*
잠	*sleep (noun)*
주무시-	*sleep (honorific equivalent of 자-)*
관련	*relation, link*
잡숴보-	*try eating (honorific form)*
잡수시-	*eat (honorific equivalent of 먹-)*
한알	*one tablet*
나아지-	*get better*
하루에	*per day*
-마다	*each, every*
식후	*after meals, after the meal*
부작용	*a side-effect*
졸음	*sleepiness, drowsiness*
같은 것	*(a) similar thing, something similar*
쉽게	*easily*
피로	*fatigue, weariness*
느끼-	*to feel*
놀라-	*to be surprised, be shocked*

NEW EXPRESSIONS

Read the expressions that are used in the next dialogue. Note their meanings.

그렇군요	*Ah, I see; it's like that, is it?*
아마 스트레스가 원인인 것 같아요.	*It seems as though it's because of stress.*
네 시간마다 한 알 씩 드세요.	*Take one tablet every four hours.*
식후에 한 알 씩 세번 드세요.	*Take one tablet three times a day after meals.*
쉽게 피로를 느껴도 놀라지 마세요.	*Don't be surprised if you feel tired very easily.*

 # Dialogue 2

두통 **NASTY HEADACHES**

회사	*company*
받-	*receive*
과로	*overwork*

10.04 Mr Pak goes to the chemist to get some medicine for a nasty headache.

1 How does the pharmacist say the following verbs in honorific form?

   a 잘 자요?
   b 약을 먹어보아요.

약사	어서 오세요.
	무슨 약을 드릴까요?
박선생	네, 두통이 아주 심한데, 두통약 좀 주시겠어요?
약사	네, 언제부터 아프기 시작했어요?
박선생	어제부터 아프기 시작했어요.
	회사에서 일을 너무 많이 하고 스트레스를 많이 받았어요.
	아마 과로하고 스트레스가 원인인 것 같아요.
약사	그렇군요. 눈은 아프지 않으세요?
박선생	네, 조금 아파요.
약사	잠은 잘 주무세요?
박선생	아니요. 머리가 너무 아파서 잘 못 자요.
약사	알겠어요. 아마 스트레스하고 관련이 있는 것 같아요. 이 약을 잡숴보세요.
박선생	하루에 몇 번씩 먹나요?
약사	두통이 심할 때는 네 시간마다 한 알씩 드시고, 좀 나아지면 식후에 한 알씩 하루 세 번 드세요.
박선생	부작용 같은 것은 없나요?
약사	이 약을 먹으면 졸음이 오니까 조심하세요.
	그리고 쉽게 피로를 느껴도 놀라지 마세요.
박선생	네, 고맙습니다.

---

2 Decide whether the following statements are true or false.

   a Mr Pak has been in pain since the morning.
   b Mr Pak's head hurts a lot, but his eyes are fine.
   c Mr Pak should take one tablet after meals (three times a day) when the pain gets a bit better.
   d The medicine has no side effects.

Language discovery 2

 Look at the following sentence. Is it in the honorific form? How can you tell? Identify the verb stem.

두통약 좀 주시겠어요?

1 ASKING POLITE QUESTIONS

Korean often uses the ending -겠어요 added to the honorific stem of verbs to ask polite questions. Examples are: 지금 가시겠어요? (*are you going now?*), 주문하시겠어요? (*would you like to order?*). It can also be used to express requests: 해 주시겠어요? (*would you do it for me?*).

2 IMMEDIATE FUTURE

The form -(으)ㄹ 거예요 puts sentences in the future tense. Korean has another future form -(으)ㄹ게요, added to the present stem of processive verbs, which expresses a more definite (rather than probable) future: something you will certainly do, are promising to do or are just about to do. It is often used in circumstances where there is no doubt about whether or not you will be able to do the thing concerned. You can only use this form to say what you yourself will do, since you have control over your own actions. You cannot say what someone else will do, since you have no control over their actions and there is therefore always a certain element of doubt about them.

3 HONORIFIC VERBS

Korean has several verbs which are only used in the honorific form (the non-honorific form is a completely different verb). In this unit you meet the verb 주무시- which is the honorific stem of the verb 자- (*sleep*). Here is a list of the common honorific verbs and their non-honorific equivalents. Notice especially the verb 있어요.

non-honorific	meaning	honorific	hon polite
자-	*sleep*	주무시-	주무세요
먹-	*eat*	잡수시-	잡수세요
있-	*exist, stay*	계시-	계세요
있-	*have*	있으시-	있으세요
죽-	*die*	돌아가시-	돌아가세요
먹-/마시-	*eat / drink*	드시-	드세요

Put the following sentences into the honorific form.

a 저녁 식사 먹어요.

b 선생님 지금 어디 있어요?

c 너무 늦게 자네요.

> **LANGUAGE TIP**
> Some verbs have specific honorific verbs which are entirely different from their non-honorific counterparts. It can be quite insulting to use the non-honorific form by mistake for an esteemed person, so it's worth getting these right.

Practice

1 This exercise is designed to help you practise the -(느)ㄴ데요 form. If we give you a Korean sentence ending in -(느)ㄴ데요, you must provide a second sentence that fits with it. If we give you the second sentence in Korean, then you are meant to make up a first sentence with -(느)ㄴ데요 along the lines of the English that we suggest.

  a 영국 대사관의 토니인데요. (Create appropriate second sentence)

  b (I've come from England) 거기서 한국말을 조금 공부했어요.

  c (I telephoned yesterday) 김 선생님 좀 바꿔 주시겠어요?

  d 어제 친구하고 여기 왔는데요. (Create appropriate second sentence)

  e (I want to buy a dictionary) 하나 보여주시겠어요?

  f 저는 김 선생님의 부인인데요. (Where has Mr Kim gone?)

2 Make up a sentence for each of the following verbs. Put the verb into the *it seems like* pattern with -(느)ㄴ 것 같아요.

  a 비가 와요.

  b 박 선생님이에요.

  c 독서를 싫어해요.

  d 동대문 시장에 갔어요.

  e 김 선생님 오세요.

  f 가방을 여기 놓았어요.

3 You have lost your jacket and the man at the lost property office asks you to describe it. (*pocket*: 주머니)

4 Join up the following sets of clauses, so that the meaning is *when A, B*. Thus, the first one will be *When you eat your food, don't talk* or, in better English, *Don't talk when you're eating*.

  a When you eat food   don't talk
  b When you park your car   take care
  c When you are going into town call me
  d When the film's over   let's go to a restaurant
  e When I arrived home   I had a beer
     (도착하-, *arrive*)
  f When you go out   let's go together

5 You have a headache and your friend, who has gone out while you were asleep, leaves you some tablets with a note about when to take them. What are his instructions?

> 심할 땐 네 시간마다
> 두 알 드세요.
> 좀 나아지면,
> 점심 때만 식전에 한 알씩
> 드세요

❓ Test yourself

1 Translate the following sentences into English.

a 어쨌든 지금 무엇을 하기로 했어요?

b 우리 여자 친구 못 봤어요? 보면 저한테 전화하세요.

c 좀 나아지면 약을 더 이상 먹지 마세요.

d 언제 졸업할 거에요? 그 다음에 무슨 계획이 있어요?

e 이 서류가 중요해요? 중요하지요! 내 면허증이잖아요!

f 데이트를 할 때 영화 보러 자주 가요.

2 Translate the following sentences into Korean.

a You've made a big mistake!

b If you go into the city late at night it's dangerous.

c Would you show me that dictionary? Where did you buy it?

d Is there a problem? Yes, I seem to have lost my medicine.

e I've had so much stress lately and I can't sleep at night.

f You've lost your bag? What was inside?

g You don't like my ideas!

h So what did you do?

SELF CHECK

	I CAN...
⚪	...say I've lost something or left it behind.
⚪	...say when and where I lost an item.
⚪	...describe items of lost property and what was inside it.
⚪	...describe an ailment and ask for medicine.
⚪	...understand instructions for taking medicine.
⚪	...form and use when clauses.
⚪	...say it seems as though something or other will happen.

한번 입어보시겠어요? / 나한테 잘 어울리니?

Would you like to try it on? / Do you think it suits me?

In this unit you will learn how to:

▶ *shop for clothes.*
▶ *comment on prices, quality and style.*
▶ *compare one thing with another.*
▶ *use informal styles of speech (used between close friends).*
▶ *use more modifiers and honorifics.*

CEFR: *Can explain likes or dislikes (A2); can use connectors to describe something as a list of points (A2); can use simple descriptive language to make statements about and compare objects (A2); can cope with less routine situations in shops (B1).*

Shopping in Korea

Korea is a shopper's paradise with fantastic 가격 (*prices*) for absolutely everything, especially if you know where to go!

The best bargains are to be found in Seoul's numerous 지하상가 (*underground shopping centres*), where prices for a T-shirt can start from as low as 5,000 won. Two of the biggest and most popular 지하상가 are located at 강남역 (*Gangnam Station*) and 고속터미널역 (*Express Bus Terminal Station*).

쇼핑 (*shopping*) hotspots near 대학교 (*universities*) offer great bargains, too. In particular, the 쇼핑 areas near 이화여자대학교 (*Ewha Woman's University*), also known as 이대, and 홍익대학교 (*Hongik University*), also known as 홍대, are popular destinations for the young and beautiful as they specialize in affordable fashion. 명동 (*Myeongdong*) is another of Seoul's coveted 쇼핑 areas that is always packed.

At the opposite end of the spectrum, luxury boutiques (both Korean and Western) and 백화점 (*department stores*) can be found in the affluent areas of Seoul such as 압구정 (*Apgujeong*), 청담동 (*Cheongdamdong*) and 강남 (*Gangnam*).

 Shinsegae was Korea's first 백화점. Where would you expect to find it in Seoul – 강남 or near 홍익대학교?

Vocabulary builder 1

CHOOSING AN OUTFIT

11.01 **Listen to the words and try to pronounce them. Try to imitate the speaker.**

셔츠	*shirt*
디자인	*design*
구식	*old style, old fashioned*
꼭	*exactly, certainly, precisely*
질	*quality*
별로	*(not) particularly*
곳	*place*
활동적	*casual, active*
활동적인	*(modifier form of the above, like an adjective)*
밝은	*bright*
청바지	*blue jeans*
멋있-	*be stylish, be handsome*
유행하-	*be popular, be in vogue*
스타일	*style*
재료	*stuff, (raw) material (also ingredients)*
퍼센트	*per cent*
면	*cotton*
어울리-	*suit (a person)*

NEW EXPRESSIONS

Read the expressions that are used in the next dialogue. Note their meanings.

내 마음에 꼭 들어 (요).	*I like it very much.*
한번 입어보시겠어요?	*Would you like to try it on?*
와, 정말 싸다.	*Wow, that's really cheap.*
에이!	*Hey!*
⋯ -한테 어울려요?	*Does it suit . . . ?*

Dialogue 1

한번 입어보시겠어요? **WOULD YOU LIKE TO TRY IT ON?**

11.02 Minho and Byongsoo go to Namdaemun market to buy some clothes.

1 Identify two examples of informal speech from the dialogue. Remember, the polite form normally ends in -요. (Hint: informal speech is used between friends.)

민호	저 셔츠 좀 봐라. 정말 좋다.
병수	그래? 내 생각에는 디자인이 좀 구식 같다.
민호	아니야. 내 마음에 꼭 들어. 아가씨, 저 셔츠 얼마예요?
점원 A	팔천원이에요.
민호	와, 정말 싸다.
병수	에이, 그런데 이거 봐. 질이 별로 안 좋아.
민호	글쎄, 그럼 다른 곳에 가볼까?

Minho and Byongsoo decide to try out the department store instead.

점원 B	어서오세요. 뭘 찾으세요?
민호	좀 활동적인 옷을 찾는데요, 좀 밝은 색으로요. 청바지하고 같이 입을 수 있는 멋있고 질 좋은 옷이요.
점원 B	이거 어때요? 요즘 아주 유행하는 스타일이에요.
민호	재료가 뭐예요?
점원 B	백 퍼센트 면이에요. 한번 입어보시겠어요?
민호	네, 고맙습니다 … 나한테 어울려요?

2 What's wrong with the shirt at the market?

3 What is the shirt at the department store made of?

Language discovery 1

Match the following sentences to the correct translation.

a 정말 좋다.
b 디자인이 좀 구식같다.
c 정말 싸다.

1 The design is a bit old-fashioned.
2 It's really nice.
3 That's really cheap.

146

1 THE PLAIN STYLE

The plain style is used between very close friends or when speaking to someone much younger than you. It can also be used when saying something to yourself out loud and it is used as a written form in notices and in books and newspapers.

Its form is very like that of the modifiers, but with some important differences. For processive verbs you add -는 (after a consonant stem) or -ㄴ (after a vowel stem) onto the verb stem for the present tense, plus the verb ending -다. Hence: 듣는다, 기다린다, 먹는다, 한다, 마신다, etc. For the past tense you simply add -다 onto the past stem of the verb: 기다렸다, 먹었다, 했다, 마셨다.

For descriptive verbs, you add -다 to the stem of the verb, either the past stem or the present stem according to whether you want a past or present meaning.

Here are some example sentences in the plain style.

민호가 시장에 간다.	*Minho goes to the market.*
민호가 시장에 갔다.	*Minho went to the market.*
민호가 사과를 먹는다.	*Minho eats an apple.*
민호가 사과를 먹었다.	*Minho ate an apple.*
오늘 날씨가 좋다.	*Today, the weather is good.*
어제 날씨가 좋았다.	*Yesterday, the weather was good.*

In addition, there are two very common ways of asking questions in the plain style.

One of these is the question particle -나 added to any verb stem (past, present, honorific) without the particle -요 on the end. Here are some examples: 뭘 먹나? (*what are you eating?*), 뭘 하나? (*what are you doing?*).

Another common question pattern is to add -니? to any verb stem: 비가 오니? 어디 갔니? meaning *is it raining?* and *where did you go?* respectively.

Here are some examples of questions in the plain style:

남대문 시장이 어디니?
Where is Namdaemun market?

오늘 아침 무슨 약을 먹었니?
What medicine did you take this morning?

You can make commands in the plain style by adding -라 to the polite style of the present tense, minus the -요. Thus, plain style commands would include: 먹어라, 해라, 가지 마라 *eat it!, do it!, don't go!* (from 하지 마세요), and so on.

Plain style suggestions can be made by adding -자 to the present stem of any processive verb: 먹자, 하자, 이야기 하자 (*let's eat, let's do it, let's talk*) and so on.

2 THE INFORMAL STYLE

Korean also has another very important system of addressing those younger than you or very close to you, in addition to the plain style. In fact, it is perhaps even more common and it is very easy.

All you have to do is take the polite style of the verb (present, past or future) and take off the -요 particle! That's all there is to it:

Match the following familiar examples to the correct translation.

a 내 마음에 꼭 들어.	**1**	But look at this.
b 그런데 이거 봐.	**2**	The quality is not very good.
c 질이 별로 안 좋아.	**3**	I like it very much.

The one exception is the copula: instead of taking the -이에요 form and taking off the -요, the informal style of the copula is -야 after a vowel, and -이야 after a consonant:

저 사람은 한국 사람이야.　　　*That person is a Korean.*

김 선생님은 의사야.　　　*Mr Kim is a medical doctor.*

3 USE OF THE PARTICLE -(으)로

The particle -(으)로 has various functions. Here is a list of its different uses.

Instruments: by, by means of

기차로 와요
come by train

손으로 만들어요
make by hand

Cause, reason: because of

교통사고로 죽었어요.
(He) died (because of / in) a traffic accident.

개인적인 이유로 거절했어요.
(I) refused for a private reason.

Stuff, raw material: from, of

이 집은 나무로 만들었어요.
This house is made of wood.

와인은 포도로 만들어요.
Wine is made from grapes.

Unit, measure, degree: by

영국에서는 파운드/킬로로 팔아요.
They sell by the pound / kilo in Britain.

Direction: towards

런던으로 갔어요.
(He) went to London.

우리 집으로 오세요.
Please come to my house.

Complete the following sentences using the appropriate form of -(으)로. Then translate the sentences into English.

a 학교까지 버스 _____ 가세요.
b 이 옷들을 면 _____ 만들었어요.
c 부산 _____ 가자!

4 MORE ON MODIFIERS

You can make modifiers with -는 for processive verbs and -(으)ㄴ for descriptive verbs. You learned how they could be used with the noun 거(것) to mean *the act of* (verb)*ing*.

In addition to this, you can use modifiers in front of any noun and, as you would expect, their function is to modify the noun, to tell you something about the noun they modify. Here is a good example:

제가 먹는 사과

Here the noun is 사과 (*apple*), and 제가 먹는 (from the verb 먹-) is modifying the noun *apple*. The meaning of the phrase is *the apple I am eating*. In English, we put the noun first, and afterwards the modifying phrase (*(which) I am eating*), but in Korean it is the other way round. The noun and its modifying phrase can then be used as part of a sentence, as with any other noun. For example, you might want to say *the apple I am eating has gone bad* or *where is the apple I am eating?* You could do this in Korean like this (the modifying phrases are in brackets and you can see that they are optional; the sentences would make perfect sense without them, but the modifying phrases show which particular apple you are talking about):

(제가 먹는) 사과가 썩었어요

(제가 먹는) 사과가 어디 있어요?

 Identify the modifiers in the following sentences.

a 좀 활동적인 옷을 찾는데요, 좀 밝은 색으로요.

b 요즘 아주 유행하는 스타일이에요.

Vocabulary builder 2

TALKING ABOUT AN OUTFIT

 11.03 Listen to the words and try to pronounce them. Try to imitate the speaker.

응	*yes* (casual form)
맞-	*to fit well*
근사하-	*look super, look good*
겨우	*only*
비슷하-	*look similar*
다르-	*be different* (polite style: 달라요)
만에	*within, in only (two or three months)*
쓰게	*usable*
되-	*become*
배	*double, (two) times*
오래	*long*
가-	*last, endure*
훨씬	*by far, far and away*

NEW EXPRESSIONS

Read the expressions that are used in the next dialogue. Note their meanings.

제가 생각해도	*it seems to me / I think*
겨우 삼만 이천원인데요 뭐.	*It's only 32,000 won (it's not much).*
적어도요	*at least*
가서 생각 좀 다시 해봐야겠어요.	*I'll have to go away and think about it.*

 Dialogue 2

나한테 잘 어울리니? **DO YOU THINK IT SUITS ME?**

11.04 Minho tries the clothes on and they have another discussion.

1 How does the shop assistant ask if Minho would like to try on a bigger size?

점원	야, 아주 멋있는데요.
민호	(to Byongsoo) 나한테 어울리니?
병수	응, 잘 어울려. 그런데 좀 작은 것 같다.
점원	좀 큰 걸 입어보실래요?
민호	네.
점원	여기 있어요.

A little while later.

병수	그게 더 잘 맞는다.
점원	야, 아주 근사해요.
민호	그런데 얼마지요?
점원	삼만 이천원이에요.
민호	뭐라고요?
점원	왜요? 싼 거에요. 겨우 삼만 이천원인데요 뭐.
병수	제가 생각해도 좀 비싼 것 같은데요.
민호	남대문 시장에서는 비슷한 게 팔천원이에요.
점원	아, 네, 남대문하고는 비슷해 보여도 질이 달라요. 남대문 시장에서 옷을 사면 두세 달 만에 못 쓰게 돼서 새 옷을 사야 되거든요.
병수	그러면 이옷이 남대문 시장 옷보다 네 배나 더 오래 가요?
점원	적어도요. 그리고 훨씬 더 잘 맞아요.
민호	음, 가서 생각 좀 다시 해봐야겠어요.

2 How much is the shirt? What is Minho's initial reaction to the price?

3 According to the shop assistant, why is the shirt from the shop better than a similar one from the market?

Language discovery 2

Look at the following examples of sentences that use *do you want to . . . ?* Translate the final sentence into English yourself.

좀 큰 걸 입어보실래요?   *Do you want to try on a bigger one?*

여기 앉을래요?   *Do you want to sit here?*

버스 탈래요?   *Do you want to get the bus?*

비빔밥 먹을래요?

1 DO YOU WANT TO / DO YOU FEEL LIKE?

The pattern -(으)ㄹ래요 can be added to the stems of processive verb bases (present tense) to ask in a casual way if someone wants to do or feels like doing something. In the phrase 한번 입어 보실래요, it is added to the honorific form of 입어보- (*to try on*) to give the meaning *would you like to try it on?* Other examples would be:

커피 마실래요?
Do you want to drink coffee, do you fancy some coffee?

노래방에 갈래요?
How about going to a noraebang?

2 ENDING SENTENCES WITH 뭐

Sometimes Koreans will add 뭐 to the end of certain sentences as a kind of afterthought. It has no real translation (despite literally meaning *what!*), and you don't need to use it yourself. It means something like *you know, isn't it* or *I think*, but you should not try to translate it or think that it has any great significance when you come across it.

3 EVEN IF IT LOOKS THE SAME

Observe this sentence from the dialogue. 남대문하고는 비슷해 보여도 질이 달라요. The rather complex construction 비슷해 보여도 is a good example of how Korean uses particles and compound verbs in quite complicated ways to build up important meanings. We will work through it slowly to see how it is formed.

The basic verb is 비슷하-, which means *is similar*. To this the verb 보이- (*to look like, to appear*) has been added to give the meaning *to look similar, to appear similar*. Other compounded verbs include those with 주- and 보-. These verbs are added onto the polite style of the main verb, with the -요 particle taken off (for example, 먹어 보세요, *please try eating it*). This example is just the same; the polite style of *is similar* is taken (비슷해요), the -요 is removed (비슷해-) and the next verb 보이- is added (비슷해 보이-).

Then the form -(어)도, which means *even though*, is also added to the polite style of the verb, minus the -요.

This means that the meaning of the entire verb set 비슷해 보여도 is *even though it looks similar, even though it appears similar*.

4 USE OF THE VERB 되-

The verb 되- means *is OK, (it) will do*, and it can be used after verbs with the particle -도 (even though), to mean *it's OK if . . .* Here are two examples:

나가도 돼요.
It's OK to go out. (lit: *Even if / even though you go out, it's OK / it will do.*)

먹어도 돼요?
Is it OK to eat this? (lit: *Even if / though I eat this, is it OK?*)

This is a very useful pattern and is often used by Koreans to ask for and to give permission.

Another meaning of the verb 되- is *becomes*. For example when used with the words 못 쓰게 (*unusable*) it means *it becomes unusable*. You can add the ending -게 onto other verb stems, and follow it with 되- to say that something becomes or comes to a particular state.

Here are some other examples:

못 먹게 됐어요.
It has become inedible. (It's gone off!)

한국 여자하고 결혼하게 됐어요.
I came to marry a Korean girl.

 Translate the following sentences into Korean using the verb 되-.

a Is it okay to get the bus here?
b I came to eat lunch with a friend.
c It's OK to go home.

5 SPEECH STYLES AND HONORIFICS

We are taking this opportunity to remind you about the essential difference between speech styles and honorifics in Korean. It is absolutely essential that you are clear about the distinction, which is why we are going over it again and giving you a few more examples.

Remember, speech styles are decided according to the person you are talking to. Mostly you will use the polite style, but in formal situations you might use the formal style, and with close friends and young people or children you might use the informal style or the plain style.

The person you are talking about, however, will govern whether or not you use an honorific. There is thus no incompatibility between honorifics and informal speech styles. Imagine you are talking to a child and asking the child where his grandad has gone. You would use the informal or plain style (because you are talking to a child) and you would use an honorific (because you are talking about grandad, who is an older, esteemed person).

When you are addressing someone as 'you' and talking about them, things will be much more straightforward. If you are asking a child what he is doing, you would use an informal style and, of course, no honorific since the person you are talking about (the child) is not an honorific person. In contrast, if you are talking to a professor and asking him what he is doing, you might use the polite or even the formal style and you would certainly use an honorific.

 Here are a couple of examples of different combinations of speech styles and honorifics. Match the sentences to the correct translation. Make sure you understand in each case the social level of the person being addressed and the social level of the person being spoken about.

a 민호, 할아버지 뭐 하시니?

b 민호, 너 뭐 하니?

c 선생님, 할아버지 뭐 하세요?

d 선생님, 민호 뭐 해요?

1 Minho, what do you do?

2 Minho, what does your grandad do?

3 Professor, what does your grandad do?

4 Professor, what does Minho do?

> **LANGUAGE TIP**
>
> You use different styles (such as the polite style, the plain style, the informal style) depending on who you are speaking to (and irrespective of who you are speaking about). You use honorifics (like - (으)시, or the honorific verbs like 주무시-) if you are talking about someone who is esteemed or of high social status (or age).

🔓 Practice

1 **Put the following sentences into the plain style.**

   a 이 웃이 정말 좋아요!
   b 비가 와요.
   c 뭘 하세요?
   d 밥을 먹고 있어요.
   e 걱정하고 있어요?
   f 조금 더 기다리면 버스가 올 거에요.
   g 밥 먹어요.
   h 어제 밤 어디 갔어요?
   i 조심했어요?

2 **Translate the following phrases into Korean using the modifier forms you have learned in this lesson.**

   a clothes made of cotton
   b the beer we drank yesterday
   c the book Mr Kim is reading
   d the shirt he is wearing
   e the film we saw last year
   f the food I hate

3 **Join the following two sets of information with -어/아도 to give the meaning *even if A, then B* (or, *even though A, B*). For example, the first will be: *Even if it looks good, it isn't*.**

   a It looks good   it isn't
   b It's expensive   it'll be tasty
   c It's raining   I want to go out
   d I don't like him   I'll have to meet him
   e It's a bright colour   it doesn't suit you
   f I've got a headache   thinking of going to a noraebang

4 **Make up a dialogue between two people arguing about which film to see on TV tonight. One of them wants to see a film which the other one says they saw last year. He wants to see a different film, but the other thinks it's on too late and that it's boring anyway. To help you, here are three phrases that you might like to use:**

   그것은 우리가 작년에 본 영화잖아요!
   두시가 너무 늦었어요? 무슨 말이에요?!
   정말 재미없는 것 같아요.

Now say the dialogue aloud using the informal style for all the verb endings and taking out any honorific suffixes you might have used.

5 **You are looking for a new bag and come across the following pair. Compare one with the other (price, quality, size, colour) and say which one you would like to buy.**

🏻 Test yourself

1 **Translate the following sentences into Korean.**

   a That person who speaks Korean well is coming.
   b I don't like those clothes you bought yesterday.
   c He's a stylish man.
   d Even though the quality is better, it's four times as expensive.
   e Can I try on those clothes you are wearing?
   f What did you say?
   g Please take care when you are driving at night, even though you haven't been drinking.
   h Do you have anything similar?

2 **Change the following sentences from the polite style to the plain style and then the informal style.**

   a 도서관 가서 책을 읽었어요.
   b 학교에선 점심 때 뭘 먹나요?
   c 민호는 학생이에요.
   d 날씨가 안좋아요. 비가 와요.
   e 여기서 700번 버스 타야돼요.
   f 어제 수영장 갔었어요.

156

SELF CHECK

I CAN...

...shop for clothes and ask if something suits me.

...comment on prices, quality and style.

...describe clothing and compare one thing with another.

...use informal styles of speech with close friends.

...use honorifics.

12 빈 방 있어요? / 수건이 너무 더러웠어요

Do you have a spare room? / The towel was too dirty

In this unit you will learn how to:
▶ *book hotels and inquire about vacancies and facilities.*
▶ *make complaints when things don't go quite as they should.*
▶ *use the formal style of speech and the future tense.*
▶ *use quoted speech and report what other people said.*

CEFR: *Can explain why something is a problem (B1); can deal with situations likely to arise whilst travelling (B1); can make a formal verbal complaint (B2); can explain a problem that has arisen and make it clear the provider must make a concession (B2).*

Accommodation

South Korea offers a variety of accommodation options to suit different needs. Although Korean also uses the word 호텔 (hotel), this is reserved for Western-style accommodation. The word 모텔 (motel) has quite different connotations in Korea. These are cheap 호텔 with small 방 (rooms) that are often used as 'love hotels'. However it is quite acceptable to treat them just as a cheap form of accommodation.

여관 are Korean-style inns, often with shared bathroom facilities. Most rooms are of the traditional Korean 온돌 (ondol) style where you sleep on a blanket on a heated floor rather than on a 침대 (bed). 민박, sometimes referred to as home-stays in English, are rooms in private houses. If you are planning to stay in more remote villages, this may be the only accommodation option available.

South Korea only has a handful of youth hostels, but most are modern with good 시설 (facilities). If you are looking for something totally different, several Buddhist 절 (temples) now offer accommodation and fascinating insights into Korean culture. Temple stays are becoming increasing popular amongst the local South Koreans too, who go to relax and unwind amidst the natural surroundings.

Which is the most appropriate accommodation option for a business partner visiting Korea?

a 모텔　　　b 절　　　c 호텔

Vocabulary builder 1

BOOKING A HOTEL ROOM

 12.01 **Listen to the words and try to pronounce them. Try to imitate the speaker.**

빈	*empty, vacant, free* (for seats and rooms)	사이에	*between*
방	*room* (침대방: *room with bed*, 온돌방: *room with bed on floor*)	(지하) 식당	*(basement) restaurant*
		배달하-	*deliver*
		직접	*direct(ly)*
		시설	*facility*
하루에	*per day*	수영장	*swimming pool*
-동안	*during*	수영하-	*swim*
묵-	*stay, lodge, spend the night*	사우나	*sauna*
		오락실	*amusements (electronic games, etc.)*
이상	*more than*		
예약하-	*reserve, book*		
할인하-	*give a discount* (할인: *discount*)	스텐드바	*bar (standing bar)*
		한식당 / 양식당	*Korean restaurant (serving Korean food) / Western restaurant*
의논하-	*discuss*		
아침식사	*breakfast* (아침: *morning, breakfast (abbreviated form)*)		
		미니바	*mini-bar*
아침하-	*have breakfast*	훌륭하-	*is excellent, great*
포함되어 있-	*be included*		

NEW EXPRESSIONS

Read the expressions that are used in the next dialogue. Note their meanings.

얼마 동안 묵으시겠어요?	*How long will you be staying for?*
좀 더 묵을지도 몰라요.	*We may stay longer (I don't know if we might . . .).*
집사람하고 좀 의논해 봐야겠어요.	*I'll have to discuss it with my wife.*
직접 식당에 가서 먹겠어요.	*We'll go to the restaurant to eat.*
오일 동안 예약하는 게 좋을 것 같아요.	*It seems like it would be a good idea to book for five nights.*

 Dialogue 1

빈 방 있어요? DO YOU HAVE A SPARE ROOM?

12.02 Mr Lee is looking for a couple of rooms in a hotel.

1 How does the guest say we might stay a little longer, we're not sure?

손님	빈 방 있어요?
주인	네 있어요. 침대방을 드릴까요, 온돌방을 드릴까요?
손님	침대방 하나하고 온돌방 하나 주세요.
주인	네 알겠습니다. 침대방은 하루에 오만원이고 온돌방은 하루에 사만 원입니다. 얼마 동안 묵으시겠습니까?
손님	우선 삼일 동안요. 그리고 좀 더 묵을지도 몰라요.
주인	오일 이상 예약하시면 5% 할인해 드리는데요.
손님	아, 그럼 우리 집사람하고 좀 의논해 봐야겠어요. 아침식사도 포함되어 있지요?
주인	네, 물론 아침식사도 포함되어 있습니다. 7시부터 10시 사이에 지하 식당에 가시면 됩니다. 그리고 이천원만 더 내시면 손님 방까지 배달도 해드립니다.
손님	아니오, 직접 식당에 가서 먹겠어요. 이 호텔에 또 무슨 시설들이 있습니까?
주인	수영장, 사우나, 오락실, 노래방, 스텐드바, 그리고 한식당과 양식당이 있습니다.
손님	방에 텔레비젼과 전화도 있나요?
주인	물론입니다. 그리고 미니바도 있습니다.
손님	오, 아주 훌륭하군요. 오일 동안 예약하는 게 좋을 것 같아요. 아마 우리 집사람도 좋아할 거예요.

2 Give as much detail as you can about the breakfast service at the hotel.

3 How many days does the guest book in the end?

160

Language discovery 1

Look again at the following dialogue extract. Then translate the sentences into Korean.

주인	얼마 동안 묵으시겠습니까?
손님	우선 삼일 동안요. 그리고 좀 더 묵을지도 몰라요.
주인	오일 이상 예약하시면 5% 할인해 드리는데요.
손님	아, 그럼 우리 집사람하고 좀 의논해 봐야겠어요.

a How long will you be staying for?
b I will have to discuss it with my wife . . .

1 THE FUTURE MARKER -겠

The future marker -겠 can be added to any present stem (normal or honorific) to make a future stem. You can then add verb endings to this (such as the polite or formal styles, or a clause ending, such as -지만) in the normal way.

The -겠 future marker is used in the ending -야겠어요. It is also used in certain idiomatic phrases like 알겠습니다 and 모르겠습니다 (*I understand* and *I don't understand*).

Although this form does express the future (it can also be used to express probability), the most common way to put a normal sentence into the future is with the -(으)ㄹ 거에요 form which you have already learned. -(으)ㄹ 거에요 is a more useful form than -겠 for most situations, and the precise difference between them is something that you do not really need to worry about for this course. It is sufficient to be able to recognize the -겠 as the future marker, and to know that it can be used to make future stems which can then be used in other constructions.

2 THE FORMAL STYLE

The formal style of speech is used in formal situations, often by officials or representatives (such as the hotel worker in the dialogue), but it can also be used by anybody when some formality is called for. It is perhaps slightly more common among men than women and, if you are a man, it is a good idea to say some sentences in the formal style occasionally, as if you always use the polite style it can sound to Koreans as though your Korean is a bit effeminate. It is quite common to mix formal and polite speech styles in this way, with some sentences in the formal style and some in the polite style.

To make statements in the formal style (that is, normal sentences which state facts, not questions, commands or suggestions), you add the ending -(스)ㅂ니다 to the stem of the verb (either the present stem, past stem, or honorific present or past stem). Note that the ending is spelt -습니다, but pronounced -슴니다. To consonant stems you add the form -습니다, and to vowel stems -ㅂ니다:

	wear	*buy*
stem	입-	사-
	입습니다	삽니다
past	입었-	샀-
	입었습니다	샀습니다
honorific	입으시-	사시-
	입으십니다	사십니다
hon past	입으셨-	사셨-
	입으셨습니다	사셨습니다

You will recognize these formal statements from expressions like 미안합니다, 죄송합니다 and 알겠습니다. All those expressions are almost always used in the formal style.

To make questions in the formal style, you add the ending -(스)ㅂ니까? as follows:

	wear	*buy*
stem	입-	사-
	입습니까?	삽니까?
past	입었-	샀-
	입었습니까?	샀습니까?
honorific	입으시-	사시-
	입으십니까?	사십니까?
hon past	입으셨-	사셨-
	입으셨습니까	사셨습니까

Commands in the formal style always go on honorific present stems, and the ending is -ㅂ시오 (pronounced rather as if it were -ㅂ시요):

stem	입-	사-
honorific stem	입으시-	사시-
formal command	입으십시오	사십시오

To make suggestions in the formal style, add -(으)ㅂ시다; this gives 입읍시다 (*let's wear it*), 삽시다 (*let's buy it*)

Note that this form can be added to an honorific stem, to express the feeling of formal style: 입으십시다, 사십시다.

3 I DON'T KNOW WHETHER

You can say that you don't know whether you will do something or other by adding -(으)ㄹ지도 모르- to a verb stem. The example from the dialogue was 좀 더 묵을지도 몰라요 (*I don't know whether we will stay a bit longer, it might be that we stay a bit longer*).

Here are a couple of other examples. Try translating them into English.

a 졸업할지도 몰라요.
b 갈 수 있을지도 모릅니다.

4 IF YOU DO, IT WILL BE OK

The sentence 가시면 됩니다 means *if you go, it will be OK*, and this pattern, one clause ending in -면, plus a form of the verb 되- is a common pattern. In the context of the dialogue, it is used to say that breakfast is available between certain times, so that if they go to the restaurant between those times, it will be OK. It can be used to ask for permission to do something: 지금 가면 돼요? (*is it OK to go now?*).

Vocabulary builder 2

MAKING A COMPLAINT

12.03 **Listen to the words and try to pronounce them. Try to imitate the speaker.**

서비스	*service*
-에	*about, concerning*
문제	*problem*
불친절하-	*be unhelpful, be unkind, be impolite*
무뚝뚝하-	*be stubborn, be blunt*
식어 있-	*be bad, have gone off, cold, be stale, etc.*
얘기하-	*talk, tell*
노력하-	*make effort, strive*
실수하-	*make a mistake* (실수: *mistake*)
발생하-	*occur, happen*
더럽-	*be dirty* (polite: 더러워요, ㅂ - verb like 가깝-, etc.)
청소하-	*clean, clean up*
불평하-	*complain*
경우	*circumstance, situation* (*occurrence*)
고장나-	*break down*
열리지 않-	*does not open*
엉망	*rubbish, awful, appalling*
요금 환불하-	*reimburse fee*

NEW EXPRESSIONS

Read the expressions that are used in the next dialogue. Note their meanings.

… -에 대해서 할 말이 있어요	*I have something to say about . . .*
	There's something I want to say about . . .
저한테 말씀하시면 안될까요?	*Wouldn't it be all right to tell me?*
	Can't you just tell me?
말씀하세요	*Please tell me, please say it (honorific)*
어제도 마찬가지였고요.	*It was exactly the same yesterday as well.*
못 알아듣겠다고 하-	*say that (one) couldn't understand*
아무 문제가 없다고 했어요.	*(She) said that there wasn't any problem.*
맛이 없는데도 말이에요.	*I'm saying (emphasis!) that the food even tasted bad.*
수건을 갈아달라고 했어요.	*I asked (her) to change the towel.*
솔직히 말해서	*honestly speaking; to tell the truth; in fact . . .*

 Dialogue 2

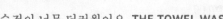

수건이 너무 더러웠어요 **THE TOWEL WAS TOO DIRTY**

지배인	*manager* (of hotel or facility)
직원	*employee*
웨이터	*waiter*
-면서	*while*
아직	*yet, still*
참	*very*
-처럼	*like*
-뿐	*only*
당장, 즉시	*immediately*
냉장고	*refrigerator*
문	*door*

164

12.04 Unfortunately, the hotel didn't turn out to be as good as it looked . . .

1 How does the guest say they have something to say regarding the hotel's service?

손님	지배인 좀 바꿔주세요.
종업원	실례지만, 무슨 일이세요?
손님	이 호텔 서비스에 대해서 할 말이 있어요.
종업원	죄송하지만 저한테 말씀하시면 안될까요?
손님	지배인한테 직접 말하고 싶은데요.
종업원	좋습니다. 잠깐 기다리세요.

A little while later.

지배인	네, 지배인입니다. 말씀하시지요.
손님	이 호텔 서비스에 문제가 많은 것 같아요. 직원들이 불친절하고 무뚝뚝해요. 그리고 오늘 아침에 식당에 갔는데 음식이 다 식어 있었어요. 어제도 마찬가지였고요.
지배인	그래요? 정말 죄송합니다. 웨이터한테 말씀하셨습니까?
손님	물론 종업원 아가씨한테 얘기했지요. 그런데 아가씨가 불친절한데다가 제 한국말을 못 알아듣겠다고 하면서 음식에 아무 문제가 없다고 했어요. 음식이 다 식었고 맛이 없는데도 말이에요.
지배인	아, 정말 죄송합니다. 항상 최선의 봉사를 하려고 노력하는데도 가끔 실수가 발생합니다. 제가 즉시 식당 종업원들에게 얘기하겠습니다.
손님	그리고 또 있어요. 오늘 아침 수건을 갈아달라고 했는데 수건이 너무 더러웠어요. 그리고 내 아들 방은 아직까지 청소도 안 했어요.
지배인	그것 참 이상하군요. 손님처럼 불평하는 경우가 지금까지 없었는데요.
손님	그것뿐이 아니에요. 내 방의 텔레비전은 고장이 났고, 냉장고 문은 열리지도 않아요. 솔직히 말해서 이 호텔 서비스하고 시설은 엉망이네요.
지배인	죄송합니다. 그렇지만 저희도 손님처럼 불평많은 사람은 필요없으니까 오늘 당장 나가 주세요. 요금은 다시 환불해드리겠습니다.

2 What was wrong with the food this morning at breakfast?

3 What is the state of the guest's son's room at the moment?

12 빈 방 있어요? *Do you have a spare room?* 165

Language discovery 2

 Look at the following sentences and their translations. What do you think the phrase -에 대해서 means?

a 이 호텔 서비스에 대해서 할 말이 있어요.
I have something to say about this hotel's service.

b 숙제에 대해서 질문이 있어요.
I have a question concerning the homework.

c 식당에 대해서 뭘 알아요?
What do you know about the restaurant?

1 CONCERNING

You can say what you are talking, discussing, writing or reading about in Korean with the construction -에 대해서 which is added to the noun which describes what it is you are talking about. Here are some examples:

정치에 대해서 이야기했어요.
(We) talked about politics.

서비스에 대해서 불평했어요.
(He) complained about the service.

날씨에 대해서 물어봤어요.
(He) asked about the weather.

2 THE FUTURE MODIFIER

Here are a few examples on the use of the future modifier -(으)ㄹ. Modifiers are added to verbs which then modify or describe the noun which they precede. Observe the following examples where we've put the modifier phrase in brackets to help you spot the pattern, and likewise its literal meaning in English:

서비스에 대해서 (할 말이) 있어요.
(words to say) I've got some things to say about the service.

(갈 시간이) 됐어요?
(time to go) Is it time to go? (lit. Has it become time to go?)

 Translate the following example into English. Identify the modifier phrase.

집에 (먹을 것이) 있어요?

3 ON TOP OF THAT

The word 게다가 means *on top of that* and you can use a similar form to add to verbs. You use the -(으)ㄴ데 or -는데 imminent elaboration form plus -다가, so that the completed forms look like 좋은데다가 (*on top of being good*); 가는데다가 (*on top of going*) and so on. Here are two examples in sentences:

이 옷이 질이 좋은데다가 싸요.
These clothes are good quality and, on top of that, they're cheap.

비가 오는데다가 추워요.
It's raining and, on top of that, it's cold.

4 QUOTATIONS AND REPORTED SPEECH

This unit introduces you to the rather complicated matter of reported speech in Korean. Reported speech is when you say what someone else said to you. For example, *He said he was going to the shops*. What the person said literally, of course, was *I'm going to the shops*, but when we report what someone said we change it to something like, *He said he was going to the shops*. This section is designed so that you will be able to recognize reported speech in Korean and use some of the forms yourself. It is not designed to teach reported speech comprehensively. If you wish to know more, you should consult an advanced grammar book. What we tell you here is more than you need to get by.

To report speech in Korean you use the plain style of the verb: 먹는다, 산다, 간다, 좋다, etc., plus -고 하-. Remember that the plain style can be formed on any verb stem – past present or future, and honorifics. Here are three examples: the first sentence gives you what the person actually said, the second one gives the reported speech form, *he said* or *he says*:

나는 집에 가요. *I'm going home.*	집에 간다고 해요 (plain style of 가- = 간다) *He says he's going home.*
사람들이 많습니다. *There are a lot of people.*	사람들이 많다고 했어요 (plain style of 많- = 많다) *He said there were a lot of people.*

Translate the following sentences into English.

a 날씨가 좋았어요.
b 김 선생님이 날씨가 좋았다고 했어요.

Note that suggestions and commands can be quoted in the same way:

| 집에 갑시다
Let's go home. | 집에 가자고 했어요
(가자 = plain style suggestion of 가-)
He suggested we go home. |
| 밥 먹어라
Eat your food! | 밥 먹으라고 했어요
He told (him/me) to eat his / my food. |

Questions are a little more complicated and you only need to be able to recognize them as having -냐- or -느냐- in them: you will then know what they are when someone uses the form.

5 WHILE

You can say that you are doing something while you are doing something else by adding -(으)면서 to the 'while' clause. For example, to say that you were talking (while you watched TV), you would say: 텔레비젼을 보면서 이야기했어요.

 Here are a couple of other examples. Translate them into English.

a 한국말 배우면서 음악을 들어요.
b 먹으면서 말해 보세요.

6 EVEN THOUGH: -는데도

The imminent elaboration form -는데 indicates that you have not finished what you are saying yet and that there is more to come. -도, added to the polite style minus -요 means *even though*. The combined 도 form -는데도 also means *even though (so and so)*, but has a stronger emphasis than simply -도. Thus, 노력하는데도 가끔 실수가 발생합니다 (from the dialogue) means *even though we (really) are trying, occasionally mistakes happen*.

The other -는데도 form from the dialogue is a way of putting special emphasis on what you have just said. You saw it in the phrase 음식이 다 식었고 맛이 없는데도 말이에요. The waiter had just told Mr Lee that there was no problem with the food, and then Mr Lee adds: *even though (despite the fact that) the food was off and was tasteless*. The 말이에요 bit on the end means something like *that's what I'm saying* and adds strong emphasis to what has just been said.

7 QUOTED REQUESTS

When you ask something to be done for your benefit (by using a compound verb with 주-, as in 해주세요 (*please do it for me*) and then report what you have just said, as in *I asked him to (do it for me)*, there is a special rule to remember. Instead of saying something like (해주라고) 했어요, you swap the verb 주- and the -라- which follows it with the verb 달라, to give 해 달라고 했어요 (*I asked him to do it for me*).

Do not worry about this pattern; this note is merely to explain what is going on in the dialogue and to enable you to recognize the form.

🔓 Practice

1 **You are thinking of sending your children to a new school in Korea and you have a meeting with one of the teachers to chat about the school. Before you go, you jot down some questions you want to ask about the school. Can you put them into Korean in full sentences?**

   a How many students? (학생: student)
   b What facilities?
   c Is it possible to study Korean and Chinese?
   d How many students studying Korean? (how many: 몇 명)
   e What time is lunch?
   f Is it OK to go home to eat at lunchtime?

2 **You go to make a booking at a hotel with the following requirements. The receptionist asks you the following questions, for which you must prepare answers in Korean.**

   a 뭘 도와드릴까요?
   b 침대방 드릴까요?
   c 아이들이 몇 살이에요? (아이: child)
   d 얼마 동안 묵으시겠어요?
   e 아침 식사 배달해드릴까요?

3 **Put the following sentences into the formal style.**

　a 무엇을 하셨어요?
　b 침대방 하나 주세요.
　c 저 사람은 김 선생님이세요?
　d 나는 백화점에 간다.
　e 라디오를 들으면서 책을 읽어요.

4 **Ask if there are the following facilities at the hotel at which you are staying.**

5 **Your hotel room has a few problems, as you can see in the picture. Make a series of complaints, making your language as strong as you can.**

Test yourself

1 Translate the following sentences into English.

   a 일주일 이상 예약하시면 10% 할인해드립니다.
   b 솔직히 말해서 그런 사람을 싫어해요.
   c 아침 벌써 먹었다고 했어요.
   d 온돌방은 하루에 이만원이에요.
   e 일곱시에 일어나시면 됩니다.
   f 요금은 다시 환불해드릴 수 없습니다.
   g 침대방 두 개 주세요.
   h 이 호텔에 대해서 할 말이 있으시면 지배인한테 말해주세요.

2 Translate the following sentences into Korean.

   a How long are you booking for?
   b I told the bank clerk immediately.
   c What facilities are there at the hotel?
   d There seem to be a lot of problems with my car.
   e My son still hasn't got up.
   f We'll go straight to the bar and have a drink.
   g Mr Kim is an impolite person.
   h It would be a good idea to stay for three nights.

SELF CHECK

I CAN...
...book a hotel room, check availability and inquire about facilities.
...ask for the manager and make a complaint.
...use the formal style of speech.
...use the future tense.
...use quoted speech and report what other people said.

13 대구 가는 기차가 있나요? / 불고기는 별로예요

Are there any trains to Daegu?/ I don't particularly like bulgogi

In this unit you will learn how to:
▶ *buy train tickets.*
▶ *ask for information about catching the train you want.*
▶ *discuss going out for meals and drinks together.*

CEFR: *Can get simple information about travel, use of public transport, and buy tickets (A2); can explain likes or dislikes (A2); can link a series of shorter, discrete simple elements into a connected, linear sequence of points (B1).*

Transport in Korea

대중 교통 (*public transport*) in Korea is first class. The 지하철 (*subway/ underground*) network, found in six major 도시 (*cities*), combined with the extensive 버스 (*bus*) and 기차 (*train*) systems, make getting around the country very easy, efficient and affordable.

Even if you are only going to be in Seoul for a few days, it usually works out cheaper and easier to buy a prepaid 교통 카드 (*transport card*). These can be bought and topped up at all 지하철 stations as well as at local convenience stores. When using a 교통 카드, you can get a 환승 할인 (*transfer discount*) on your journeys when transferring from one 버스 or 지하철 to the next. Make sure to beep your 교통 카드 each time you get on and off to get your 할인 (*discount*)!

Travelling by 택시 (*taxi*) in Korea is reasonably inexpensive and another popular form of 교통 (*transport*). 택시 are generally easy to flag down, except in the hour or so after the 대중 교통 system shuts down for the night. Most 택시 now also provide 동시통역 (*simulataneous interpreting*) services on the phone, making them very foreigner friendly. However, traffic is notoriously heavy within the 도시 and on the 고속도로 (*motorway*), so be aware of this before you travel.

How many different types of 교통 are mentioned here? List them.

Vocabulary builder 1

BUYING TRAIN TICKETS

13.01 Listen to the words and try to pronounce them. Try to imitate the speaker.

대구	*a Korean city*
완행	*slow train* (also called 무궁화)
직행	*fast train, express train* (also called 새마을호)
가격	*price*
좌석	*seating, places*
남-	*be left (over), remain*
자리	*seat*
함께	*together*
확인하-	*check, confirm*
흡연석	*smoker (compartment)*
금연석	*no smoking compartment*
원하-	*want, require*
부탁하-	*make a request*
편도	*single*
왕복	*return*
홈	*platform*
출발하-	*depart* (출발: *departure*)

NEW EXPRESSIONS

Read the expressions that are used in the next dialogue. Note their meanings.

뭘 도와드릴까요?	*How can I help you?*
얼마 남지 않았습니다.	*There are only a few left.*
출발 시간 전에 전광판을 봐주세요.	*Please look at the electronic notice board before departure.*

 Dialogue 1

대구 가는 기차가 있나요? **ARE THERE ANY TRAINS TO DAEGU?**

13.02 Mr Pak is trying to buy tickets to go to Daegu over the weekend.

1 How does Mr Pak ask if he can book four tickets?

매표원	뭘 도와드릴까요?
박선생	오늘 저녁 대구 가는 기차가 있나요?
매표원	네, 두 가지가 있는데요, 완행은 5 시 30 분이고 직행은 7 시 45 분이에요.
박선생	시간은 얼마나 걸려요?
매표원	직행은 3 시간 걸리고, 완행은 4 시간 30 분 걸립니다.
박선생	가격은요?
매표원	완행은 만 팔천원이고, 직행은 사만 오천원입니다. 직행은 좌석이 얼마 남지 않았습니다.
박선생	네 자리를 함께 예약할 수 있을까요?
매표원	잠깐만 기다려보세요. 확인 좀 해보겠습니다. 아, 네. 네 자리가 있군요! 흡연석을 원하세요, 금연석을 원하세요?
박선생	금연석으로 부탁합니다.
매표원	편도를 드릴까요, 왕복을 드릴까요?
박선생	왕복으로 주세요.
매표원	언제 돌아오시겠어요?
박선생	일요일 저녁에요.
매표원	6 시 30 분 기차가 있는데, 완행이에요. 일요일 저녁에는 직행 기차는 없는데요.
박선생	그러면 일요일 오후에는요?
매표원	2 시 30 분에 직행 기차가 있어요.
박선생	그거 좋군요. 그걸로 주세요.
매표원	모두 삼십육만원입니다.
박선생	몇 번 홈에서 기차가 떠나지요?
매표원	아직 모릅니다. 출발 시간 전에 전광판을 봐주세요.
박선생	네, 알겠어요. 고맙습니다.

2 Decide whether the following statements are true or false.

 a Mr Pak books seats for the smoking area.
 b The 6.30 p.m. train on Sunday is an all-stopping service train.
 c One return ticket costs 80,000 won.
 d The train will depart from platform five.

Language discovery 1

 Look again at the following dialogue extract. Find two examples of Mr Pak making a request.

매표원	흡연석을 원하세요, 금연석을 원하세요?
박선생	금연석으로 부탁합니다.
매표원	편도를 드릴까요, 왕복을 드릴까요?
박선생	왕복으로 주세요.
매표원	언제 돌아오시겠어요?
박선생	일요일 저녁에요.

1 MAKING REQUESTS

Koreans have a word for *favour* (as in *do a favour for someone*), 부탁 as used in the following sentence: 금연석으로 부탁합니다. To say *I have a favour to ask*, you say either (제가) 부탁 있어요 and then say what the request is or else say the request, and then add 부탁합니다 or 부탁해요 (*please, I ask you to do it as a favour*).

2 -을까요 TO ASK QUESTIONS

-을까요 has previously been introduced as a pattern meaning *shall we?* It is also sometimes used to ask a question: 네 자리를 함께 예약할 수 있을까요? (*is it possible to book four seats together?*). There are several patterns like this in Korean where certain verb endings do not always have their basic meaning. The context will always make clear to you which is the correct meaning and in most cases -(으)ㄹ까요 does mean *shall we?* and is used to make suggestions.

 Translate the following sentences into English. Read them carefully to see which meaning of -을까요 is being used.

a 저녁 같이 먹을까요?
b 비빔밥 먹을 수 있을까요?
c 여기 앉을까요?

3 *BEFORE* AND *AFTER*

The nouns 전 and 후 mean *before* and *after*, respectively. They can be used with nouns, as in 출발 시간 전에 (*before the time of departure*), or 식사 후에 (*after the meal*). They can also be used with verbs, although in a slightly different way.

To say *before* (verb) you add -기 전에 to the stem, as in the following examples: 시작하기 전에 (*before we begin . . .*) or 학교에 가기 전에 (*before (I / you) go to school*).

To say *after* (verb) you add -(으)ㄴ 후에 (or -(으)ㄴ 다음에, which has the same meaning) to the verb stem of a processive verb. This -(으)ㄴ is the past modifier which you have already learned (the present modifier, you will recall, is -는, as in 가는), e.g. 먹은 후에 (*after eating*); 학교에 간 다음에 (*after going to school*).

 Translate the following sentences into English.

a 식사 하기 전에 앉으세요.
b 식사 하신 후에 집에 가세요.
c 점심 전에 오세요.
d 점심 후에 가세요.

 # Vocabulary builder 2

AFTER-WORK PLANS

 13.03 **Listen to the words and try to pronounce them. Try to imitate the speaker.**

계획	*plan(s)*
부르-	*call*
밥 먹-	*have a meal*
그냥	*simply, just*
딱 질색이에요	*hate, is awful (to me)*
-기만 하세요	*just do (verb)*
별로 없-	*have almost none, scarcely have any*
인천	*Korean port near Seoul*
싱싱하-	*be fresh*
생선	*fish*
회	*raw meat*
따르-	*follow*
-(으)ㄹ 수 밖에 없-	*there is nothing for it but to (verb)*

NEW EXPRESSIONS

Read the expressions that are used in the next dialogue. Note their meanings.

일 끝나고	*after finishing work*
아직 계획 없어요.	*I don't have any plans yet.*
좋은 생각이네요.	*That's a good idea.*
우리 둘만 가요?	*Is it just the two of us going?*
그냥 소주 한 잔 하려고요.	*We were just thinking of having a soju.*
저는 불고기는 별로예요.	*I don't really like bulgogi.*
노래하는 건 딱 질색이에요.	*I really hate singing.*
노래하지 말고 듣기만 하세요.	*Don't sing, just listen instead.*
그냥 해본 소리예요.	*I was just saying it (don't take it too seriously).*
소주나 먹을 수 밖에 없겠네요.	*There's nothing for it (no alternative) but to eat soju.*
한턱 낼게요.	*I'll pay (for everyone).; It's on me.*

Dialogue 2

불고기는 별로예요 I DON'T PARTICULARLY LIKE BULGOGI

어이	*hey!* (used to call close friends and colleagues)
그리고 나서	*after that*
별로	*not particularly, not really (fond of)*
말고	*not, instead of* (when suggesting an alternative)
에이	*hey, come off it!*
게다가	*on top of that*

Read the following Dialogue and answer the questions below.
Some colleagues are discussing what they will do after work.

1 How does Mr Yun ask his colleagues what they're doing after work today?

윤선생	오늘 저녁 일 끝나고 뭐 할 거예요?
백선생	일 끝나고요? 모르겠어요. 아직 계획없어요.
윤선생	저녁이나 같이 먹으러 갈까요?
백선생	좋은 생각이네요. 그런데 우리 둘만 가요?
윤선생	다른 사람도 부르지요. 김 선생하고 이 선생한테 얘기해볼까요?
백선생	좋지요. 어이, 김 선생, 이 선생! 오늘 저녁 밥 먹으면서 소주 한 잔 어때요?
김선생	좋아요. 그런데 어디로 갈 거예요?
윤선생	글쎄요, 그냥 불고기하고 소주 한잔하려고요. 그리고 나서 노래방에도 가고요.
김선생	술 마시는 건 좋은데, 저는 불고기는 별로예요. 그리고 노래하는 건 딱 질색이에요.
백선생	아, 그럼 불고기 말고 다른 거 먹으면 되잖아요. 그리고 노래하지 말고 그냥 듣기만 하세요.
김선생	그거 괜찮은 생각이네요. 그런데 오늘 돈이 별로 없는데 …
윤선생	걱정 마세요. 오늘 저녁은 내가 한턱 낼게요.
김선생	아 그럼, 좋습니다.
백선생	이 선생은 어때요? 같이 가시겠어요?
이선생	글쎄요, 저도 가고 싶은데, 저는 인천에 가서 싱싱한 생선회를 먹고 싶은데요.
백선생	에이, 인천은 너무 멀어요. 그리고 생선회는 요즘 너무 비싸고요.
윤선생	게다가 저는 생선회를 못 먹어요.
이선생	좋아요, 좋아. 그냥 해본 소리예요. 오늘은 저도 따라가서 불고기에 소주나 먹을 수밖에 없겠네요.

2 Why is Mrs Kim hesitant about joining the others? What doesn't she like doing?

3 Who's offered to pay for the evening?

4 What does Mr Lee want to eat?

Language discovery 2

 Complete the following extract from the dialogue using an ending to mean *afterwards*.

불고기하고 소주 한잔 하려고요. 그리_____ 노래방에도 가고요.

1 MORE WAYS OF SAYING *AFTERWARDS*

You can add the ending -고 나서 to any present tense processive verb base to mean *after* (verb):

일하고 나서 술 한 잔 합시다.
After finishing work let's have a drink.

-고 나서 can be abbreviated to -고서, and sometimes even to just -고.

2 INFORMAL SENTENCES

With Korean, you can add particles to the end of verbs in colloquial speech to give extra nuances to what you are saying. You can also make incomplete sentences which can be completed simply by adding the polite particle -요. You do not need to worry about learning rules for this kind of thing, since in most circumstances you will want to use a more formal and grammatical style of speaking when you begin to speak Korean in Korea. It is very useful to recognize what is going on in colloquial speech, however, and as you spend more time speaking with Koreans you will quickly learn to do this kind of thing for yourself.

VERBAL CONFUSION

To a non-native speaker, Koreans sometimes seem to play fast and loose with their verb endings, mixing and matching particles and endings. Try not to be fazed by this. The main thing is to recognize what the basic verb is in the sentence, e.g. whether it's a statement, a question or a suggestion, and what the basic drift of the sentence is. In your own speech, you can keep things simpler!

You can miss out the rest of this section if you wish, as the explanation may seem a bit complicated. Your main task should be to completely familiarize yourself with the dialogue, almost to the extent of being able to say it by heart. For the adventurous, however, here are two sentences from the dialogue with an explanation of how they have been constructed.

소주 한 잔 하려고요.

This -(으)려고 pattern has the meaning with the intention of. Normally it is used in the pattern (clause A)-으려고 (clause B), as in 한국말 배우려고 책 샀어요, but here the pattern is simply (clause A)-으려고. Clause B has been omitted in casual speech and the polite particle added to round the construction off. The full form would have been something like 소주 한잔 하려고 어느 술집이나 갈까 해요 (we were thinking of going to some pub or other to have a drink), but this is cut down to what would translate as to have a drink – or, in better English, we were just thinking of going for a drink and is made into a sentence simply be adding -요 to the -(으)려고 pattern.

그리고 나서 노래방에도 가고요.

This means after that (we were thinking of) going to a noraebang too. The -고 at the end is the clause ending -고 that normally means and when you are going to add another clause. However, in this case, the meaning is as well, in addition. This sentence is being added to the one that has been said previously to indicate that this is also part of the plan as well. Then the particle -요 is added to round it all off.

3 NEGATIVES WITH 별로

Sentences with negative verbs in them (with 안 and 못) can be modified by inserting the word 별로 in them, to mean not particularly. This will be clearer with examples.

고기를 별로 안 좋아해요.
I don't particularly like meat.

별로 가고 싶지 않아요.
I don't particularly want to go.

별로 재미 없어요.
It's not particularly interesting.

The dialogue also has a 별로 sentence in it, which is slightly different. 저는 불고기는 별로예요. This is a more colloquial form, putting the copula onto the end of the word 별로. But you can see that it is in a sense an abbreviated form of 저는 불고기는 별로 좋아하지 않아요, so the pattern is essentially the same. You should stick to the full form with a negative verb most of the time and leave the colloquial, abbreviated form to native speakers.

4 NOT ONE THING, BUT ANOTHER INSTEAD

You can stay instead of (noun), or not (noun) by putting the word 말고 after the noun, as you can see in these examples.

Match the following sentences to the correct translation.

a 불국사 말고 산에 가는 게 어때요?
b 잡지 말고 신문을 읽는 거 좋아해요.
c 사과 말고 고기 삽시다.

1 Let's not buy apples, let's buy meat. / Instead of apples, let's buy meat.
2 It's not magazines, it's newspapers I enjoy reading.
3 How about going to the mountain instead of Bulguksa?

You can use a similar pattern to say *instead of* (verb). Simply add -지 말고 (this is the same -지 that you use in the long negative, or in -지 마세요). Look at the following examples.

Match the following sentences to the correct translation.

a 노래하지 말고 듣기만 하세요.
b 커피 마시지 말고 차나 드세요.
c 왜 공부하지 말고 이야기만 하라고 해요.

1 Don't sing (do a song), just listen (instead).
2 Why are you staying just talking and not studying (instead)?
3 Don't drink coffee, have some tea or something instead.

5 JUST DOING SOMETHING

The sentence 듣기만 하세요 means *just listen!* The form -기만 하- added to processive verbs means *just* (verb) or *only* (verb). Here are examples:

말하지 않고 먹기만 했어요.
We didn't say anything, we just ate.

듣기만 해요?
Are you only listening (rather than participating)?

6 THERE'S NOTHING FOR IT, BUT TO . . .

When you feel you have no option but to do something or other, or that you are obliged to do something, you can use the pattern -(으)ㄹ 수밖에 없-. Here are examples:

갈 수밖에 없어요.
There's nothing for it but to go. / I'll have to go.

비싸지만 살 수밖에 없어요.
Although it's expensive, there's nothing for it but to buy it.

🔓 Practice

1 For each of the following, say that you will go out before doing them and then that you will go out after doing them.

  a (Eating) lunch.
  b Telephoning your mother.
  c Having fun (놀-).
  d Reading the newspaper.

2 Look at the following information about train availability and then answer the questions.

  a 밤 늦게 대구에 가고 싶어요.
     기차가 몇 시에 출발해요?
  b 서울에 가는 직행은 몇 시에
     떠나요?
  c 언제 도착해요?
  d 대전에 가는 완행 있어요?
  e 부산에 가는 완행 기차
     있어요?

열차(기차) 시간표			
목적지	출발	도착	
서울	8:00	11:00	직행
대구	20:00	23:30	직행
부산	7:00	12:00	완행
광주	13:00	18:00	완행
서울	10:00	15:00	완행
대전	14:00	16:00	직행

3 Make up three sentences saying that there is nothing for it but to . . .

  a go home
  b pay the money
  c get up at six in the morning

4 Make up a set of sentences, each one using the following sets of information and using (noun)-말고 or (verb)-지 말고. For example, for the first one you could make up a sentence which said *I want to eat fruit, not meat.*

Test yourself

1 Translate the following sentences into English.

a 좌석이 얼마 남지 않았어요.

b 다른 거 먹으면 안돼요.

c 왕복을 드릴까요?

d 등산하는 건 딱 질색이에요.

e 제가 갈 수밖에 없겠네요.

f 그냥 야구하려고요.

g 오늘 오후 목포에 가는 기차 있어요?

h 그거 괜찮은 생각이네요.

2 Translate the following sentences into Korean.

a Buy something to eat before the departure time.

b Shall we have a talk to your parents?

c I'd like to go, too, but it's a long way.

d Can I book three seats together?

e Let's go to Inchŏn, not to Seoul.

f What shall we do after finishing work?

g When are you going to come back?

h Do you like eating raw fish?

SELF CHECK

I CAN. . .
...ask for train tickets to a specific destination.
...buy tickets, specifying the type of ticket required.
...ask how long a journey takes and where the train departs.
...ask someone what they are doing after work this evening.
...discuss where to go and what to do.

14 복습
Review

Introduction

So, you have virtually reached the end of this course. This unit contains more exercises which practise the situations and grammar you have been learning in the last six units. Most of these exercises are Korean to English or English to Korean translations, since that is the best way to check that you have really mastered the material in the units. Make sure you are comfortable with the topics in the list that follows and be sure to revise the grammar notes for any of the major patterns you are not quite happy with. It would be a good idea also to read through all the dialogues in the units once again. You will find there are things that you felt a bit uneasy about at the time that are now clearer to you and you are sure to understand more fully what is going on grammatically in the dialogues. Even though you have reached the end of the course, you will find that simply reading through the dialogues every so often will help you to retain the things you have learned.

Topic revision

The following list shows the main topics that have been covered in the last six units. You should feel capable of handling these topics at a simple level should you need to when you are in Korea. If you feel unsure about a particular topic, you should go over the dialogue again more thoroughly, and revise the expressions and vocabulary that go with it. Of course there will still be many things that you are not able to say in Korean, but with the tools we have given you you should be able to succeed in carrying out many language tasks, some at quite a high level, and should have a more fascinating and enjoyable experience as a result whenever you visit Korea or communicate with Korean people.

1 advanced phone conversations
2 cancelling appointments
3 dating and talking about other people
4 describing what you did
5 buying presents
6 retorting
7 police officers and traffic offences
8 lost property
9 describing objects
10 feeling ill
11 getting medicine
12 buying and comparing clothes
13 trying on clothes
14 booking into a hotel and asking about facilities
15 complaining
16 train journeys
17 arranging to go out

Practice

1 **Translate the following into English.**

a 어머니가 영화를 좋아하시니까 아버지 대신 극장에 가면 돼요.

b 스트레스가 원인인 것 같아요.

c 사실 아주 중요한 서류가 들어 있어요.

d 청바지가 못 쓰게 됐어요.

e 우리 집사람이 아마 알고 있을 거에요.

f 내일 저녁 일 끝내고 산에 갈 계획 있어요?

g 당신은 내 의견을 항상 좋아하지 않아요.

h 우리 방문은 열리지도 않아요.

i 도서관이 어디인지 좀 가르쳐 주시겠어요? (도서관 = library)

j 그렇게 술을 많이 마셨어요?

k 요즘 아주 유행하는 스타일이에요.

l 면허증 좀 보여주세요.

2 For each of the following pictures make up a question which asks if someone has ever tried doing them. Then make up an answer which says *yes, I have* and another which says *you did it yesterday, as a matter of fact.* (*dance*: 춤 추-)

3 Make up an appropriate response to the following questions or requests.

a 김 선생님 좀 바꿔주세요.

b 영화구경을 좋아하세요?

c 데이트할 때 보통 어디 가세요?

d 이 청바지 길이 어때요?

e 약속을 자주 취소하는 사람이세요?

4 Translate the following into Korean.

a I really didn't see the sign.

b You can wear it with jeans.

c I'm ringing to cancel my appointment.

d Is there a telephone and TV in the room?

e The service is rubbish!

f We bought him socks last year.

g It looks a bit small.

h I thought so.

i I'd like to go to Inchŏn and eat raw fish.

j What does your car look like?

k Would you write a letter for me?

l My head hurts so much I can't sleep.

5 Your friend has a new girlfriend and you quiz him about her. Make up questions to complete the following fact file:

Name:	
Age:	
Occupation:	
Father's name:	
How met?	
What do together?	
Likes / Dislikes:	

6 Translate the following into English.

a 잘못하면 아주 위험해요.
b 복동씨한데 전할 말이 있어요?
c 손님방까지 배달해드립니다.
d 어제 여기 왔었는데요. 잠바를 놓고 갔어요.
e 아가씨가 질이 좋다고 했어요.
f 여자 친구 생겨서 매일 나가는 것 같아요.
g 이야기하지 말고 듣기만 하세요.
h 식후에 한 알씩 하루 두 번 드세요.
i 이거 봐. 질이 별로 안 좋아.
j 혹시 어디 갔는지 아세요?
k 새 텔레비젼은 어떨까요?
l 남대문에서는 비슷한 게 두 배나 더 싸요.

7 Complete the following dialogue.

A	내일 저녁에 시간 있어요?
You	(*No, an urgent matter has come up. Why?*)
A	그냥 나가고 싶었는데요.
You	(*How about Monday?*)
A	월요일날은 아버지 생신이에요.
You	(*Really? Will there be a party?*)
A	아니요. 그냥 식당에 가서 같이 저녁 하는 거예요.
You	(*What are you going to buy for him?*)
A	양말요. 항상 양말 사요.
You	(*How about Tuesday? Do you have time then?*)
A	네, 좋아요. 나이트 클럽 갈까요? (나이트 클럽: *night club*)
You	(*That's a good idea.*)

8 Change the dialogue in Question 7 using the informal and plain styles of speech.

9 Put the following sentences into the formal style.
  a 지금 어디 가세요?
  b 주문했어요?
  c 일곱시에 일어나요.
  d 빨리 해주세요.
  e 저 사람은 불친절한 사람이에요.

10 The following pictures tell what you did last Saturday. Make up an account of what you did, putting in as many details as you can according to what the pictures suggest.

11 Translate the following into Korean.

a I started meeting her often from that time.

b Don't be surprised even if you have no energy (strength).

c You help this time.

d Although it might look similar, it isn't.

e Be (more) careful from now on.

f We'll go straight to the restaurant and eat.

g It's turned out well then. Goodbye!

h This evening I'll pay.

i What time did you leave our department store?

j Mistakes do happen.

k Shall I introduce you?

l Would you like to try it on?

Translation of dialogues

UNIT 1

Where are you off to?

Sangmin	Jaemin! Hello/How are you!
Jaemin	Hello! How have you been getting along?
Sangmin	Fine. Where are you going?
Jaemin	Right now I'm off to the city centre.
Sangmin	What are you going to do in the city centre?
Jaemin	I'm going to buy some bread.
Sangmin	I'm also going to buy bread in the city centre.
Jaemin	Let's go together!
Sangmin	Yes, let's go together.

Cheers!

Sangmin	Excuse me/Waiter! Do you have any soju?
Waiter	Yes. We have. Soju, beer, western spirits – all of them.
Sangmin	Well then, give us a beer and one soju, please.
Waiter	Yes. I understand.
Sangmin	And we also need some snacks/side dishes. What do you have?
Waiter	Fruit, squid, dry snacks, p'ajon – we've got all of those.
Sangmin	Then give me some fruit and some squid, please.
Waiter	Here you are. Enjoy it! (Good appetite!)
Sangmin	Thank you.
Sangmin	Cheers!

UNIT 2

Long time, no see!

Mr Pak	Mr Kim! How are you?
Mr Kim	Ah, Mr Pak! Hello there!
Mr Pak	Long time, no see!
Mr Kim	Yes, that's right. It's really been a long time.
Mr Pak	How have you been getting along?
Mr Kim	Yes, fine. How's business these days?

Mr Pak	It's so-so.
	This is my wife.
Mr Kim	Oh, really? Pleased to meet you. I've heard a lot about you.
Mr Pak's wife	Pleased to meet you. I'm Yunhuy Jang.
Mr Kim	I'm Jinyang Kim. I'm pleased that I've met you.

It's not me!

Mr O	Excuse me!
Mr Lee	Yes?
Mr O	Are you the Korean language teacher?
Mr Lee	No. I'm not a Korean language teacher. I'm a Japanese language teacher.
Mr O	Ah, I'm sorry. Isn't this the Korean department's office?
Mr Lee	No, this isn't the Korean department. This is the Japanese department.
Mr O	Right. Where is the Korean department office, please?
Mr Lee	It's over there.
Mr O	Excuse me, is this the Korean department's office?
Mr Kim	Yes. What brings you here? (Can I help you?)
Mr O	I've come to meet the Korean language teacher.

UNIT 3

Sorry, wrong number!

Tony	Hello? I'm sorry, but can I speak to Mr Kim, please?
Mr Pak	There is no such person here.
Tony	Isn't that 389 2506?
Mr Pak	No. You've dialled the wrong number.
Tony	I'm sorry.
Tony	Hello? I'm sorry, but can I speak to Mr Kim, please?
Mr Kim's wife	Wait a moment, please.
Mr Kim	Yes. Speaking.
Tony	Ah, hello. I'm Tony from the British embassy.
Mr Kim	Ah, hello! Long time, no see!
Tony	Do you have any free time this lunchtime?
Mr Kim	Yes, I do.
Tony	Then I'd like to buy you lunch.
Mr Kim	Yes, fine. Let's meet at 12 in front of Lotte Hotel.
Tony	Great. So, I'll see you in a little while.

Are you ready to order yet?

Waiter	Welcome! Please take a seat over here.
Mr Kim	Thank you.
Waiter	Would you like anything to drink?
Mr Kim	We'll have some beer first, please.
Mr Kim	Do you like Korean food?
Tony	Yes, I like it a lot, but I can't eat spicy food so well.
Mr Kim	Then let's eat pulgogi or kalbi.
Tony	Yes, fine. And I'd like to eat some naengmyon as well.
Waiter	Would you like to order?
Tony	Pulgogi for two people and two dishes of naengmyon, please.
Waiter	Would you like water naengmyon or pibim naengmyon?
Tony	Water naengmyon, please.
Waiter	Enjoy your meal!
Tony	Waiter! More water and more kimchi, please.

UNIT 4

How much is it altogether?

Assistant	What are you looking for?
Chris	Do you have dictionaries?
Assistant	Yes. A Korean-English dictionary?
Chris	Yes, I'd like both a Korean–English dictionary and an English–Korean dictionary.
Assistant	Here you are.
Chris	How much is it?
Assistant	Each volume is 10,000 won; 20,000 won all together.
Chris	Do you have Chinese character dictionaries also?
Assistant	We have three kinds of Chinese character dictionary.
Chris	The cheapest one, please.
Assistant	Just a moment … here it is.
Chris	Thank you. How much is it altogether?
Assistant	The Chinese character dictionary is 30,000 won … therefore altogether it's 50,000 won.
Chris	The cheapest one is 30,000 won? How much is the most expensive one, then?! 100,000 won?!
Assistant	Oh, I'm sorry; I've made a mistake. It's 30,000 won altogether. Would you like a receipt?
Chris	Yes please.

Assistant	Okay. Here it is. Goodbye!
Chris	Goodbye.

Finding the way

Mr Pak	Excuse me, can you tell me where the bank is around here?
Bank Clerk A	If you go left at that post office over there, there is the Kiop bank.
Mr Pak	Thank you.
Mr Pak	I'd like to change some English money into Korean money.
Bank Clerk B	We don't deal with foreign currency at this bank. Please go to the Korea Exchange Bank.
Mr Pak	Where is there a Korea Exchange Bank?
Bank Clerk B	Go towards Chongno. At the crossroads in Chongno, if you go right there is a Korea Exchange Bank.
Mr Pak	Is it far from here?
Bank Clerk B	No. It's about five minutes on foot.

UNIT 5

Is this the bus for Dongdaemun market?

Mr Kim	Excuse me, is there a bus for Dongdaemun market here?
Mr Lee	I don't have a clue, I'm not from Seoul.
Mr Kim	Excuse me, is there a bus to Dongdaemun market from here?
Mrs O	No. You can't get a bus to Dongdaemun market from here. But if you get bus number 20 it will take you to Namdaemun market.
Mr Kim	Namdaemun market? What is there at Namdaemun market?
Mrs O	What is there? There's nothing they don't sell at Namdaemun market.
Mr Kim	Are there more goods than at Dongdaemun market?
Mrs O	In my opinion Namdaemun market has more goods than Dongdaemun, and is more interesting. However, they don't sell monkeys at Namdaemun market. They do sell them at Dongdaemun.
Mr Kim	Is that true?! Although … I don't need a monkey.
Mrs O	Then take the number 20 bus.

Mr Kim	Where do I get it?
Mrs O	Take it at the stop straight across the road.
Mr Kim	How much is the fare?
Mrs O	My, you must be a real stranger here (country bumpkin)! It's 1,100 won.
Mr Kim	Thank you.
Mrs O	Hurry up. The bus is coming!

This fruit doesn't look too good!

Minja	How much are the apples here?
Clerk A	One box is 30,000 won.
Minja	That's too expensive. Will you cut the price a bit?
Clerk A	Okay, you can take a box for 28,000 won.
Minja	It's still expensive.
Clerk A	Then go and try somewhere else! Bad luck all morning (today, since the morning)!
Minja	These apples don't look too good (fresh). Some of them have gone bad.
Clerk B	Really? Then I'll cut the price a bit for you.
Minja	How much will you give me them for?
Clerk B	Just give me 31,000 won.
Minja	What?! That's even more expensive than the stall next door!
Clerk B	All right. Then just give me 27,000 won.
Minja	Please cut me a bit more off the price.
Clerk B	All right, then! Just pay 25,000 a box.
Minja	Thank you. Three boxes please.

UNIT 6

Off to the mountains

Mr Kim	The weather's really good today.
Tony	Yes. The weather's better in Korea than in England.
Mr Kim	What are you going to do tomorrow? If you don't have anything on, shall we go to the mountains?
Tony	I do want to go, but tomorrow I decided to go shopping at Dongdaemun market with my wife.
Mr Kim	How about next Sunday, then?
Tony	Next Sunday I'm thinking of going to Pulguksa with some friends from university.

Mr Kim	Next Sunday won't do either, then. When would be okay?
Tony	The Sunday after that would probably be fine.
Mr Kim	All right. Then let's go that following Sunday.
Tony	I like mountain climbing too. But there aren't many mountains in Britain so I haven't been able to do much. By the way, which mountain shall we go to?
Mr Kim	Dobongsan mountain would be convenient.
Tony	Then shall we meet at the entrance to Dobongsan mountain?

I've got a nasty headache!

Jaehoon	I'm going into town. Shall we go together?
Yongtae	I don't know … I don't feel too good.
Jaehoon	You don't feel well *again*? You're always pretending to be ill!
Yongtae	No I'm not. That's not true. Today I really am ill.
Jaehoon	What is it this time?
Yongtae	I've got a nasty headache. My head hurts.
Jaehoon	Is that all? Don't worry – it's perhaps because the weather is hot.
Yongtae	I don't think so. I have stomach ache as well.
Jaehoon	Is it bad?
Yongtae	Yes. It hurts a lot.
Jaehoon	Then let's go to the chemist to buy some medicine.
Yongtae	I can't. I have no energy (strength). Besides, my legs hurt.
Jaehoon	Your legs, too? It seems like your whole body hurts! Is there anywhere that doesn't hurt?
Yongtae	Shut up! Don't make fun of me. I need some medicine.
Jaehoon	I've got a cure-all medicine here – it's alcohol! It's better than medicine, you know!
Yongtae	Don't make jokes. I can't drink alcohol. I really need to go to the hospital.

UNIT 8

She's just gone out

Mr Yun	Hello?
Jaemok	Hello. Can I speak to Chongmin, please?
Mr Yun	Yes, hold on, please.

(A little while later)

Mr Yun	I'm sorry, she was here until a little while ago, but she has just gone out.
Jaemok	Oh dear. Have you any idea where she might have gone?
Mr Yun	I don't have a clue. Just a moment. Maybe my wife will know.
Mrs Yun	Tonight Chongmin has gone out to see a movie with her boyfriend.
Jaemok	Really? That's strange, she was supposed (lit: *decided*) to meet me this evening …
Mrs Yun	Oh dear. Well, she's gone out on a date with a different guy and she won't be back until late.
Jaemok	Oh well, it's turned out well then – I was just ringing up to cancel. Something came up today.
Mrs Yun	Oh really? It has turned out well. Do you have a message for Chongmin?
Jaemok	No, I don't. Goodbye.

What did you do last night?

Yongtae	Taegyu, how are you doing?!
Taegyu	Hi there! How are things?
Yongtae	Nowadays I'm a bit busy. I've (just) got a girlfriend, so I'm even more busy!
Taegyu	I thought so. What's her name?
Yongtae	She's called Kim Chongmin. She graduated last year from Seoul National University. Now she's working for Hyundai cars.
Taegyu	How did you meet?
Yongtae	My friend did an introduction for me. At first I didn't like her that much, but a month later we met by chance at a party. We started meeting regularly from then on.
Taegyu	And now you're meeting her and dating nearly every day, are you?
Yongtae	More or less!
Taegyu	I tried to ring you last night, but you'd gone out then too. Where did you go last night?
Yongtae	Last night? I don't remember. I expect we went somewhere or other.
Taegyu	You don't remember?! Had you drunk so much?!

Yongtae	You mean *me* drinking? (lit: *who was drinking*?) You're the one who drinks every day (on the contrary).
Taegyu	Anyhow, where did you go?
Yongtae	We went to a noraebang, my girlfriend really likes noraebangs.
Taegyu	Where did you go after coming out of the noraebang?
Yongtae	We played a bit of table tennis.
Taegyu	Is that all? Tell me honestly!
Yongtae	It's true! Nothing happened!

UNIT 9

We bought him that last year!

Wife	It's Grandad's birthday tomorrow.
Husband	What, already?
Wife	Yes. We're going to have to decide what to buy him.
Husband	Can't you decide? I'm busy.
Wife	I always decide. Please help this time.
Husband	All right. Why don't we buy him a jumper?
Wife	He's got ten already. He doesn't need another one.
Husband	What about a shirt then?
Wife	He doesn't need a shirt either.
Husband	A book?
Wife	You know he doesn't like reading.
Husband	Since Grandma likes reading it would be okay if she read it instead!
Wife	Don't joke. Try making a better suggestion.
Husband	What about an umbrella?
Wife	He doesn't go out when it rains.
Husband	Some socks, then?
Wife	We bought him that last year.
Husband	How about a new electric razor?
Wife	We bought him that the year before. Besides, he doesn't shave himself properly (*frequently*).
Husband	You see?! You don't like my suggestions. You'd better decide, like I said at first!

I'm sorry, I really didn't know!

Policeman	Excuse me. Please show me your driving licence.
Driver	Why? What's the matter?
Policeman	You really don't know?

Driver	What are you talking about?
Policeman	Just look at the cars parked here. The cars have all been parked in the same direction.
Driver	So what?
Policeman	Okay then, didn't you see that red one-way signpost over there?
Driver	Ah, it's a one-way street! I'm sorry. I really didn't know.
Policeman	You've committed a serious offence. It's very dangerous and there is a large fine if you go into a one-way street the wrong way.
Driver	I really didn't see the sign. Please let me off this once.
Policeman	Be careful from now on. The fine is 50,000 won.
Driver	Thank you very much and keep up the good work.

UNIT 10

What did you do with it?

Customer	Excuse me, I was here yesterday with some friends and I left my bag behind.
Employee	Just let me go and have a look. Can you describe your bag?
Customer	Yes . . . it's very big, black and made of leather.
Employee	There's a briefcase. Is that it?
Customer	No, it's not a briefcase.
Employee	No, we don't seem to have anything. Was there anything important inside?
Customer	Yes, actually. There were some important documents, some books and my bank cards.
Employee	Please wait a moment. I will ask the manager.
Manager	Hello, how can I help you?
Customer	I've lost my bag – yesterday I ate here and left it behind (*put it down and left*).
Manager	What time did you leave the restaurant?
Customer	About 11 p.m., I think.
Manager	Around closing time ... Ah yes, I remember now. There was a bag when we were cleaning this morning.
Customer	What did you do with it?
Manager	I sent it to the police station. They are keeping it there.
Customer	Can you tell me where the police station is?
Manager	Yes, go out of the restaurant and turn left and it's on the third (*small*) street on your right.
Customer	Thank you very much. Goodbye.

Nasty headaches

Pharmacist	Hello, can I help you?
Mr Pak	Yes, I've got a very bad headache; I wonder if you could give me some medicine.
Pharmacist	Yes, certainly. When did you get it?
Mr Pak	It came yesterday. I've been working very hard and have had a lot of stress – probably overwork and stress is the reason.
Pharmacist	It could be. Do your eyes hurt at all?
Mr Pak	Yes, they do a bit.
Pharmacist	Have you been able to sleep?
Mr Pak	No, my head hurts too much, and so I can't sleep.
Pharmacist	I see. It's probably linked to stress, then. I recommend these tablets.
Mr Pak	How often should I take them?
Pharmacist	You can take one every four hours while it's very bad. When it gets a bit easier, then just take one tablet after meals three times a day.
Mr Pak	Are there any side-effects?
Pharmacist	When you take the medicine you will feel drowsy so take care. Don't be surprised if you feel tired easily.
Mr Pak	Okay. Thank you very much.

UNIT 11

Would you like to try it on?

Minho	Look at that shirt; it's really nice.
Byongsoo	Well, I think the design is a bit old-fashioned.
Minho	No, I like them. Agassi, how much are those shirts?
Clerk A	8,000 won.
Minho	Wow, that's really cheap.
Byongsoo	Yeah, but look at it, the quality's not very good.
Minho	Oh, I don't know. Shall we go and look somewhere else then?
Clerk B	Welcome! What are you looking for?
Minho	Yes, I'm looking for casual shirts. (*Something in*) a bright colour. Something stylish and good quality which I can wear with jeans.
Clerk B	What about these? This style is very popular at the moment.

Minho	What is it made of?
Clerk B	100% cotton. Would you like to try one on?
Minho	Yes, please ...
	Does it suit me?

Do you think it suits me?

Clerk	Ah, that looks very nice.
Minho	Do you think it suits me?
Byongsoo	Yes. But it seems/looks a bit small.
Clerk	Would you like to try a bigger one?
Minho	Yes, please.
Clerk	Here you are.
Byongsoo	That looks a bit better.
Clerk	Ah, that looks super.
Minho	By the way, how much is it?
Clerk	32,000 won.
Minho	What?
Clerk	Why? That's a very good price. Only 32,000 won.
Byongsoo	It sounds a bit expensive to me!
Minho	At Namdaemun they had a similar one for only 8,000 won.
Clerk	Ah yes, at Namdaemun. It looks the same, but the quality is very different. If you buy clothes at Namdaemun, they become unusable in just two or three months, so you have to buy new ones.
Byongsoo	Well, I don't know. Do you reckon this shirt will last four times as long, then?
Clerk	Oh, at least. And it will be a much better fit.
Minho	Mmm. I'll go and think about it, I think.

UNIT 12

Do you have a spare room?

Guest	Do you have any free rooms, please?
Owner	Yes, we do. Would you like beds or sleeping on the floor?
Guest	One with bed and one with floor sleeping.
Owner	Certainly. It will be 50,000 won for the room with a bed, and 40,000 for the room with floor sleeping. How many nights are you staying?
Guest	Three nights, please. We may stay a little longer than that (I don't know).

Owner	If you book for five nights or more, we offer a 5% discount.
Guest	Oh, I'll talk about that with my wife. Is breakfast included in the price?
Owner	Yes, breakfast is included. Between 7 and 10 a.m. please go to the basement restaurant. Or you can have breakfast brought to your room for 2,000 won extra per person.
Guest	No, we'll go to the restaurant, thank you. What other facilities does the hotel have?
Owner	We have a swimming pool, a sauna, a games room, a noraebang, a bar, a Korean restaurant and a western one.
Guest	Is there a TV and a phone in the rooms?
Owner	Of course, and there is also a mini-bar.
Guest	Oh, that's excellent. It would be better to book for five nights, then. My wife will probably like that.

The towel is dirty and the food is cold

Guest	Excuse me, I'd like to speak to the manager, please.
Employee	Excuse me, but is there a problem?
Guest	Yes, I have something to say about the hotel service.
Employee	Is there any chance you can tell me what the problem is?
Guest	I'd like to speak to the manager direct about it.
Employee	Very well, sir. Hold on a moment please.
Manager	Hello, I'm the manager. What is the problem?
Guest	It seems that there are many problems with the service at this hotel. The staff are unfriendly and unhelpful; this morning we went in for breakfast and the food was cold. Yesterday it was the same.
Manager	Really? I'm very sorry to hear that. Did you speak to the waitress about it?
Guest	Of course I spoke to the waitress! She was impolite, and while saying that she couldn't understand my Korean, she said that the food was fine. It wasn't; it was cold and the taste was awful.
Manager	I'm extremely sorry, sir. We always try to do our best, but sometimes mistakes happen. I'll make sure that I speak to the kitchen staff right away.

Guest	And that's not all. This morning I asked for my towel to be changed and the new towel was very dirty and they still haven't cleaned my son's room.
Manager	This is strange. We don't usually get any complaints like this.
Guest	Even that is not all. The television in our room has broken down and the fridge door won't even open. I have to say that quite frankly the service and facilities are rubbish.
Manager	I'm sorry but we also don't need guests like you who complain so much in our hotel. Please leave right away. We will refund your money.

UNIT 13

Two to Taegu

Ticket seller	Can I help you?
Mr Pak	Are there any trains to Taegu this evening, please?
Ticket seller	Yes, there are two trains, a slow one at 5.30, and a fast one at 7.45.
Mr Pak	How long do they take?
Ticket seller	The fast one takes three hours, the slow one four hours 30 minutes.
Mr Pak	What about the price?
Ticket seller	Yes, the slow one is 18,000 won, the fast 45,000 won, and we only have a few seats left for the fast one.
Mr Pak	Can we book four seats together?
Ticket seller	Please wait a minute. Just let me check … yes, that's fine. There are four seats available. Non-smoking or smoking?
Mr Pak	Non-smoking, please.
Ticket seller	Would you like single tickets or return?
Mr Pak	No, return please.
Ticket seller	When are you coming back?
Mr Pak	Sunday evening.
Ticket seller	There's a train at 6.30; but it's a slow one. There is no fast train on Sunday evening.
Mr Pak	What about Sunday afternoon?
Ticket seller	Yes, there's one at 2.30.
Mr Pak	That'll be okay. We'll take the fast one, please.

Ticket seller	That will be 360,000 won altogether, please.
Mr Pak	What platform does the train go from?
Ticket seller	I don't know yet. Before the time of departure look at the electronic notice board.
Mr Pak	Okay, thank you very much.

I don't want to go there!

Mr Yun	What are you doing after work this evening?
Mr Paek	After work? Don't know. I haven't got anything planned.
Mr Yun	What about going out for a meal?
Mr Paek	Sounds a good idea. Just the two of us?
Mr Yun	We could invite some others. What about Mrs Kim and Mrs Lee?
Mr Paek	Yeah, sure! Hey, Mrs Kim, Mrs Lee! Do you fancy going out for a meal tonight?
Mrs Kim	Okay, but where are we going to?
Mr Yun	We could go and eat pulgogi, and of course we could drink soju and then go out to a noraebang or something.
Mrs Kim	I like drinking, but I don't particularly like pulgogi, and I hate singing.
Mr Paek	Well you don't have to eat pulgogi, you can have something else. And you can just listen instead of singing.
Mrs Kim	Yeah, that's fair enough. But I don't have much spare cash right now.
Mr Yun	Don't worry. I'll buy.
Mrs Kim	Yes, okay then. That's nice of you.
Mr Paek	What about you, Mr Lee, would you like to come?
Mrs Lee	I would like to go, but I'd prefer to go out to Inchŏn and eat raw fish, though.
Mr Paek	No, it's too far and it's too expensive.
Mr Yun	Besides, I can't eat raw fish.
Mrs Lee	Okay, okay, it was only an idea. I guess I'll just have to come and eat pulgogi and soju!

Key to exercises

PRONUNCIATION GUIDE

Consonants

25 hotel **26** computer **27** television **28** taxi **29** lemon **30** ice cream **31** hamburger **32** sandwich **33** orange juice **34** tomato **35** tennis **36** camera

UNIT 1

Eating and drinking in Korea

소주 (Korean vodka) and 막걸리 (rice wine)

Dialogue 1: Where are you off to?

1 안녕하세요? **2** 가요 **3** Jaemin is going to the town centre. **4** in order to buy bread **5** They agree to go to the town centre together to buy bread.

Language discovery 1

In Korean, the surname comes before the first name (opposite order), and there is no space between the first and last names.

4 a 가요 **b** 해요 **c** 사요

Dialogue 2: Cheers!

1 건배 **2** 주세요. This happens twice in the dialogue. **3** soju, beer and Western spirits **4** two **5** fruit and squid

Language discovery 2

있어요? **a** 맥주 있어요? **b** 안주 있어요? **c** 과일 있어요?

Practice

1 a 빵 있어요. **b** 맥주 있어요. **c** 술집 있어요. **d** 과일 있어요.

2 a 학교에 가요. **b** 감사합니다. **c** 안녕하세요. **d** 네, 잘 지냈어요. **e** 맥주 마시러 술집에 가요. **f** 그럼 맥주하고 소주 주세요.

3 a 가요. 지금 학교에 가요. **b** 있어요? 소주 있어요? **c** 사요. 뭐 사요? **d** 먹어요. 김 선생님 빵 먹어요. **e** 없어요. 오징어 없어요. **f** 해요. 뭐 해요? **g** 앉아요. 앉아요!

4 a 아저씨, 오징어 주세요. **b** 아저씨, 위스키 주세요. **c** 아저씨, 물 주세요.

5 a one soju, one beer and some dry snacks. **b** squid, fruit, western spirits and one beer

6 a

A	안녕하세요? 어디 가요?
B	네, 안녕하세요. 가게에 가요.
A	나도 가게에 가요. 같이 가요.
B	네. 같이 가요. 그 다음에 술 (or, 맥주) 마시러 술집에 가요.

b

A	잘 지냈어요?
B	네. 잘 지냈어요.
A	*(to the waiter)* 아저씨, 맥주 하나하고 소주 하나 주세요.
Waiter	네. 알겠어요.
A	그리고 안주도 주세요. 뭐 있어요?
Waiter	과일하고 오징어하고 마른 안주 있어요.
A	그럼 과일 주세요.

Test yourself

1 a 지금 일본에 가요. **b** 아저씨, 맥주 있어요? **c** 뭐 사러 가게에 가요? **d** 양주하고 오징어 주세요. **e** 그리고 안주도 주세요. **f** 나도 가게에 가요. **g** 맥주하고 마른 안주하고 밥 다 있어요. Or, 마른 안주하고 맥주하고 밥 다 있어요.

2 a 뭐 사러 가게에 가요? Or, 가게에서 뭐 사요? **b** 김 선생님, 안녕하세요! **c** 그 다음에 뭐 해요? **d** 지금 시내에 가요? **e** 어디 가요? **f** 맥주하고 과일하고 빵 – 다 있어요! **g** 밥도 주세요 **h** 오징어 여기 있어요. 맛있게 드세요! **i** 양주 없어요. 그럼 맥주 하나 주세요. **j** 파전하고 소주 하나 주세요.

UNIT 2

Meeting, greeting and addressing others

b, **d**

Dialogue 1: Long time, no see!

1 우리 집사람이에요 **2** so-so **3** He says that he's heard a lot about her. Her name is Yunhee Chang.

Language discovery 1

The title always comes after the name. The full name or only the surname precedes 선생님. The full name or first name only precedes -씨.

2 a 이에요 **b** 예요 **c** 이에요 **d** 예요

4 a 는 **b** 은 **c** 는 **d** 은

Dialogue 2: It's not me!

1 실례합니다, 실례지만 **2** in the Japanese department **3** to see the Korean teacher

Language discovery 2

The verb ending -합니다 is a polite ending and the ending -지만 adds the meaning *but*.

4 a 는, 은 **b** 가, 는 **c** 이, 는

6 a 네, 장윤희 아니에요. **b** 아니요, 여기가 김선생님 사무실이에요.
c 네, 오징어가 아니에요.

7 a 술집이 어디예요?, 술집이 어디 있어요? **b** 사무실이 어디예요?,
사무실이 어디 있어요?

Practice

1 a 씨, 도, 에 **b** 러, 에, 요 **c** 은 **d** 가 **e** 는, 이

2 a 오 선생님 안녕하세요! 회사는 어때요? **b** 미세스 조, 안녕하세요!
사업은 어때요? **c** 박 선생님 안녕하세요! 가족은 어때요? **d** 태규씨
안녕하세요! 학교는 어때요? **e** 미스 박, 안녕하세요! 건강은 어때요?

3 a 이것이 오징어에요. / 이것이 오징어가 아니에요. **b** 이것이
책이에요. / 이것이 책이 아니에요. **c** 이것이 사과에요. / 이것이
사과가 아니에요. **d** 이것이 신문이에요. / 이것이 신문이 아니에요.
e 이것이 잡지예요. / 이것이 잡지가 아니에요.

4 a 미국 사람이세요? 네, 미국 사람이에요. 아니요, 미국 사람이
아니에요. **b** 이 선생님이세요? 네, 이 선생님이에요. 아니요, 이
선생님이 아니에요. **c** 중국 선생님이 아니세요? 네, 중국
선생님이에요. 아니요, 중국 선생님이 아니에요. **d** 백 선생님 아들이
아니에요? 네, 백 선생님 아들이에요. 아니요, 백 선생님 아들이
아니에요. **e** 학교 선생님이 아니세요? 네, 학교 선생님이에요. 아니요,
학교 선생님이 아니에요.

5 a 박상민이에요. 아, 그래요? 만나서 반갑습니다. **b** 요즘 학교는
어때요? **c** 실례합니다. 일본말 선생님이세요? **d** 아저씨, 오징어
있어요? 오징어 어때요? 좋아요. **e** 한국학과 사무실이 아니에요? 네,
아니에요. **f** 저는 우 선생님이 아니에요. 아, 그래요? 죄송합니다.
g 우리 중국말 선생님이세요. 그래요? 말씀 많이 들었어요. **h** 일본
가게예요? **i** 나도 한국 선생님 만나러 가요. **j** 박 선생님 부인 만나러
왔어요. **k** 한국 학과가 어디예요? **l** 학교 사무실이 어디예요?

6

A	안녕하세요?
B	아! 안녕하세요?
A	오래간만이에요.
B	네, 그래요. 진짜 오래간만이에요.
A	잘 지냈어요?
B	네. 잘 지냈어요. 요즘 사업은 어때요?
A	그저 그래요. *(signalling to his son)* 우리 아들이에요.
B	아! 그래요. 반갑습니다.

7 여기는 중국학과 사무실이 아니에요. 중국말 선생님이 없어요.

Test yourself

1

A	Excuse me, are you Mr Pak?
B	No, I'm not Mr Pak. Mr Pak is the Chinese teacher. This is the Chinese department office.
A	Ah, I'm sorry. Excuse me, but could you tell me where the Korean department is?
B	It's over there. I'm going to see (meet) a teacher (someone) at the Korean department also.
A	Let's go together then.

2 네, 오래간만이에요. 잘 지냈어요? / 요즘 좋아요. / 사무실에 가요. / 저기에요. / 김 선생님 만나러 가요.

3 안녕하세요, 이에요, 선생님, 우리, 예요

UNIT 3

Eating out in Korea

by calling out 여기요! to a passing waiter

Dialogue 1: Sorry, wrong number!

1 김 선생님, Mr Kim. He asks to speak to Mr Kim: 죄송하지만 김선생님 좀 바꿔주세요. **2** Tony meant to call 389-2056. The phone number is made up of seven Sino-Korean numbers. **3** Tony from the British embassy **4** Tony asks if Mr Kim is free at lunchtime today; he wants to buy Mr Kim lunch. **5** Outside Lotte Hotel at 12 o'clock.

Language discovery 1

a 공 **b** 이 **c** 삼 **d** 오 **e** 육 **f** 팔 **g** 구

1 a 84 **b** 475 **c** 69,221

2 Mr Kim drinks beer well, but I drink whisky well.

3 a 물 좀 주세요 **b** 책 좀 읽어 주세요 **c** 라디오 좀 켜 주세요

4 a true **b** false - 먹어요 is an example of the polite ending

Dialogue 2: Would you like to order?

1 Mr Kim suggests eating bulgogi or kalbi. He says 불고기나 갈비를 먹읍시다. **2** He likes Korean food very much but cannot eat spicy food very well. **3** Yes, he says 네, 좋아요. **4** Tony asks the waitress for more water and kimchi.

Language discovery 2

a 네, 좋아요. **b** 한국 음식 좋아하세요?

1 The first means that Mr Kim is a good man, a good guy. The second means that you (or whoever) actually likes him.

2 a Let's go to school or to the embassy. **b** Let's drink soju or beer or something.

3 a 책 못 읽어요, I can't read books. **b** 비빔 냉면 못 먹어요, I can't eat 비빔냉면.

Practice

1 a 박 선생님하고 미세스 김 만나고 싶어요. **b** 빵하고 과일 사고 싶어요. **c** 불고기하고 갈비 먹고 싶어요. **d** 영어 선생님하고 일본말 선생님 기다리고 싶어요. **e** 맥주하고 위스키 마시고 싶어요. **f** 오징어하고 냉면 주문하고 싶어요. Second part: 박 선생님이나 미세스 김 만나고 싶어요; 빵이나 과일 사고 싶어요, etc.

2 김 선생님: 오팔이-오구이공; 재민: 이구일-육사팔이; 의사: 육육육-공이삼일; 피터: 공일육이삼-이구육공; 박 선생님: 공일오일육팔칠구일공이.

3 a 나는 일본 대사관에 못 가요. **b** 지금 점심 먹으러 식당에 못 가요. **c** 재민씨는 상민씨 못 기다려요 (or 기다리세요). **d** 상민씨 매운 거 못 먹어요. **e** (중국 대사관 앞에서) 미세스 장 못 만나요. **f** 백화점에 못 가요.

4 a 가세요, 갑시다 **b** 주문하세요, 주문합시다 **c** 보세요, 봅시다 **d** 앉으세요, 앉읍시다 **e** 기다리세요, 기다립시다 **f** 사세요, 삽시다 **g** 만나세요, 만납시다 Second part: e.g. 김 선생님 잠깐 기다리세요. 열시에 학교에 갑시다.

5 The first sentence says something is good (irrespective of whether or not you personally like it) and the second says that you like it (irrespective of its quality).

6 a 중국말로 말합시다. **b** 백화점에 갑시다. **c** 맥주나 와인 마십시다 **d** 미국에 가고 싶지만 못 가요. **e** 위스키 좋지만 못 마셔요. **f** 김 선생님한테 전화하고 싶지만, 잘못 걸었어요.

7 a 97 **b** 53 **c** 207 **d** 867 **e** 34495

8 열두시에 학교 앞에서 만납시다.

Test yourself

1 a 한국 음식 좋아하세요? **b** 저는 힐튼 호텔의 상민이에요. **c** 열시에 학교 앞에서 만납시다. **d** 오늘 점심에 시간이 있어요? **e** 우선 물 좀 주세요. **f** 매운 거 잘 못 먹어요. **g** 갈비 삼 인분하고 냉면 두 그릇 주세요.

2 a I like spicy food, but I can't eat Korean (well). Or, Although I like spicy food, I can't eat Korean. **b** Excuse me, where is the British embassy? **c** Please sit down over here (at this side). Would you like anything to drink? **d** Do you have (some/free) time? Let's meet later, then. **e** Mr Kim? Just a moment . . . I'm sorry, but there is no such person here. You've misdialled. **f** Is that 863-0542?

UNIT 4

South Korean currency

on five – on the 100 won coin and on all four notes

Dialogue 1: How much is it altogether?

1 Chris says 한영사전하고 영한사전 둘 다 주세요. **2** It is 10,000 won. The shop assistant says each book is 10,000 won per volume: 한 권에 만원씩. **3** 30,000 won **4** yes

Language discovery 1

The underlined words are counters for the nouns (book, money/won, type and money/won, respectively) mentioned.

2 a pure **b** Sino-Korean **c** Sino-Korean **d** pure

3 a Water is 15,000 won per bottle. **b** Dictionaries are 60,000 won per three volumes.

5 a 제일 맛있는 음식 **b** 제일 시원한 물 **c** 제일 싼 사전

Dialogue 2: Finding the way

1 The bank clerk says to turn left (to in the leftward direction) at the post office. **2** Mr Pak wanted to exchange English money into Korean money. The bank clerk tells Mr Pak their bank doesn't do/offer exchange services: 우리 은행은 외환 업무를 안해요. **3** The Exchange Bank is in the direction of Jongno. Mr Pak must turn right at the Jongno crossroads. It is roughly give minutes away by foot.

Language discovery 2

으로 means to, towards, in the direction of . . .

2 a 에서 **b** 에 **c** 에 **d** 에서

3 a If you go left at the crossroads, there is a bank. **b** If you go in this direction, it takes five minutes.

Practice

1 a 그런, 다른, 가세요 **b** 가면 **c** -지만, 사전 **d** 여기서, 오십분 **e** 저는, 의 **f** 우체국, 오른, 은행 **g** 종류가 **h** 모두, 드릴까요 **i** 이에요, 사업 **j** 비싼, 싫어요

2 a 여보세요. 김 선생님 좀 바꿔주세요. **b** 내일 시간 있으세요? **c** 거기 한국 대사관 아니에요? **d** 우리 집사람이에요. **e** 영어 사전 있어요? **f** 한국 음식 좋아하세요? **g** 맥주 마시고 싶어요?

3 a 한 권에 백원씩이에요. 그러니까 모두 사백원이에요. **b** 한 잔에 칠백원씩이에요. 그러니까 모두 천 사백원이에요. **c** 한 개에 이천원씩이에요. 그러니까 모두 만이천원이에요. **d** 한 병에 천 오백원씩이에요. 그러니까 모두 사천 오백원이에요. **e** 한 상자에 육천원씩이에요. 그러니까 모두 만 팔천원이에요.

4 a 서, 으로, 이 **b** 이, 에, 에서 **c** 을, 으로 **d** 은/이, 를 **e** 는, 을, 나 **f** 는, 이 **g** 을, 이나 **h** 가 **i** 에, 이에요

5 a 책 세 권, 책 여덟 권, 책 스물두 권. **b** 일일, 삼일, 육십칠일. **c** 한 사람, 일곱 사람, 서른네 사람. **d** 오징어 세 마리, 오징어 아홉 마리, 오징어 열 네 마리. **e** 두 병, 열 병. **f** 개 아홉 마리, 개 한 마리. **g** 천 원, 만 원.

6 a 마른 안주 안 주문해요. **b** 오분 안 걸려요. **c** 맥주 안 드세요. **d** 선생님 안 기다리세요. **e** 책 안 읽어요.

7

Clerk	뭘 찾으세요?
Child	우유 있어요?
Clerk	네, 있어요.
Child	우유 두 병하고 **빵** 좀 주세요.
Clerk	여기 있어요.
Child	얼마에요?
Clerk	삼천원이에요.
Child	맥주하고 고기하고 사과하고 김치도 있어요?
Clerk	네, 있어요.
Child	얼마에요?

Test yourself

1 a film **b** what (him) **c** none **d** word **e** bread

2 a 실례지만, 여기 식당 있어요? **b** 냉면 못 먹어요. 갈비도 못 먹어요. **c** 얼마에요? 한 접시에 이천원…, 그러니까 모두 육천원이에요. **d** 여기서 왼쪽으로 가세요. 오분 가면, 종로사거리가 있어요. 왼쪽으로 가세요. 은행이 오른쪽에 있어요. **e** 제일 싼 거 얼마에요? **f** 걸어서 십분쯤 걸려요. **g** 여기 한국 외환은행 지점이 없어요. **h** 돈을 좀 바꾸고 싶어요. 오만원쯤 있어요. 한국에 열 가지 종류의 김치가 있어요. **j** 한국말 사전을 드릴까요? **k** 어떤 종류를 드릴까요? **l** 제일 싼 거 주세요. **m** 김 선생님이 나쁜 사람이에요? **n** 우체국에 가세요? 좋아요. 안녕히 가세요.

UNIT 5

Markets

남대문 시장 and 동대문 시장

Dialogue 1: Is there a bus going to Dongdaemun market?

1 Mr Lee is unable to help because he isn't from Seoul. He says, 서울 사람이 아니라서 잘 모르겠어요, because I am not from Seoul I don't really know. **2** The number 20 bus goes to Namdaemun market. Mrs O says 이십 번 버스를 타면 … **3** Namdaemun has a wider, better choice of goods and it is more interesting. **4** a monkey **5** You should catch the bus at the bus stop on the opposite side of the road. The fare is 1,100 won.

Language discovery 1

-라서 means since

2 a 에도 **b** 에서는 **c** 에는

4 a 시장이 학교보다 (더) 재미있어요. **b** 갈비가 불고기보다 더 비싸요.

6 a 오늘은 남대문 가고 내일은 동대문 가요. **b** 20번 버스를 타고 은행 앞에서 내려요. **c** 점심에는 비빔밥을 먹고 보리차를 마셔요.

Dialogue 2: This apple doesn't look too good!

1 Apples are 30,000 won per box. The expression used by the shopkeeper is 한 상자에 삼만 원이에요. **2** The apples don't look fresh and some have gone off. **3** Minja eventually pays 25,000 won per box of apples. She buys three boxes altogether.

Language discovery 2

만 is the particle for only.

4 a 한테서 **b** 에게/께 **c** 에게서 **d** 한테

Practice

1 a 아니요. 남대문 시장이 동대문 시장보다 더 재미있어요. **b** 동대문 시장에서 원숭이는 안 팔아요. **c** 이십번 버스를 타면 남대문 시장에 가요. **d** 네. 남대문 시장에는 안 파는 게 없어요. **e** 바로 길 건너편 정류장에서 타요.

2 a 아니요. 나는 못 가요. **b** 남대문 시장 앞에서 김 선생님 만나요. **c** 그럼 다른 데에 가보세요. **d** 삼백 오십원이에요. **e** 한국 좋아하지만 한국말 재미없어요.

3 a 김 선생님(의) 개군요! **b** 오 선생님 부인이시군요! **c** 일본 책이군요! **d** 한국 외환 은행이군요! **e** 형준이군요! **f** 중국말 선생님이시군요!

4 a 한국 음식이 일본 음식보다 더 맛이 있어요. **b** 여기는 거기보다 더 많아요. **c** 기차는 버스보다 더 빨라요. **d** 김 선생님이 박 선생님보다 재수 더 좋아요. **e** 남대문 시장이 동대문 시장보다 더 비싸요.

5 The acceptable sequences are: a, c, d, h.

6 a 이 사전이 비싸네요. **b** 태규가 오네요. **c** 뭘 하네요! **d** 이 신문이 정말 재미있네요.

7

한국 사람 안녕하세요. 한국 사람이에요? 실례지만 여기 루브르 박물관 가는 버스가 있어요?

일본 사람 저 한국 사람 아니에요. 일본 사람이에요.

한국 사람 죄송합니다.

일본 사람 루브르 박물관 여기서 멀지 않아요. 버스 (탈) 필요 없어요. 걸어서 칠 분 걸려요.

한국 사람 고맙습니다. 안녕히 계세요.

일본 사람 안녕히 가세요.

8 오십칠 번 버스가 학교에 가는 버스에요. 십팔번 버스는 시내에 가요.

Test yourself

1 a Wow, it's expensive here! Let's go and try next door (at the next door shop). **b** They do sell them here, but if you go somewhere else (to a different place) it's cheaper. **c** Where do you catch a bus for (going to)

Seoul city centre? **d** I haven't had any luck all morning! **e** Japan is more expensive than Korea. Mind you (however . . .), Korea is expensive too. **f** There are more English people in Korea than I thought. **g** I'll cut the price for you. You can take a box for 13,000 won. **h** Would you like to order? **i** Since this isn't Korea (since we're not in Korea) there are few places selling kimchi. **j** You want to know if we've got monkeys? Go and try at Tongdaemun market!

2 a 이 사람이 박 선생님이고 저 사람 강 선생님이에요. **b** 어머니는 책 읽고 아버지는 텔레비를 봐요. **c** 고기 못 먹고 사과도 못 먹어요. **d** 십일번 버스가 남대문 시장에 가고, 이십번 버스는 동대문 시장에 가요. **e** 상준(도) 버스 타고 명택도 버스 타요.

UNIT 6

Hobbies and pastimes

baseball 야구, basketball 농구, football 축구, taekwondo 태권도, folk wrestling 씨름, golf 골프, skiing 스키, mountain climbing 등

Dialogue 1: Shall we go mountain climbing?

1 He says 쇼핑하기로 했어요. He is going to go to Dongdaemun market with his wife tomorrow. **2** He is thinking about going to Bulguksa with classmates from university. He says 갈까 해요. **3** They agree to go mountain climbing on Sunday in two weeks' time. **4** He likes mountain climbing but he hasn't been mountain climbing many times because there aren't a lot of mountains in England.

Language discovery 1

The verb ending used to indicate the future tense is -(으)ㄹ 거예요.

2 a 동창하고 학교 가기로 했어요. **b** 여기에 앉기로 했어요. **c** 신문 읽기로 했어요.

3 a 대사관에 갈까 해요. **b** 소주 마실까 해요.

4 a Shall we play basketball? **b** Shall we eat kalbi? **c** Shall we send a letter to our friend?

Dialogue 2: I've got a headache!

1 He isn't feeling very well. He says 몸이 좀 좋지 않아요. **2** He thinks he should take medicine and thinks he should go to the hospital. He says 가야겠어요. **3** He suggests alcohol!

Language discovery 2

To say you will have to do something, you need to use the verb ending -야겠어요.

2 a 가르쳐요 **b** 그려요 **c** 펴요

3 a 바빠요 **b** 써요

4 여기에서 기다리지 마세요, 쇼핑하지 마세요

5 a I can't eat Kimchi. **b** I don't eat Kimchi. **c** I can't eat Kimchi.
d I don't eat Kimchi.

6 a I have a dictionary at school but I've come to buy another one.
b I am free tomorrow but Jaemin is busy.

Practice

1 내일은 쇼핑할까 해요. 할 일이 많아서 너무 바빠요. 대학 동창하고
골프 하기로 했어요. 등산을 안 좋아해요.

2

A	머리가 아파요.
B	많이 아파요?
A	그래요. 많이 아파요.
B	그럼 약을 사러 약국에 갑시다.
A	나는 못 가요. 다리도 아파요.
B	아! 여기 두통약이 있어요.
A	그래요? 고마워요.

3 a 놀리지 마세요 (or 시끄러워요) **b** 안 되겠네요 (or 재수 없네요!)
c 전신이 다 아프군요 **d** 뭐라구요? (or 시끄러워요) **e** 시끄러워요.
f 착각했어요. **g** 그렇지 않아요. **h** 아닌 것 같아요. **i** 걱정하지 마세요.
j 뭐라구요?

4 a 빨리 탑시다. **b** 시간은 있- **c** 안 좋아요. **d** 같이 갈까요? **e** 그 사람
부인이 안 좋아요.

5 a 고기를 좋아하지 않아요. **b** 지금 가지 못 해요. **c** 주문하지 않아요.
d 이 사과가 싱싱하지 않아요. **e** 버스 타지 못 해요.

6 머리가 아파요. 다리도 아파요. 음식을 못 먹어요.

Practice

1 a 아플 거에요 **b** 먹을 거에요 **c** 없을 거에요 **d** 가기로 했어요
e 사기로 했어요 **f** 먹기로 했어요 **g** 볼까 해요 **h** 할까 해요 **i** 갈까 해요
j 갈까요? **k** 만날까요? **l** 탈까요?

2 a 게다가 **b** 글쎄요 **c** 그렇지만 (그래도) **d** 그렇지만 **e** kŭrigo 그리고

UNIT 7

Practice

1 a Then let's go together. **b** Do you have (free) time today at lunchtime? **c** It's really been a long time (since we've seen each other). **d** I'm not the Japanese language teacher. **e** I'm sorry. I made a mistake. **f** Next Monday will perhaps be OK. **g** Since I'm not from Seoul either, I really don't know. **h** So your whole body hurts, then?! Is there anywhere that doesn't hurt? **i** I'd like to change English currency into Chinese. **j** And I'd like to eat some naengmyon as well. **k** Give us some dried snacks and some Korean pancake, please. **l** You can take them for 20,000 won a box.

2 a 세시에요 **b** 여덟 시 반이에요. Or, 여덟시 삼십 분이에요. **c** 열 시 사십오분이에요. **d** 곱시 이십분이에요. **e** 여섯시 십분이에요. **f** 여덟 시 십오분이에요.

3 a 해요, 하고, 합시다. **b** 닫아요, 닫고, 닫읍시다. **c** 팔아요, 팔고 팝시다. **d** 바빠요, 바쁘고, 바쁩시다. **e** 움직여요, 움직이고, 움직입시다.

4 a 산에 갑시다. **b** 운동하러 산에 가요. **c** 유월 십이일에 갑시다. **d** 여덟 시에 만납시다. **e** 교회 앞에서 만납시다.

6 E.g. 어디 가요? 가게에 가요. 뭐 사러 가게에 가요? 오징어 사러 가요.

7 a 박 선생님은 7 시 30 분에 일어나요. **b** 힐튼 호텔에서 이 선생님의 부인을 만나요. **c** 중국 음식을 먹어요. **d** 영화 보러 극장에 가요. **e** 11시에 자요.

8 a 축구를 좋아하지 않아요. 테니스 좋아해요. **b** 아니요, 매운 거 잘 못 먹어요. 갈비 먹을 수 있어요. **c** 아니요, 많이 안 봐요. 그렇지만 라디오를 많이 들어요. **d** 잘 못 불러요. 음악을 잘 들어요. **e** 아니요, 중국말 배우지 않아요. 영어 배워요.

9 a 교회에서 영국 대사관은 멀지 않아요. **b** 이 근처에 한국외환은행이 없어요. 상업은행은 있어요. **c** 학교가 은행 옆이에요. **d** 제과점이 멀어요. **e** 네. 우체국은 대사관보다 더 멀어요. **f** 학교에 가려면 걸어서 사십오 분쯤 걸려요. **g** 우체국은 제과점 옆이에요.

11 a 나도 영어를 공부하러 학교에 가요. **b** 가게 밖에서 만납시다. 나중에 봐요. **c** 맛있게 드세요. (많이 드세요) **d** 정말 병원에 가야겠어요. **e** 그럼 만오천원만 내세요. **f** 십오분쯤 걸려요. **g** 요즘 사업은 어때요? **h** 제일 싼 거 주세요. **i** 요즘 날씨가 좋아요. **j** 한국 대사관에서 박 선생님을 만나러 왔어요. **k** 매운 거 못 먹어요. **l** 우체국 가는 버스가 여기 서요?

UNIT 8

Dating culture in Korea

meeting

Dialogue 1 : She's just gone out.

1 He says 여보세요. **2** 우리 집사람이 아마 알고 있을 거예요.
3 He speaks to Mr Yun and his wife. **4** She has gone out to see a film with her boyfriend. **5** She says Chongmin probably won't return until late at night.

Language discovery 1

a 우리 집사람이 아마 알고 있을 거예요. **b** 아마 밤 늦게까지 안 들어올거예요. Probability is expressed by using the verb ending -을 거예요

2 a I eat bibimbap. I am eating bibimbap **b** I am eating bibimbap.
c I don't eat bibimbap. I'm not eating bibimbap. **d** I'm not eating bibimbap.

4 a 바꿨어요 **b** 나갔어요 **c** 전화했어요 **d** 돌아왔어요

5 a 갈비 먹으려고 식당에 갔어요 **b** 학교 가려고 버스 타요

7 a Something has come up today, so I cannot keep the appointment. (lit: a busy matter has come up) **b** My head hurts, so I cannot drink.

Dialogue 2: Where did you go last night?

1 He was introduced to her by a friend. He says, 소개해 주었다.
2 He asks 어제 밤에 어디 갔었어요? **3** She works at Hyundai, a car company. **4** They went to karaoke and then went to play some table tennis.

Language discovery 2

The construction -기 시작했어요 implies the meaning start to do something.

1 a 커피 마시기 시작했어요. **b** 태규가 학교를 가기 시작해요.

2 a 오늘 점심 사주세요. **b** 이 우산 좀 빌려 주세요.

Practice

1 a 해주세요. **b** 쇼핑해주세요. **c** 점심 사주세요. **d** 김 선생님한테 전화해주세요 (or 해 주시겠어요?) **e** 약을 사주세요. **f** 시작해주세요.

2 a 오늘 학교에 못 가요. 머리가 아프거든요. **b** 일요길 날에 시내에 못 가요. 다른 약속이 있거든요. **c** 오늘 밤 탁구 못 쳐요. 팔이 아프기 시작했거든요. **d** 노래방에 가요? 나는 안 가요. 노래방을 싫어하거든요. **e** 재민씨 못 가요? 그럼 잘 됐네요. 나도 못 가거든요.

3 a 대학 동창회가 있어요. **b** Friday, 10th, June. **c** 집사람하고 쇼핑하려고 해요. **d** 도봉산에 가려고 해요. **e** From Friday, 17th June. **f** 토니하고 점심을 먹었어요.

4 a Please try the soup! (Have a taste of . . .) **b** 불국사 한번 가보세요. **c** Even though you're busy, go and see. **d** Have you never tried playing table tennis? Then have a go! **e** 재민씨 아직 안 왔어요? 그럼 조금 더 기다려 보세요

5 a 바쁜 일이 생겨서 못 가요. (or 갈 수 없어요) **b** 집에 음식이 없어서, 식당에 가요. **c** 사업이 안 좋아서, 돈이 없어요. **d** 밖에 나가서 기다립시다. **e** 상민씨 집에 가서 뭘 할까요? **f** 시내에 가서 과일 좀 사 오세요.

6 테니스 해봤어요? 농구 해봤어요? 신문 읽어 봤어요? 영국 음식 먹어 봤어요?

Test yourself

1 a 학교에 갔어요. **b** 맥주 많이 마셨어요. **c** 약속을 못 지켰어요. **d** 친구를 만났어요. **e** 영화를 보고 싶었어요. **f** 도봉산에 갈까 했어요.

2 아침에 …, -기로 했어요 …, 그렇지만 …, 생겨서 …, 그러니까 …, 하려고 …, 했어요 …, 지켰어요

3 a 약속을 취소하려고 전화했어요. 일이 생겼거든요. **b** 상민씨는 탁구 치러 방금 나갔어요. **c** 처음에는 김치가 그렇게 마음에 들지 않았는데 (or 김치를 별로 좋아하지 않았는데), 익숙해졌어요. **d** 언제 졸업했어요? **e** 술집에서 우연히 만났어요. **f** 이상하네요! 크리스는 벌써 돌아왔어요. **g** 어제밤에 뭐 했어요? 솔직히 말해보세요.

UNIT 9

Gift giving in Korea

a

Dialogue 1: We bought him that last year!

1 무엇을 사드릴까 결정해야겠어요. **2** Grandfather already has 10 jackets. **3** Last year they gave him socks and the year before last they bought him a new electric shaver.

Language discovery 1

a 1 **b** 2

2 a I was worried I might be late for school. **b** I wonder whether or not my younger sister will do her homework. **c** Decide what you want to eat quickly.

3 a 내일 비빔밥을 먹어야겠어요. **b** 저녁에 동대문 시장 가야겠어요.

4 a I can't get back home today. **b** Can you read those Chinese characters?

5 할아버지는 독서를 싫어하시잖아요? – You know Grandfather doesn't like reading; 할머니는 독서를 좋아하시니까 대신 읽으시면 되잖아요 – Grandmother likes reading so she can read it instead; 할아버지는 비 올 때 나가지 않으시잖아요 – Grandfather doesn't go out when it rains; 작년에 사드렸잖아요 – We bought him that last year; 그건 재작년에 사드렸잖아요 – We bought him that the year before last.

Dialogue 2: I'm sorry, I really didn't know!

1 The policeman and driver use the honorific speech form. This is because they do not know each other and a certain level of respect is required. **2** He is driving the wrong way on a one-way street. This is very dangerous and the fines can be huge. **3** He says he honestly didn't see the signpost.

Language discovery 2

a 하셨어요 **b** 봐주세요 **c** 조심하세요

1 a Please sit there. **b** Where are you going? **c** When did you come? **d** What did you buy at the market?

3 a 1 **b** 4 **c** 3 **d** 2

Practice

1 a 파티에 선생님이 오실까(봐) 걱정이에요. **b** 음식이 모자랄까(봐) 걱정이에요. **c** 김 선생님이 안 오실까(봐) 걱정이에요. **d** 여자 친구가 당신을 안 좋아할까(봐) 걱정이에요. **e** 비가 올까봐 걱정이에요.

2 a 약을 사야겠어요. **b** 취소하려고 전화해야겠어요. **c** 사전을 사야겠어요. **d** 돌아가야겠어요. **e** 신문을 봐야겠어요.

3 a 무엇을 살까 결정해야겠어요. **b** 무엇을 입을까 결정해야겠어요. **c** 어디 앉을까 결정해야겠어요. **d** 무엇을 주문할까 결정해야겠어요. **e** 주말에 어디 갈까 결정해야겠어요.

4 a 나도 올 수 있어요? **b** 이거 먹을 수 있어요? **c** 나를 내일 만날 수 있어요? **d** 일본말을 말할 수 없어요. **e** 돈이 없어서 살 수 없어요. **f** 여기 주차할 수 없어요.

5 a 어제 샀잖아요! **b** 아니요, 벌써 결혼했잖아요! **c** 벌써 했잖아요! **d** 읽기 싫어하잖아요! **e** 우리 집사람이에요. 어제 만났잖아요!

6

A	내일이 오빠 생일이에요.
	뭘 사드릴까 정해야겠어요.
B	청바지를 사드릴까요?
A	청바지는 벌써 열 벌이나 갖고 있어요.
B	그러면 책은 어떨까요?
A	오빠는 책을 싫어해요.
B	그럼 만년필은요?
A	만년필도 더 이상 필요 없어요.
B	그럼 씨디는?
A	작년에 사드렸잖아요.

Test yourself

1 김 선생님 대학교 선생님이세요. 런던 대학교에서 한국말을 가르치시고 일본말도 가르치세요. 매일 아침 공원에 가서 산책하세요. 개하고 같이 가세요. 공원은 아주 좋아요. 김선생님의 개는 고기를 잘 먹어요. 작년부터 부인도 가끔 산책하기 시작하셨어요. 부인도 가시면 둘이 식당에 가서서 커피 한잔 마시세요.

2 a I'll have to call him today. **b** You can't drink alcohol in this restaurant. **c** Have you had a cup of coffee? Shall I buy you a coffee? **d** Can you watch a film with us? I really like watching films. **e** I'll have to decide what to eat at lunch.

UNIT 10

Chemists

외과

Dialogue 1: What did you do with it?

1 없는 것 같은데요. **2** 영업 끝날 때쯤 ⋯ **3** Around 11 p.m. **4** The bag is at the police station. When you go out of the restaurant, turn left and it is on the third alley on your right.

Language discovery 1

The particle 들 forms the plural form of a noun.

3 a It seems like the weather is bad in England. **b** This house seems to be nice.

4 a 민호가 빵을 먹을 것 같아요. **b** 선생님이 TV를 보실 것 같아요; **a** 1 **b** 3 **c** 2

Dialogue 2: Nasty headaches

1 a 잘 주무세요? **b** 약을 잡숴보세요.

2 a false **b** false **c** true **d** false

Language discovery 2

Yes, it is in the honorific form. You can tell as the verb ending includes -시-. The verb stem is 주-, meaning to give.

3 a 저녁 식사 잡수세요, 저녁 식사 드세요. **b** 선생님 지금 어디 계세요? **c** 너무 늦게 주무시네요.

Practice

1 a 내일 시간 있어요? **b** 영국에서 왔는데요. **c** 어제 전화했는데요. **d** 가방을 놓고 갔어요. **e** 사전을 사고 싶은데요. **f** 김 선생님 어디 가셨어요?

2 a 비가 오는 것 같아요. **b** 그 사람은 박 선생님인 것 같아요. **c** 독서를 싫어하는 것 같아요. **d** 동대문 시장에 간 것 같아요. **e** 김 선생님 오시는 것 같아요. **f** 가방을 여기 놓은 것 같아요.

3 아주 크고 검정색이고 가죽으로 만들었어요.

4 a 음식을 먹을 때 이야기(말)하지 마세요. **b** 주차할 때 조심하세요. **c** 시내에 갈 때 나한테 전화해주세요. **d** 영화가 끝날 때 식당에 갑시다. **e** 도착했을 때 맥주 하나 마셨어요. **f** 나갈 때 같이 갑시다.

5 Take two tablets every three hours while it's very bad. When it gets a bit better, then take one tablet before meal only at lunchtime.

Test yourself

1 a Anyhow, what have you decided to do now? **b** Didn't you see my girlfriend? If you see her (please) give me a call. **c** If you get a bit better don't take the medicine any more. **d** When will you graduate? What plans have you got after that? **e** Are these papers important? Of course they're important! It's my driving licence, stupid! **f** When we have a date, we often go to see a movie.

2 a 큰 실수를 하셨어요. **b** 밤 늦게 도시에 가면 위험해요. **c** 그 사전 좀 보여 주시겠어요? 이거 어디서 사셨어요? **d** 무슨 문제가 있나요? 네. 내 약을 잃어버린 것 같아요. **e** 요즘 스트레스를 너무 많이 받아서 밤에 잠을 잘 수 없어요. **f** 가방을 잃어버리셨어요? 뭐가 들어 있나요? **g** 내 생각을 좋아하지 않잖아요. **h** 그래서 뭘 하셨어요?

UNIT 11

Shopping in Korea

강남 (Gangnam)

Dialogue 1: Would you like to try it on?

1 Any two from: 저 셔츠 좀 봐라; 정말 좋다; 디자인이 좀 구식 같다; 내 마음에 꼭 들어; 정말 싸다; 이거 봐; 질이 별로 안 좋아; 다른 곳에 가볼까? **2** It's not very good quality. **3** 100% cotton

Language discovery 1

a 2 **b** 1 **c** 3

2 a 3 **b** 1 **c** 2

3 a -로; Go to school by bus. **b** -으로; I made these clothes from cotton. **c** -으로; Let's go to Busan!

4 a (좀) 활동적인, (좀) 밝은 **b** (요즘 아주) 유행하는

Dialogue 2: Do you think it suits me?

1 좀 큰 걸 입어보실래요? **2** The shirt is 32,000 won. Minho is surprised at the price and thinks it's expensive. **3** The assistant says they may look similar, but the quality is different. Clothes from the market will only last two to three months. The shop assistant says the shirt from the store also fits Minho better.

Language discovery 2

Do you want to eat bibimbap?

4 a 여기서 버스 타도 돼요? **b** 친구랑 점심 먹게 됐어요. **c** 집에 가도 돼요.

5 a 2 **b** 1 **c** 3 **d** 4

Practice

1 a 이 옷이 정말 좋다. **b** 비가 온다. **c** 뭘 하나? **d** 밥을 먹고 있다. **e** 걱정하고 있나? **f** 조금 더 기다리면 버스가 올 거다. **g** 밥 먹는다. **h** 어제 밤 어디 갔니? **i** 조심했니?

2 a 면으로 만든 옷. **b** 어제 우리가 마신 맥주. **c** 김 선생님이 읽고 있는 책. **d** 그 사람이 입고 있는 셔츠. **e** 작년에 우리가 본 영화. **f** 내가 싫어하는 음식.

3 a 좋아 보여도, 안 좋아요. **b** 비싸도, 맛이 있어요. **c** 비가 와도, 나가고 싶어요. **d** 그 사람을 좋아하지 않아도, 만나야겠어요. **e** 밝은 색이라도, 어울리지 않아요. **f** 머리가 아파도, 노래방에 갈까 해요.

4

A	무슨 영화를 볼까요?
B	____를 봅시다.
A	그건 우리가 작년에 본 영화잖아요.
	____를 봅시다.
B	그건 시간이 너무 늦어요.
A	열두 시가 너무 늦어요? 무슨 말이에요?!
B	그래도 그 영화는 정말 재미 없는 것 같아요.
A	무슨 영화를 볼까?
B	____를 보자.
A	그건 우리가 작년에 본 영화잖아.
	____를 보자.
B	그건 시간이 너무 늦어.
A	열두시가 너무 늦어? 무슨 말이야?!
B	그래도 그 영화는 정말 재미없는 것 같아.

Test yourself

1 a 한국말을 잘 하는 사람이 와요. **b** 어제 산 옷을 좋아하지 않아요. **c** 그 사람은 멋있는 사람이에요. **d** 질이 더 좋아도 네 배나 비싸요. **e** 당신이 입고 있는 옷을 입어볼 수 있어요? **f** 뭐라구요? **g** 술 마시지 않았어도 밤에 운전할 때 조심하세요. **h** 비슷한 거 있어요?

2 a 도서관 가서 책을 읽었다; 도서관 가서 책을 읽었어 **b** 학교에선 점심 때 뭘 먹니?; 학교에선 점심 때 뭘 먹어? **c** 민호는 학생이다; 민호는 학생이야 **d** 날씨가 안좋다. 비가 온다; 날씨가 안좋아. 비가 와 **e** 여기서 700번 버스 타야된다; 여기서 700번 버스 타야돼. **f** 어제 수영장 갔었다; 어제 수영장 갔었어

UNIT 12

Accomodation

c

Dialogue 1: Do you have a spare room?

1 좀 더 묵을지도 몰라요. 2 Breakfast is included in the price per day. Guests need to go to the basement restaurant between 7 a.m. and 10 a.m. If you pay an extra 2,000 won, breakfast can be delivered to the guest's room. 3 five days

Language discovery 1

a 얼마 동안 묵으시겠습니까? **b** 우리 집사람하고 좀 의논해 봐야겠어요.

3 a I don't know whether I'll graduate (or not). **b** I don't even know if I'll be able to go or not.

Dialogue 2: The towel was too dirty

1 이 호텔 서비스에 대해서 할 말이 있어요. **2** It was cold.
3 It hasn't even been cleaned yet.

Language discovery 2

-에 대해서 follows a noun and means regarding, concerning, about.

2 (thing to eat) is there anything to eat at home?

4 a The weather was good. **b** Mr Kim said that the weather had been good.

5 a I listen to music while I study Korean. **b** Please tell me while you're eating.

Practice

1 a 학생이 몇 명입니까? **b** 무슨 시설들이 있습니까? **c** 한국말하고 중국말을 공부할 수 있습니까? **d** 몇 명이 한국말을 공부합니까? **e** 점심 시간은 몇 시입니까? **f** 점심 시간에 밥 먹으러 집에 가도 됩니까?

2 a 빈 방 있어요? **b** 네. 침대방 주세요. **c** 일곱 살하고 다섯 살이에요. **d** 삼일 동안이요. **e** 아니요. 직접 식당에 가서 먹겠어요.

3 a 무엇을 하셨습니까? **b** 침대방 하나 주십시오. **c** 저 사람은 김 선생님이십니까? **d** 나는 백화점에 갑니다. **e** 라디오를 들으면서 책을 읽습니다.

4 a 이 호텔에 사우나 시설이 있습니까? **b** 아침 식사를 배달해 줍니까? **c** 이 호텔에 수영장이 있습니까?

Test yourself

1 a If you book for more than a week, we'll give you a 10 % discount. **b** To be (perfectly) honest, I hate people like that. **c** He said that he had (or, he has) already eaten breakfast. **d** A room with a floor mattress is 20,000 won per day. **e** It will be OK if you get up at 7 o'clock. **f** We can't give you a refund (of the fare). **g** Two rooms with (Western) beds, please. **h** If you've got something to say (comments to make) about this hotel, please speak to the manager.

2 a 며칠 동안 예약하셨습니까? **b** 즉시 은행원한테 얘기했습니다. **c** 이 호텔에 무슨 시설들이 있습니까? **d** 내 차에 문제가 많은 것 같아요. **e** 내 아들은 아직까지 일어나지 않았어요. **f** 우리는 즉시 바에 가서 술 마실 거에요. **g** 김 선생님은 불친절한 사람이에요. **h** 삼일 동안 묵는 게 좋겠어요.

UNIT 13

Transport in Korea

four: 지하철 (subway/underground), 버스 (bus), 기차 (train), 택시 (taxi)

Dialogue 1: Are there any trains to Daegu?

1 네 자리를 함께 예약할 수 있을까요? **2 a** false **b** true **c** true **d** false

Language discovery 1

금연석으로 부탁합니다; 왕복으로 주세요.

2 a Shall we eat dinner together? **b** Is is possible to eat bibimbap?
c Shall we sit here?

3 a Please sit down before you eat your meal. **b** Please go home after
you have eaten your meal. **c** Please come before lunch. **d** Please go after
lunch.

Dialogue 2: I don't particularly like bulgogi

1 오늘 저녁 일 끝나고 뭐 할 거예요? **2** She doesn't particularly like
bulgogi and hates singing at karaoke. **3** Mr Yun **4** He wants to eat fresh
sashimi.

Language discovery 2

-고 나서

4 a 3 **b** 2 **c** 1; **a** 1 **b** 3 **c** 2

Practice

1 a 점심 먹기 전에. 점심 먹은 다음에. **b** 어머니한테 전화하기 전에.
어머니한테 전화한 다음에. **c** 놀기 전에. 논 다음에. **d** 신문을 읽기
전에. 신문을 읽은 다음에.

2 a 20.00 (10 p.m.) **b** 8.00 **c** 11.00 **d** No, there isn't. **e** Yes, there is.

3 a 집에 돌아갈 수밖에 없어요. **b** 돈을 낼 수 밖에 없어요.
c 아침 여섯시에 일어날 수밖에 없어요.

4 a 나는 고기 말고 과일 먹고 싶어요. **b** 나는 수영 말고 농구하고
싶어요. **c** 나는 신문 말고 소설책 읽고 싶어요. **d** 나는 노래하지 말고
음악 듣고 싶어요.

Test yourself

1 a There are not many seats left. **b** You can't eat something different.
c Would you like a return ticket? **d** Mountain climbing is really awful.
(I really hate it . . .) **e** It looks as if I'll have to go, then. **f** We were just
going to have (intending to have) a game of baseball. **g** Is there a train
going to Mokp'o this afternoon? **h** That's a decent idea (surprise!).

2 a 출발 시간 전에 (or 출발하기 전에), 먹을 거를 사세요. **b** 부모님한테 얘기할까요? **c** 나도 가고 싶지만, 너무 멀어요. **d** 세 자리를 함께 예약할 수 있어요? **e** 서울 말고 인천에 갑시다. **f** 일 끝난 다음에 뭘 할까요? **g** 언제 돌아오시겠어요? **h** 생선회 좋아하세요?

UNIT 14

Practice

1 a Since Mum likes watching films, she can go to the cinema instead of Dad. **b** It's probably due to stress. **c** In fact (actually) there were some very important papers inside. **d** (My) jeans have worn out (become unusable). **e** My wife will perhaps know. **f** Tomorrow evening after work I'm planning to go to the mountains. **g** You never like my ideas (or, opinions). **h** The door to our room doesn't even open. **i** Could you tell me where the library is, please (lit: could you teach me . . .)? **j** Did you drink so much alcohol (as that)? **k** It's a very popular style nowadays. **l** Show me your driver's licence, please.

2 a 야구 해보셨어요? 네. 해봤어요. 사실은 어제 해봤어요. **b** 수영 해보셨어요? 네. 해봤어요. 사실은 어제 해봤어요. **c** 탁구 해보셨어요? 네. 해봤어요. 사실은 어제 해봤어요. **d** 춤 춰보셨어요? 네. 해봤어요. 사실은 어제 해봤어요.

3 a 죄송하지만 여기 그런 사람 없어요. **b** 아니요, 싫어합니다. **c** 데이트할 때는 보통 극장이나 공원에 가요. **d** 별로 좋지 않은 것 같아요. **e** 아니요, 약속을 잘 지켜요.

4 a 정말로 표지판을 못 봤어요. **b** 청바지하고 같이 입을 수 있어요. **c** 약속을 취소하려고 전화했어요. **d** 방에 전화하고 테레비가 있어요? **e** 서비스가 엉망이에요. **f** 작년에 그 사람한테 양말을 사주었어요. **g** 좀 작은 것 같아요. **h** 그런 줄 알았어요. **i** 인천에 가서 생선회를 먹고 싶어요. **j** 차가 어떻게 생겼어요? **k** 편지 한 장 써 주시겠어요? **l** 머리가 너무 아파서 잠을 못 자요.

5

Name: 이름이 뭐에요?
Age: 몇 살이에요?
Occupation: 직업이 뭐에요?
Father's name: 아버지 이름이 뭐에요?
How met: 어떻게 만났어요?
What do together: 함께 (같이) 뭘 해요?
Likes/dislikes: 뭘 좋아해요?
뭘 싫어해요?

6 a If you do it wrong (if you don't do it properly), it's very dangerous.
b Do you have a message for Poktong? **c** We deliver it to your room
(lit: the guest's room). **d** I was here yesterday. I left my jumper. **e** The girl
said that it was good quality. **f** I've got a new girlfriend and it seems as if
we're out every day. **g** Don't talk; just listen. **h** Take one tablet twice a day
after meals. **i** Look at this! The quality's pretty bad. **j** You wouldn't know
where he/she has gone, would you? **k** How would a new television be?
l A similar thing is about twice as cheap at Namdaemun.

7 아니요, 바쁜 일이 있어요. 왜요?; 월요일은 어때요?; 그래요? 파티가
있어요?; 아버지한테 뭘 사 드릴까요?; 화요일은 어때요? 그때는 시간
있어요?; 좋은 생각이에요.

8

Informal style:

A	내일 저녁에 시간이 있어?
You	아니. 바쁜 일이 있어. 왜?
A	그냥 나가고 싶었는데.
You	월요일은 어때?
A	월요일 날은 아버지 생신이야.
You	그래? 파티가 있어?
A	아니. 그냥 식당에 가서 같이 저녁 하는 거야.
You	아버지한테 뭘 사 드릴 거야?
A	양말. 항상 양말 사.
You	화요일은 어때? 그때는 시간 있어?
A	응. 좋아. 나이트 갈까?
You	좋은 생각이야.

Plain style:

A	내일 저녁에 시간이 있니?
You	아니다. 바쁜 일이 있다. 왜?
A	그냥 나가고 싶었는데.
You	월요일은 어떠니?
A	월요일 날은 아버지 생신이다.
You	그래? 파티가 있니?
A	아니다. 그냥 식당에 가서 같이 저녁 하는 거다.
You	아버지한테 뭘 사 드릴 거니?
A	양말. 항상 양말 산다.
You	화요일은 어떠니? 그때는 시간 있니?
A	응, 좋다. 나이트 갈까?
You	좋은 생각이다.

9 a 지금 어디 가십니까? **b** 주문했습니까? **c** 일곱시에 일어납니다.
d 빨리 해주십시오. **e** 저 사람은 불친절한 사람입니다.

10 아침 일곱시에 일어났어요. 아침을 먹은 다음에 아홉 시에 교회에
갔어요. 열두 시에 여자 친구하고 같이 점심을 먹었어요. 세시에
기차를 타고 부산에 갔어요. 일곱시에 영화를 봤어요

11 a 그때부터 그 여자를 자주 만나기 시작했어요. **b** 힘이 없어도
놀라지 마세요. **c** 이번에는 당신이 도와주세요. **d** 비슷해 보여도
비슷하지 않아요. **e** 지금부터 더 조심하세요. **f** 지금 (즉시) 식당에
가서 밥 먹을 거에요. **g** 그럼 잘 됐네요. 안녕히 계세요. **h** 오늘 저녁은
내가 낼게요 (or 살게요). **i** 우리 백화점을 몇 시에 떠나셨어요?
j 실수가 발생합니다. **k** 당신을 소개할까요? **l** 입어보시겠어요?

Korean–English vocabulary

The Korean words have been listed alphabetically. Look back, if necessary, to the introduction to the Korean writing system at the front of the book to find the alphabetical order for consonants and vowels.

Here are some simple steps to follow when looking up your Korean word:

▶ Take the first syllable block of the word. Observe its letters.
▶ Look up the letters in the chronological order. The first letter will always be a consonant, the second will always be a vowel, and if there is a third letter this will be another consonant.

가-	*go* (verb stem)
가게	*shop*
가격	*price*
가는	*going to, bound for*
가르치-	*teach*
가방	*a briefcase, a bag*
가보-	*go and see, visit (a place)*
가요	*go (stem plus polite ending -요)*
가져가-	*take*
가족	*family*
가죽	*leather*
가지	*kind, example (counter for the noun 종류)*
갈-	*change (a towel, a platform, clothes etc.)*
갈비	*marinated and fried meat, usually beef or pork*
갈아입-	*change clothes*
갈아타-	*change (platform, trains etc.)*
갖고 계시-	*have, possess (for honorific person; polite style = 갖고 계세요)*
같-	*be the same, be similar; seem like*
같은	*same*
같은 것	*(a) similar thing, something similar*
같이	*together*
거	*thing, object, fact (abbreviation of 것)*
거기	*over there (nearer than 저기)*
거의	*nearly, almost*
걱정	*worry, concern*
걱정하-	*be worried*
걱정하지 마세요	*don't worry! (colloquial form: 걱정마세요)*

건	thing, object (abbreviation of 것 + topic particle)
건강	health
건너편	opposite side
걸려요	it takes (polite style)
걸리-	takes (time duration)
걸어서	on foot
걸었어요	dialled (past tense of 걸-, irregular verb)
검정	black
게다가	on top of that
겨우	only
결정하-	decide
경우	circumstance, situation
경찰	policeman
경찰서	police station
계시-	exist (honorific of 있- in its existential there is / are meaning
계획	plan(s)
-고	and (to join clauses)
-고 나서	after (added to verb stems)
고맙습니다	thank you
고장 나-	break down
고장 났어요	be broken down
골목	alley, small road
곳	place
과로	overwork
과일	fruit
관련	relation, link
교회	church
구식	old style, old fashioned
국	soup
권	volume (measure word)
그-	that one (nearer than 저)
그 다음에	after that
그건	that thing (topic)
그것 보라고!	you see!
그냥	simply, just
그래도	however, nevertheless, but still
그래요(?)	really (?), is it / it is so (?)
그러니까	therefore, because of that
그러세요?	so what?
그런	such a, that (particular)
그런 편이에요	(we) tend to be so / do so (it's usually like that etc.)
그럼	then, in that case

그렇게	*like that*
그렇지 않아요	*of course not*
그릇	*dish*
그리고	*and (also)* (used to begin a sentence)
그리고 나서	*after that*
그저 그래요	*so-so*
근사하-	*look super, look good*
근처	*district, area, vicinity*
글쎄요	*I dunno, I'm not sure, who knows?*
금연석	*non-smoking compartment*
기다리-	*wait*
-기로 했어요	*decided to*
-기만 하세요	*just do* (verb)
기억	*memory*
길	*road, route*
김치	*classic Korean side dish, marinated cabbage*
-까지	*until*
깎아주-	*cut the price* (for someone's benefit)
꼭	*exactly, certainly, precisely*
꼭	*without fail, definitely*
꾀병	*a feigned illness*
꾀병을 부리지요	*you're making it up!* (feigning an illness)
끝나-	*finish*
끝내-	*finish* (verb stem, to finish something)
나	*I / me*
-나	*approximately, about; or*
나가-	*go out*
나아지-	*get better*
나오-	*come out*
날씨	*weather*
남-	*be left (over), remain*
남대문	*Great South Gate* (in Seoul), *Namdaemun*
남자친구	*boyfriend*
남편	*husband*
내	*my*
내-	*pay*
내일	*tomorrow*
냉면	*thin noodles with vegetables*
냉장고	*refrigerator*
너무	*too (much)*
넣-	*put down, leave*
네	*yes*
노래	*song*

노래방	*karaoke singing room*
노래하-	*sing*
노력하-	*make effort, strive*
놀라-	*to be surprised, be shocked*
놀리-	*make fun of*
놀리지 마세요	*don't joke, don't kid me, don't tease*
농담	*joke* (noun)
농담하-	*jokes* (verb)
누가	*who?* (subject form)
누구	*who?*
눈	*an eye*
느끼-	*to feel*
늦게	*late*
다	*all, everything*
다르-	*be different* (polite style = 달라요.)
다른	*another, different*
다리	*leg*
다시	*again*
다음	*after, next*
달	*month*
당신	*you* (often between husband and wife)
당장	*immediately*
대구	*Korean city*
대사관	*embassy*
대신	*instead, on behalf of*
대학	*university*
대학교	*university*
대해서	*about, concerning* (noun에 대해서)
더	*more*
더 이상	*any more*
더럽-	*be dirty* (polite = 더러워요, ㅂ - verb like 가깝- etc.)
더워서	*because it is hot, because you're hot*
데	*place*
데이트하-	*to date*
-도	*too, also* (particle, attaches to nouns)
도봉산	*Dobongsan* (Korean mountain in Seoul)
도와주-	*to help*
독서	*reading*
돈	*money*
돌아오-	*come back, return*
동대문	*Great East Gate (in Seoul), Dongdaemun*
동안	*during*
동창	*colleague* (or fellow student)

되-	*become*
두	*two (pure Korean number)*
두통	*headache*
둘	*two (when you mean the two of them, both)*
드릴까요	*would you like? (lit: shall I give you?)*
들어 있-	*be contained, be included*
들어오-	*to enter*
등산	*mountain climbing*
디자인	*design*
따라	*follow*
딱 질색이에요	*hate, is awful (to me)*
때	*time (when)*
또	*again; moreover, also*
똑	*exactly, precisely (often used with 같-)*
-러	*in order to*
-마다	*each, every*
마른 안주	*dried snacks*
마시-	*drink*
마음	*mind, heart*
마음에 (꼭) 들어요	*I (really) like it*
마음에 들지 않아요	*I don't like (her) (마음에 안 들어요)*
마찬가지에요	*be the same, be identical*
만	*10,000*
-만	*only*
만나-	*meet (stem)*
만나서 반갑습니다	*pleased to meet you*
만들-	*make (ㄹ- irregular verb like 팔-, 놀- etc.)*
만들었어요	*be made of (past tense of 만들-, ㄹ- irregular verb)*
만병통치약	*cure-all medicine, miracle cure*
-만에	*within, in only (two or three months)*
많-	*is many (ㅎ is not pronounced, polite style = 만나요)*
많이	*much, many, a lot*
많지 않아서	*since there aren't many*
말	*language*
말씀	*words, speech*
말씀 많이 들었어요	*I've heard a lot about you*
말씀하-	*speak, say (of someone honorific, often in phrase 말씀하세요!)*
말씀하세요	*please tell me, please say it (I'm listening!) (honorific)*
말하-	*speak, say*
말한 대로	*as (I) said, like (I) said*
맛이 없는데도 말이에요	*I'm saying (stress) that even the food tasted bad*
맛이없-	*be tasteless, be unpleasant (to eat)*

맞-	to fit well (맞 + 는다)
매운	spicy
매일	every day
맥주	beer
머리	head
먹-	eat
멀어요	is far (polite style, irregular stem)
멋있-	be stylish, be handsome
면	cotton
-면	if
면도(를) 하-	shave
-면서	while
면허증	(driving) licence
몇	what (number)?
몇 시	what time
모두	altogether, everything, everyone
모르-	not know (stem)
모르겠어요	I don't know
몰라요	I don't know
몸	body
못	cannot
못 알아듣겠다고 하-	say that (one) couldn't understand
무뚝뚝하-	be stubborn, be blunt
무슨	what (kind of), what, which
무엇	what (full form of 뭐)
묵-	stay, lodge, spend the night
문	door
문제	problem
물	water
물건	goods
물냉면	thing noodles in cold soup, spicy and refreshing!
물어보-	ask
뭐	what?
뭘	what (object form)
미국	America
미니바	mini-bar
바꾸-	change
바로	directly
바쁘-	is busy
바쁜	busy
반갑습니다	pleased to meet you
받-	to receive
발생하-	occur, happen

234

밝은	bright
밤	night
밥	rice (cooked rice)
밥먹-	have a meal
방	room
방금	just now
방향	direction
배	double, (two) times
배	stomach
배달하-	deliver
백화점	department store
버리-	throw away
버스	bus
번	number
번	time (as in first time, second time, many times)
벌	(counter for clothes)
벌금	a fine, a penalty
별로	not particularly, not really (+ negative)
별로 없-	have almost none, scarcely have any
별일	a special matter, something particular
별일 없으면...	if you don't have anything special on...
병원	hospital
보-	see, look (sometimes = meet)
보관하-	keep
보내-	send
-보다	more than
보여주-	to show
봐요	see, look (polite style, irregular)
봐주세요	please look at
부르-	call
부작용	a side-effect
부탁하-	make a request
-부터	from
분	minute
불고기	Korean spiced marinated beef
불국사	Bulguksa (Korean Buddhist temple, near Gyeongju)
불친절하-	be unhelpful, be unkind, be impolite
불평하-	complain
비가 오-	rains, is raining
비빔	mixed
비슷하-	look similar
비싸-	is expensive
비싼	expensive (adjective)

빈	*empty, vacant, free* (of seats and rooms)
빌려주-	*lend*
빌리-	*borrow*
빨간	*red*
빨리	*quickly*
빵	*bread*
-뿐	*only*
사-	*buy* (verb stem)
사거리	*crossroads*
사과	*apple*
사람	*person*
사랑하-	*love*
사무실	*office*
사실	*fact (the fact is. . .)*
사업	*business*
사요	*buy* (stem plus polite ending -요.)
사우나	*sauna*
사이	*between*
사장(님)	*manager* (honorific form)
사전	*dictionary*
산	*mountain*
상업	*trade*
상업은행	*Commercial Bank* (lit: trade bank)
상자	*box*
색	*colour*
생각	*thought*
생각	*idea*
생각나-	*remember, it comes to mind*
생기-	*to occur, happen, take place; look like*
생선	*fish*
생신	*birthday* (honorific form)
생일	*birthday* (normal form)
서-	*stop* (stem)
서류	*document*
서비스	*service*
서울	*Seoul*
세	*three* (pure Korean)
셔츠	*shit*
소개하-	*to introduce*
소주	*soju, Korean wine / vodka*
손님	*customer*
솔직히	*frankly, honestly*
솔직히 말해보세요	*tell me the truth!*

솔직히 말해서	*honestly speaking; to tell the truth; in fact ...*
쇼핑(하-)	*shopping (do / go shopping)*
수건	*towel*
수건을 갈아달라고 했어요	*I asked (her) to change the towel*
수고하세요	*work hard! (said to someone doing their job)*
수영장	*swimming pool*
수영하-	*swim*
술집	*pub*
쉽게	*easily*
스타일	*style*
스탠드바	*bar (standing bar)*
스트레스	*stress*
시	*o'clock*
시간	*time, hour*
시끄러워요!	*shut up!, be quiet!*
시내	*town centre*
시설	*facility*
시작하-	*begin, start*
시장	*market*
식-	*get cold*
식당	*restaurant*
식사하-	*have meal*
식어 있-	*be cool, get cold*
식후	*after meal*
신문	*newspaper*
실례지만...	*excuse me, but...*
실례합니다	*excuse me, please*
실수	*mistake*
실수하-	*make a mistake*
싫어하-	*to dislike*
심하-	*be serious*
싸-	*is cheap*
싼	*cheap (adjective)*
썩었어요	*has gone bad, has gone off (polite style, past tense)*
쓰-	*write*
쓰게	*usable*
-씩	*each, per*
아!	*ah!*
아가씨	*waitress! lit. = girl, unmarried woman*
아니에요	*is not (opposite of -(이)에요, negative copula)*
아니요	*no*
아들	*son*
아마	*perhaps, probably*

아저씨	waiter!
아주	very
아직	yet, still
아침	morning; breakfast (abbreviated form)
아침식사	breakfast
아침하-	have breakfast
아파요	hurts (polite style)
아프-	hurts (stem)
아픈	hurting, painful (adjective)
안	not (used to make verbs negative)
안 파는 거	something which is not sold, not available
안녕히 가세요	goodbye (to someone who is leaving)
안녕히 계세요	goodbye (to someone who is staying)
안주	snacks or side dishes for drinks
앉-	sit (stem)
알	tablet
알겠습니다	I understand; OK, right, fine (formally)
알아들-	understand (ㄹ/ㄷ verb like 듣-, listen; 알아들어요, 알아듣고 etc.)
앞에서	in front of
약	medicine
약국	chemist, drugstore
약사	pharmacist, chemist
약속	appointment
약을 먹어야겠어요	I'll have to take some medicine
양말	socks
양식당	Western restaurant
양주	spirits, western alcohol
얘기하-	talk, tell
어느	which one
어디	where?
어디 가는지 아세요?	do you know where (she) has gone?
어딘가	somewhere or other
어때요?	how is it?
어떤	certain, some (as a question word = which?)
어떨까요?	how would it be?
어떻게 생겼어요?	what does it look like?
어떻게?	how?
어서 오세요	welcome!
어울리-	suit (a person)
어이	hey! (used to call close friends and colleagues)
어제도 마찬가지였고요	it was exactly the same yesterday as well
어쨌든	anyway

언제	when
얼마	how much
얼마 남지 않았습니다	there are only a few spaces left
얼마 동안	how long?
얼마 동안 묵으시겠어요?	how long will you be staying?
업무	business, service
없는것 같은데	it doesn't look as though there is anything / are any
엉망	rubbish, awful, appalling
-에	at (a certain time)
-에	each, per
-에	to (preposition, attaches to nouns)
-에	about, concerning
-에 대해서	about, concerning
-에게	to
-에서	location particle (place in which something happens); from
에이	hey, come off it!
여기	here
여기서	from here (abbreivation of 여기에서)
여보세요	hello (on the telephone)
여자친구	girlfriend
열	ten (pure Korean number)
열두	twelve (pure Korean number)
열리지 않-	does not open
영국	England/ish, Britain/ish
영수증	receipt
영업	business
영한	English-Korean
영화	film, movie
옆	next door
예	yes (politer form of 네)
예약하-	reserve, book
오-	come (stem)
오늘	today
오락실	amusements (electronic games, etc.)
오래	long
오래간만이에요	long time no see!
오른	right
오징어	squid
오히려	rather, on the contrary
온돌방	room with bed on floor
와!	wow!
와요	come (polite style form)

와인	*wine*
완행	*slow train*
왔어요	*came (past tense form)*
왕복	*return*
왜요?	*why?*
외환	*exchange*
외환은행	*Korea Exchange Bank*
왼	*left*
요금	*fee, fare*
요즘	*nowadays*
요즘 사업은 어때요?	*how is business these days?*
요즘 재미가 어떠세요?	*how are you doing?, how are things these days?*
우너숭이	*monkey*
우리	*we / our*
우리 둘만 가요?	*is it just the two of us going?*
우산	*umbrella*
우선	*first*
우연히	*by chance, coincidentally*
우체국	*post office*
우회전	*right turn*
우회전한 다음에	*after doing a right turn*
운전수	*a driver*
원	*won (unit of Korean currency)*
원인	*reason, cause*
원하-	*want, require*
웨이터	*waiter*
위험하-	*be dangerous*
유행하-	*be popular, be in vogue*
-으로	*towards, in the direction of (-로 after vowels)*
은행	*bank*
은행원	*bank clerk*
음료수	*drink*
음료수 하시겠어요?	*would you like something to drink?*
음식	*food*
응	*yes (casual form)*
-의	*belonging to*
의견	*suggestion, opinion*
의논	*discussion*
의논하-	*discussion*
이	*two*
이-	*this one (+ noun), this noun*
이따가	*in a little while*
-이랑	*with (-랑 after vowel)*

이렇게	like this
이름	name
이번	this time
이상	more than
이상하-	is strange, bizarre
이상하네(요)	(it is) strange!
-이요	(used to check information, *you mean?*)
-인분	portion
인천	Korean port near Seoul
일	matter, business, work
일 끝내고	after finishing work
일방통행	one way
일방통행로	one-way street
일본	Japan
일본말	Japanese langauge
일요일	Sunday
일요일날	Sunday (longer form)
일찍	early
일하-	work (verb stem)
읽-	read
잃어버리-	lose
입구	entrance
있-	1 *exist, there is / are* (stem) 2 *have* (stem)
있어요	as above, polite style
있으시-	*have* (honorific of 있- in its meaning of possession)
자-	sleep
자동차	car
자리	seat
자주	often, frequently
작년	last year
잔	cup
잘	good, well (adverb)
잘못	wrongly, mis-
잠	sleep (noun)
잠깐	a little (while)
잠깐 기다리세요	please wait a moment
잠바	jumper
잡수시-	eat (honorific equivalent of 먹-)
잡쉬보-	try eating (honorific form)
잡지	magazine
재료	stuff, (raw) material
재미있-	is interesting, is fun
재수	luck

재수없-	have no luck, have bad luck
재작년	the year before last year
저	me
저-	that one (a long way away, old English yon)
저...	er ..., hm ...
저기	(over) there
저녁	evening
저런	oh dear! oh my!
저희	humble form of 우리 our, my
적어도	at least
전	before
전광판	electronic noticeboard
전기 면도기	electric shaver
전신	the whole body
전에	previously
전하-	communicate
전할 말	something to say / pass on / communicate
전화	telephone
전화하-	telephone (verb stem)
점심	lunch
정도	decide
정류장	bus stop
정말	really
정하-	extent, about (approximatel)
제	my (humble form)
제 생각에는	in my opinion
제과점	bakery
제일	the most
조금	a little, a bit
조금 전	a little while ago
조심하-	be careful, be cautious
졸업하-	to graduate
졸음	sleepiness, drowsiness
좀	a little; please
종로	Jongro (one of the main streets in Seoul, north of the Han river)
종류	type, sort, kind
종업원	waiter, assistant
좋-	good (stem)
좋아요	good, fine, OK (polite style)
좋아하-	like (stem)
좋은 생각이네요	that's a good idea
좋지 않-	is not good (from 좋-)

좌석	*seating, places*
좌회전	*left turn*
좌회전한 다음에	*after doing a left turn*
죄송하지만	*I'm sorry, but; excuse me, but . . .*
죄송합니다	*I'm sorry; I apologize; excuse me*
주-	*give* (stem)
주무시-	*sleep* (honorific equivalent of 자-)
주문하-	*order* (stem)
주세요	*please give* (polite request form)
주차하-	*to park*
주차한	*parked*
중국	*China*
중요하-	*be important*
중요한	*important* (modifier form, like an adjective)
즉시	*immediately*
-지 마세요	*please don't*
지금	*now*
지배인	*manager* (of hotel or facility)
지점	*branch*
지하	*basement*
지하 식당	*basement restaurant*
직원	*employee*
직접	*direct(ly)*
직행	*fast train, express train*
진짜	*really*
질	*quality*
질색이-	*(really) hate*
집	*house*
집사람	*wife*
제	*number* (time)
쪽	*side*
차	*car* (short form)
참	*very*
창구	*window, cashier window*
찾-	*look for*
찾아보-	*to have a look, to look for*
-처럼	*like*
처음	*at first*
청바지	*blue jeans*
청소하-	*clean, clean up*
촌사람	*country bumpkin, yokel*
출발	*departure*
출발하-	*depart*

취소하-	*cancel*
치-	*to play* (tennis, table tennis, etc.)
침대	*bed*
침대방	*room with bed*
카드	*card*
큰	*big*
타-	*take* (transport), *travel on* (transport)
탁구	*table tennis*
파는 거	*item for sale, items sold*
파전	*Korean-style pancake*
파티	*party*
팔아요	*sell* (polite style form, stem is irregular)
팔지만	*they sell, but . . .*
퍼센트	*per cent*
편도	*single* (ticket, way)
편지	*letter*
편하-	*is comfortable, is convenient*
포함되어 있-	*be included*
표	*ticket*
표지	*a sign, a signpost*
표지판	*a signpost*
피로	*fatigue, weariness*
필요없-	*is not necessary, is not needed, has no need of*
필요있-	*is necessary, is needed*
필요하-	*is needed*
하-	*do* (verb stem)
-하고	*and*
하나	*one*
하러	*in order to do*
하루	*one day* (duration)
하루에	*per day*
학과	*department* (of college / university)
학교	*school*
한	*one* (pure Korean, when used with a counter or measure word)
한 (숫자/시간) 쯤	*about, around* (number / time) *approximately*
한국말	*Korean language*
한국	*Korea(n)*
한식당	*Korean restaurant* (serving Korean food)
한영	*Korean–English*
한자	*Chinese characters*
-한테	*to, for* (a person)
할말	*something to say*

할머니	grandma
할아버지	grandfather
할인	discount
할인하-	give a discount
함께	together
항상	always
해요	do (stem plus polite ending -요, irregular form)
했어요	did (past tense form of 하-, do)
현대 자동차	Hyundai car (company)
호텔	hotel
혹시	maybe, perhaps, possibly
혼자	alone, on one's own
홈	platform
확인하-	check, confirm
환불하-	reimburse
활동적인	modifier form of the below (like an adjective)
활동적	casual, active
회	raw meat
회사	company
후	after
훌륭하-	is excellent, great
훨씬	by far, far and away
흡연석	smoker (compartment)
힘	strength, energy

English–Korean vocabulary

about, concerning	에; -에 대해서
about / around, approximately	한 (number / time), -쯤
after (after, next)	후, 다음
again (moreover, also)	다시, 또
all, everything	다
almost, nearly	거의
alone	혼자
altogether, everything, everyone	모두
always	항상
and	-하고
and (to join clauses)	-고
and (also) (used to begin a sentence)	그리고
apple	사과
appointment, promise	약속
area, district, vicinity	근처
at (a certain time)	-에
bag, briefcase	가방
bank (bank clerk)	은행 (은행원)
basement	지하
bed; (room with a bed)	침대; 침대방
(– on the floor, Korean style)	온돌방
beer	맥주
before	전
begin, start	시작하-
big	큰
birthday (honorific form)	생일 (생신)
black	검정
blue jeans	청바지
body	몸
borrow	빌리-
boy / girlfriend	남자/여자 친구
bread	빵
break down	고장 나-
breakfast	아침식사
breakfast (abbreviated form); (to have breakfast)	아침; 아침 먹-
bus	버스

bus stop	정류장
business	사업
busy	바쁘-
buy (verb stem)	사-
by far, far and away	훨씬
call	부르-
cancel	취소하-
car	자동차
car (short form)	차
careful / cautious	조심하-
change (clothes / trains etc.)	바꾸- (갈아입-/타-)
cheap	싸-
check, confirm	확인하-
China	중국
Chinese character	한자
church	교회
clean, clean up	청소하-
colour	색
come (out)	오- (나오-)
comfortable / convenient	편하-
company	회사
complain	불평하-
cotton	면
country bumpkin, yokel	촌사람
cup	잔
customer	손님
dangerous	위험하-
decide	정하-
deliver	배달하-
depart	출발하-
department (store)	학과 (백화점)
departure	출발
design	디자인
dictionary	사전
different	다르-
directly	직접/바로
discount	할인
dish	그릇
dislike	싫어하-
district, area, vicinity	근처
do (verb stem)	하-
document	서류

door	문
double, times	배
drink	마시-
driver	운전수
during	동안
each, every (each, per)	-마다, (-씩)
early	일찍
easy, easily	쉽-, 쉽게
eat	먹-
eat (honorific) (try eating) (honorific form)	잡수시-; 잡숴보-
effort, strive	노력하
embassy	대사관
employee	직원
empty	빈
energy, strength	힘
England, Britain	영국
English–Korean	영한
entrance	입구
every day	매일
everything, everyone, altogether	모두
eye, snow	눈
exactly, certainly, precisely	꼭, 똑
exchange (Korea ExchangeBank)	외환 (은행)
excuse me, sorry, but . . .	죄송하지만
excuse me, please	실례합니다
exist, there is / are (honorific)	있- (계시-)
expensive	비싸-
express train	직행
evening (time as well as meal)	저녁
everything, all	다
family	가족
feel	느끼-
film, movie	영화
(at) first	처음
fish	생선
food	음식
(on) foot	걸어서
frequently, often	자주
(in) front of	앞에서
from (location particle, place in which something happens)	-부터, (-에서)
fruit	과일

give	주-
go (out)	가- (나가-)
good (stem)	좋-
good, fine, ok (polite style)	좋아요
good, well (adverb)	잘
goodbye (to someone who is leaving)	안녕히 가세요
goodbye (to someone who is staying)	안녕히 계세요
graduate	졸업하-
grandfather, old men in general	할아버지
grandma, old women in general	할머니
handsome	멋있-
have (stem)	있-
have (honorific form)	있으시-
head	머리
health	건강
hello (on the telephone)	여보세요
help	도와주-
here (from here)	여기 (여기서)
hospital	병원
house	집
how?	어떻게
how is it?	어때요?
however, nevertheless, but still	그래도
how much, long?	얼마, (동안)
hurts (polite style)	아파요-
hurts (stem)	아프-
hurting, painful (adjective)	아픈
husband	남편
if	-면
important	중요하-
in order to do	하러
interesting, fun	재미있-
introduce	소개하-
Japan (Japanese language)	일본 (말)
joke	농담(하-)
jumper	잠바
just, simply	그냥
just now	방금
kind, type, example	가지
Korea	한국

Korean–English	한영
Korean language	한국말

language, word (to speak / say)	말 (말하-)
last year	작년
lately, nowadays	요즘
least	적어도
left	왼
leg	다리
lend	빌려주-
letter	편지
like (adjective)	-처럼
like (stem), I like (polite form)	좋아하-, 마음에 들어요
like that	그렇게
like this	이렇게
little (while, time); in a little while	잠깐; 이따가
little, a bit (quantity)	조금
little, please	좀
look, see (sometimes to meet)	보-
look for	찾-
look, to look for	찾아보-
lose	잃어버리-
love	사랑하-
lunch	점심

magazine	잡지
make	만들-
manager (honorific form)	사장 (님)
many (h is not pronouced)	많-
market	시장
maybe, perhaps	혹시
me (humble form)	나 (저)
medicine (pharmacist), (drugstore)	약 (약사) (약국)
meet (stem) (pleased to meet you)	만나- (만나서 반갑습니다)
mind, heart	마음
minute	분
mis-, wrongly	잘못
mixed	비빔
money	돈
month	달
more (any more)	더
more than	이상,-보다
morning	아침
most	제일

mountain (climbing)	산 (등산)
my (humble form)	제
name	이름
needed (not needed)	필요하-/있-(없-)
nevertheless, however, but still	그래도
newspaper	신문
next	옆
night	밤
no	아니요
noodles in cold soup	물냉면
not (opposite of -(i)eyo)	아니에요
not know (stem)	모르-
now	지금
nowadays, lately	요즘
number (times)	-째
number (time as in 'first time', etc.)	번
o'clock	-시
office	사무실
often, frequently	자주
OK, right, fine (formal)	알겠습니다
one	하나
one day	하루
only	-만, -뿐
opinion (in my) (humble form)	제 생각에는
opposite side	건너편
order; would you like to order?	주문하-; 주문하시겠어요?
our, we	우리
our, we (humble form of wuri)	저희
over there	고기
park	주차하-
particularly (not), (not)really (negative)	별로
per, each	-에
perhaps, probably	아마
person	사람
place	곳
plan	계획
play (tennis, piano etc.)	치-
please don't . . .	-지 마세요
please give (polite request form)	주세요
police (man/station)	경찰서
portion	-인분

post office	우체국
previously	전에
price	가격
problem	문제
promise, appointment	약속
pub	술집
quality	질
quickly	빨리
rains, is raining	비가 오-
really (colloquial)	진짜
really	정말
really(?), is it(?), is that so(?)	그래요(?)
read	읽-
reason, cause	원인
receipt	영수증
receive	받-
red	빨간
refrigerator	냉장고
request	부탁하-
reserve, book	예약하-
restaurant	식당
return (tickets)	왕복
rice, cooked (uncooked)	밥 (쌀)
right (direction)	오른
road	길
room	방
same / identical	마찬가지
school	학교
seat	자리
see, look	보-
shave	면도 (-를 하-)
shop	가게
sit (stem)	앉-
side	쪽
side dish for drinks or snack	안주
simply, just	그냥
single (ticket, way)	편도
sleep	자-
sleep (honorific)	주무시-
smoker (compartment)	흡연석
non-smoking compartment	금연석

snow	눈
socks	양말
soft drinks	음료수
something to say	할 말
son	아들
song, 'karaoke' singing room	노래(하-), 노래방
(I'm) sorry, I apologize,	죄송합니다
so-so	그저 그래요
soup	국
spicy	매운
spirits, western alcohol	양주
squid	오징어
start, begin	시작하-
stay, lodge, spend the night	묵-
stomach	배
stop (verb stem)	서-
strange, bizarre	이상하-
strength, energy	힘
stylish/handsome	멋있-
suit (a person)	어울리-
Sunday	일요일
swim (swimming pool)	수영하- (수영장)
take (time duration)	걸리-
take, travel on (transport)	타-
talk, tell	얘기하-
tasty / tasteless	맛이 있-/없-
teach	가르치-
telephone	전화
telephone (verb stem)	전화하-
thank you	감사합니다/고맙습니다
that one (long way away)	저
that one (nearer than cho-)	그
(over) there	저기
therefore, because of that	그러니까
thing, object, fact	거 (abbreviation of 것)
this one (1 noun), this noun	이
thought, idea (remember, it comes to mind)	생각 (나-)
three (pure Korean)	세
ticket	표
time, hour	시간
times/double	배
to (preposition, attaches to nouns)	-에

to / for (a person)	-에게; -한테
today	오늘
together	함께; 같이
tomorrow	내일
too, also (particle)	-도
too (much)	너무
towards, in the direction of	으로
towel	수건
town centre	시내
turned out well, it's all for the best	잘 됐네요
two	두, 이
umbrella	우산
understand	알아듣-; 알아들어요
unfortunately	안 되겠네요
university	대학, 대학교
until	-까지
USA	미국
very	아주, 참
vicinity, area, district	근처
wait	기다리-
wait a moment (please)	잠깐 기다리세요
waiter!	아저씨
waitress! (lit: girl, unmarried woman)	아가씨
want, require	원하-
water	물
we, our	우리
weather	날씨
welcome!	어서 오세요
well, good (adverb)	잘
what (object form) (full form)	뭐 (뭘) (무엇)
what (kind of, which) (number)	무슨, 몇
when	언제
where	어디
which one?	어느
while, a little	잠깐
who? (subject form)	누구 (누가)
wife (not a polite form)	집사람
window	창구
with (irang after consonants)	-랑
word, language (to speak/say)	말 (말하-); 말씀 (polite form)

work, matter, business	일
worry (to)	걱정 (하-)
write	쓰-
wrongly, mis-	잘못
yes	네
yet, still	아직
year before last	재작년
you (often between married couples)	당신; 여보